Scheming for Youth

Scheming for Youth
A study of YTS in the enterprise culture

DAVID LEE, DENNIS MARSDEN,
PENNY RICKMAN AND JEAN DUNCOMBE
(in collaboration with Kenneth Masters)

Open University Press
Milton Keynes · Philadelphia

Open University Press
Celtic Court
22 Ballmoor
Buckingham MK18 1XW

and

1900 Frost Road, Suite 101
Bristol, PA 19007, USA

First Published 1990

British Library Cataloguing in Publication Data

Scheming for youth: a study of the YTS in the enterprise culture
1. Great Britain. Unemployed young persons. Employment programmes:
Youth Training Scheme
I. Lee, David
331.3'412042

ISBN 0-335-15193-0
ISBN 0-335-15192-2 (pbk)

Library of Congress Cataloging-in-Publication Data

Scheming for youth: a study of YTS in the enterprise culture/
by David Lee . . . [et al.].
       p.   cm.
Includes bibliographical references.
ISBN 0-335-15193-0   ISBN 0-335-15192-2 (pbk.)
1. Occupational training – England. 2. Youth – Employment – England.
3. Free enterprise. I. Lee, David.
HD5715.5.G72E547   1990
331.3'42592'0941 – dc20   89-22987
                                      CIP

Typeset by Scarborough Typesetting Services
Printed in Great Britain by St Edmundsbury Press,
Bury St Edmunds, Suffolk

For

Rebecca
Suzanna
Jack
Michelle
Daniel
Sarah
Ben
Daisy
Rosie
Millie
Aimee
Emily
James
Michael

Contents

Preface

This book is based upon nearly six years of research into the workings of the Youth Training Scheme (YTS) in a town in South-East England. We argue that the emphasis of the scheme upon so-called 'free-market forces' severely limits its effectiveness as a means of training young workers and providing them with opportunities to improve their personal circumstances through paid work.

In the face of official claims that YTS is a resounding success, there is an obvious risk that such a critical conclusion will be dismissed as the rubbishing of sensible policies by subversive intellectuals in the name of so-called social science. It is therefore important to say that we applaud many of the aims of the New Training Initiative from which YTS developed. It is right for a civilized society to ensure that young people's early years at work are regulated by some standard of training in useful and marketable skills, which will enable them to live prosperous and independent lives and to adapt intelligently to changes. It is important, too, that the vocational should be given a new strength and respectability. British schooling has for too long been impoverished by rigid and elitist ideas of academic worth which have created socially harmful divisions between the 'educated' and the 'trained'. No political position has a monopoly on 'vocationalism'. Long before Lord Young, for example, Karl Marx envisaged a 'polytechnical' education based on direct experience of productive labour.

The argument is not about ends but means. The automatic association of the efficient with the unregulated action of markets has been taken too seriously for too long. We argue here that leaving training to market forces, both under YTS and before it, has resulted in underprovision, skill shortages and the waste of young people. We live in a complicated world in which the need for a balance of intervention and market forces cannot be wished away by dogma from the right or left.

While we have been doing the work reported here, we have become increasingly anxious about the general future of independent enquiry. We therefore attach all the more importance to the role of non-governmental foundations like the Leverhulme Trust, to whom we are greatly indebted for five years' generous support under conditions which allowed us the maximum freedom to develop our ideas in whatever direction our findings pointed.

We are also grateful to David Ashton, David Raffe and Adrian Sinfield for backing, encouragement and frequent advice throughout the project. Dan Finn, Derek Betts, Ken Roberts and Sally Dench, among others, gave generously of their time. Phil Brown gave invaluable advice on how to make our manuscript more publishable. John Skelton of the Open University Press was enormously patient and helpful.

Michael Hardey worked on the project between 1983 and 1986. Fiona Devine, Ros Chapman, Sarah Marsden and John Cresswell helped with the Leavers Survey and Joy Alsopp tried hard to make us efficient. Shelley Pennington and Rebecca Lee transcribed interviews, Lance Rickman designed our questionnaire cover and Bea Rickman helped with its distribution. Sue Hutson transcribed first drafts, and Ben Marsden gave helpful comments on comprehensibility. The DEC10 collapsed regularly, but the services of the Essex University Computing Support staff were excellent throughout the project. Our colleagues in the Sociology Department got in our way, gossiped about us endlessly, but also provided much needed intellectual stimulus, friendship and support. Adrienne Lee did some coding, much brow-mopping and, despite good cause, never got cross with any of us. Finally our grateful thanks go to the many people, administrators, educators, trainers and trainees, who must remain anonymous but who co-operated willingly in our research. We have tried to report what they said to us honestly and accurately. Inevitably, we did not always share their view of what was going on because, as we have tried to show here, individual experiences of YTS formed part of a wider pattern with its own logic. Nevertheless, we hope our informants will feel that we have been fair. No criticism of a personal nature is intended.

List of abbreviations

AMB	Area Manpower Board
ATC	Accredited Training Centre
ATO	Approved Training Organization
B(T)EC	Business (and Technical) Examinations Council
CBI	Confederation of British Industry
CITB	Construction Industry Training Board
DE	Department of Employment
DES	Department of Education and Science
EITB	Engineering Industry Training Board
ET	Employment Training
FE(U)	Further Education (Unit)
HCITB	Hotels and Catering Industry Training Board
ITB	Industrial Training Board
JTS	Job Training Scheme
LCU(S)	Large Companies Unit (Schemes)
MSC	Manpower Services Commission
NAFTE	National Association of Teachers in Further and Higher Education
NALGO	National and Local Government Officers' Association
N(C)VQ	National (Council for) Vocational Qualifications
NHS	National Health Service
NTI	New Training Initiative (1982)
NTP	New Training Programme (pilot YTS)
OTF	Occupational Training Family
RSA	Royal Society of Arts
RTITB	Road Transport Industry Training Board
TEC	Training and Enterprise Council
TFS	Training for Skills

TOC   Training Occupational Category
TUC   Trades Union Congress
TVEI   Training and Vocational Education Initiative
YOP   Youth Opportunities Programme
YTG   Youth Task Group
YTS 1   Youth Training Scheme (one-year version)
YTS 2   Youth Training Scheme (two-year version)
YWS   Young Workers Scheme

Part One
Introduction

Chapter 1
Youth training and market forces

In 1983, through the Youth Training Scheme (YTS)*, young people became a major target of Mrs Thatcher's free-market revolution and its moral programme. Her government's aim is to create an 'enterprise culture' of self-reliance and self-help, opening up economic and social policy to competition and market forces. In line with this, it has attacked union and legal controls on young workers' wages, arguing that they price young people out of the market. Schools have been accused of failing to teach pupils the work skills and discipline needed in industry.

But it is YTS which most fully embodies the essence of Thatcherism. YTS aims to give school leavers opportunities to price themselves back into jobs by lowering their wage aspirations, by giving them valuable skills, and by developing the right attitudes to work. Trainees' allowances are set low to match their trainee status and to keep down public spending. Skills training must be done in the most 'natural way', through the free market, by employers on their own premises.

In this book, we have taken seriously the claim that organizing youth training through YTS will give young people marketable skills, with improved job chances and a more positive outlook on work and society. We describe the development of YTS between 1983 and 1988 in a town in South-East England which we call 'Southwich'. Various aspects of YTS have been studied before in isolation, but our research is probably unique in using a range of methods to follow the development of the Scheme both in the round and over its whole lifetime. We have explored the value of YTS as a training programme, where it fitted in the local economy and society, how it affected the lives of trainees, and also its impact on the behaviour of the managing agents, employers, careers officers and FE teachers who helped to recruit and train young people. The only omission is that, because there were very few black young people in Southwich, our findings rarely relate

* For an explanation of abbreviations used in this book, see the list of abbreviations on pages xi–xii.

directly to the issue of racial discrimination in YTS, though it undoubtedly exists elsewhere (see, for example, Finn, 1987: 185–6) and our analysis could be applied to it.

In 1983, YTS was portrayed as part of the solution to Britain's long-standing problem of skill shortages. There is no doubt that, by international standards, British school leavers are badly educated and poorly trained (Barnett, 1986: ch. 11; Lindley, 1983; Taylor, 1982: ch. 4). In its latest White Paper, the government described how training in Britain this century has compared unfavourably with that of our major competitors (DE, 1988: 28–9). YTS was supposed to help the young unemployed to get jobs, improve the productivity of the whole workforce and thus help end Britain's cycle of skill shortages and low growth.

With a vast public expenditure, YTS expanded rapidly, and since 1985 it has catered for about 45 per cent of all 16-year-old school leavers and a growing proportion of 17-year-olds (about 30 per cent in 1988 (*Employment Gazette* September 1987: 462)). Reviewing this in the White Paper, the government claims that YTS is now a 'resounding success' (DE, 1988: 46). Ministers publicize model schemes and make great play with the trainees' rates of success in getting jobs.

Yet there is still scepticism about these claims, based on the past experience of trade unions and the workforce. During the inter-war years government 'training' schemes absorbed the unemployed but devalued training and skills and fostered hostile industrial relations (Rees and Rees, 1982; Sheldrake and Vickerstaff, 1987). In the late 1970s, the Youth Opportunities Programme (YOP) had reawakened suspicion because its placements in small and peripheral workplaces gave no training, and by 1981 the employment rate of YOP 'trainees' had fallen to only one in three (Youthaid, 1981; Raffe, 1984). So the rhetoric of 'training' rather than jobs had a familiar ring. Its critics, especially in the labour movement, saw YTS as a further part of a Conservative government strategy to massage the unemployment statistics, undermine union activity and attack the living standards of the unemployed (Finn, 1987). Was YTS to be just another in the 'alphabet soup' of schemes whose names were changed with predictable regularity as soon as they became discredited?

More recently, YTS has been seen as spearheading a programme of 'workfare', where the unemployed must work for state benefits. Employers, trade unions, and the Treasury (the last on grounds of the possible extra expense) all opposed the government's original plan to make YTS compulsory by the threat of withdrawal of benefits from school leavers who 'unreasonably' refuse a YTS place. But benefit rules for young people and adults are being continually tightened and since September 1988 jobless school leavers who refuse a YTS place have been unable to claim social security, making the Scheme workfare in all but name. Meanwhile, state support for adults increasingly depends on their accepting places on YTS lookalikes such as the Job Training Scheme (JTS) and, more recently, Employment Training (ET).

Frequent controversial policy changes have made research on YTS difficult, because those responsible for the Scheme's success are suspicious of independent scrutiny and research runs the risk of being too short-term and narrow in its focus. At the same time a large and growing body of research on school leavers and trainees has shown how the structure and impact of YTS varies between regions and types of programme, and also according to young people's lives and plans. Relatively little has been written about how national YTS policy is modified to fit different localities or its impact on whole local populations. It has been argued that there remains a need for 'a deeper qualitative understanding' of young people's and others' experiences of YTS in different localities (Raffe and Smith, 1987).

Our research, funded by a generous grant from the Leverhulme Trust, was intended to help to fill this gap, but from the first we had to acknowledge several basic problems. Because the Manpower Services Commission (MSC) 'kept moving the goal posts' (as the managing agents put it), YTS was at once controversial and constantly changing. This affected what those involved were able and willing to tell us about the training. We decided that where experts have failed we could hardly hope to observe and measure the YTS training process itself; carried out in numerous small workplaces, it was at best spasmodic, at worst non-existent. But in any case, attempts to 'monitor' it were likely to provoke suspicion or unreal specially-arranged sessions.

We also recognized the difficulty of capturing the impact of YTS alone upon the values and attitudes of young people as they moved through training and into the labour market during their transition from school to adulthood. They, too, sometimes had a vested interest in presenting the outcomes of YTS in a good (or bad) light. Also, because in Southwich the Scheme absorbed virtually the whole of a particular stratum of young people, there was no matching group of *non*-trainees to compare with those who went through YTS training.

Clearly, to gain a comprehensive view of YTS in Southwich we had to adopt as broad a range of methods as resources would allow (see the Appendix for details). In 1982–3 we observed some of the pilot schemes for YTS in the local FE college, we interviewed staff and distributed question-naires, and we observed co-ordinating meetings. We carried out two postal surveys of the whole cohort of Southwich's 16-year-old school leavers, late in 1984 when they met the first full-blown YTS schemes, and again in late 1985 when they had been in the local labour market for a year. From among them we also interviewed over 200 trainees across the full range of YTS schemes, during 1984 and again in 1985 after they had left YTS. (These ex-trainees were later followed up by phone and post in 1988.) In 1984, 1986 and 1988 we interviewed virtually all the local managing agents to chart the development of one-year YTS (YTS 1) from its inception well into the two-year scheme (YTS 2) which began in 1986. During this time we also observed managing agents' meetings involving FE staff, MSC and the Careers Service. We watched some recruitment interviews at the Careers Office, and we interviewed Careers Service staff and also some of the smaller employers who provided work placements.

From 1987, a further grant from Leverhulme enabled us to explore YTS 2, which was claimed by the government to be a major upgrading in training quality, guaranteed by a new system of skills accreditation, National Vocational Qualifications (NVQ). YTS 2 now met the quite different social and economic climate of the late 1980s, with the local Southwich economy booming and educational opportunities increasing, but the numbers of young people in the age group falling. Rather than repeat our overall strategy we focused on the more marginal schemes where our earlier research had revealed that training was most precarious. To check on YTS 2 claims for quality, we visited over 50 placements from a range of schemes and interviewed the trainees (singly and in groups). We also interviewed the managing agents, employers and tutors who provided training, and we observed a range of off-the-job training, finally completing our research only in 1988. Unfortunately, despite formal discussions with officials (and informal help throughout from research staff at headquarters), our early reception by the MSC locally was frosty. It was not until almost the end of our study that we were able to have meaningful informal discussions with new local MSC staff.

Overall, we have tried to judge the success of market- and employer-led training in YTS by its own ideals of efficiency and enterprise. Southwich offered a good test-bed where YTS *training* could be judged in relation to an expanding economy, rather than under the constraints of economically depressed regions. Indeed Southwich epitomized Britain's recent economic 'miracle', its prosperity reliant on new small businesses and burgeoning financial and consumer services. Yet there were plenty of jobless school leavers for YTS to absorb, because Southwich schools had poorer exam passes and fewer pupils staying on than in comparable towns. If privatized training and market forces failed in Southwich then they are unlikely to succeed elsewhere.

To understand the workings of YTS in practice we have used the concept of a 'surrogate' labour market, where YTS outcomes are determined by a mix of market forces and state intervention which differs in different parts of the country. The tinge of the spurious in the name 'surrogate' is intended because, despite its free-market rhetoric, YTS creates extra training places by public intervention.

We also argue that the seemingly old-fashioned questions of 'political arithmetic' concerning the inequalities of opportunity which stem from social background cannot be ignored in the enterprise culture. Sharp social inequalities could actually hamper efforts to increase the supply of skilled labour and to spread the fruits of enterprise downwards. YTS itself has official goals of promoting equal opportunities and compensating for disadvantage. So we have asked which young people from what sorts of social backgrounds and with what educational attainments join the various

YTS schemes, and what improvement in life chances (if any) does YTS bring? Do the opportunities provided by YTS really compensate for bad schooling, racial and sexual discrimination or a deprived social background? In fact, we show that YTS in Southwich was drawn into the rapid socio-economic changes of the 1980s, and so what made it a good test-bed also made it interesting in the light of academic debates about economic and social change in Britain, including controversies over the surviving influence of social class (Marshall *et al.*, 1988: ch. 1).

This book follows YTS up to 1988. Chapter 2 shows how Southwich provided a good test-bed for YTS, by comparing the official YTS administrative blueprint and assumptions with Southwich's economy, society and young people. Chapter 3 describes how YTS undermined vocational training at the FE college. Part Two outlines our approach to YTS as a 'surrogate' youth labour market. The managing agents describe how the 'demand' for trainee labour was built up and how schemes recruited and organized. We conclude by suggesting a model of the unequal 'segmentation' of opportunities shown by YTS. Part Three then draws on our postal surveys and trainee interviews to compare these opportunities with the 'supply' of trainees from various backgrounds. We describe their recruitment, their views on work placements, their work careers after leaving YTS, their social attitudes, and their verdicts on YTS three years later. Part Four describes our research on YTS 2, which shows how market forces are further undermining not only YTS training but also the new NVQ intended to assess and guarantee its quality. Part Five argues that the case for training by market forces is not supported by our research.

Chapter 2
The YTS blueprint in Southwich

This chapter begins with a brief history of YTS and an outline of its administrative structure. Supporters of YTS have exaggerated the extent to which it represented a real break with the assumptions of past youth training policies, and we will describe how it continued a long British tradition of voluntarism and market forces in training. Underlying the blueprint of YTS was a simple version of 'human capital theory' which ignored existing criticisms that so-called free markets do not operate in the way YTS intends. We argue that this blueprint and its underlying assumptions provide an ideal opportunity to test the Thatcher government's passionate belief in the benefits of opening up all areas of public life to market forces. And we show why Southwich offered such a good test-bed of how these assumptions worked out in practice.

The origins of YTS 1 and YTS 2

Although YTS was the Conservatives' main response to the youth un-employment crisis of the early 1980s, it grew out of the Youth Opportunities Programme (YOP) devised under Labour by the MSC. The MSC (a quango with equal representation from employers, unions and education) was originally set up by the Heath government to oversee employment and training, but the MSC's priorities had shifted as the number of young people without work began to rise, the ill-fated YOP being one result. In 1979, the newly-elected Conservative government, seeking to get rid of all quangos, threatened to abolish the MSC, cutting its budget for three years. But by 1983, rising youth unemployment and the inner-city riots had persuaded the government to save it, and its activities shifted more rapidly from traditional training and employment services to special unemployment measures.

Initially, by guaranteeing a place to all 16-year-old school leavers still unemployed at Christmas, YOP was adapted to help to lower young people's expectations and wages, and to take jobless school leavers off the register (Finn, 1987: 131–42). But YOP had attracted criticism as a source of cheap labour and the TUC, among others, called for its upgrading. Research, including the MSC's own, found a high proportion of placements in small firms, many of poor quality or exploitative, and with rising youth unemployment fewer trainees found jobs. Pressure mounted to transform YOP into a national scheme offering a year of real training. This idea underlay the MSC's *New Training Initiative* (MSC, 1981a; 1981b) and the pilot schemes for the New Training Programme, NTP or 'super-YOP'. In response, in December 1981 a Government White Paper announced £1 billion to fund a new one-year Youth Training Scheme (DE, 1981), to be worked out by a task group.

The *Youth Task Group Report* (MSC, 1982) was intended to cover employed as well as unemployed young people, and it proposed 13 weeks of training off the job, with the rest of the year spent on employers' premises learning job-related skills. Design and oversight of individual schemes would be delegated to 'managing agents' under contract to the MSC. These could be private sector organizations (including Chambers of Commerce and private training associations) or statutory bodies such as local authorities, FE colleges and Industrial Training Boards (ITBs). Of the three proposed modes of funding the largest, Mode A, gave managing agents a block grant towards training costs and to cover trainees' weekly allowances (originally £25, though the government wanted less). Modes B1 and B2, aimed at disadvantaged youth, could be funded like Mode A or else the managing agents, mostly local education authorities and colleges, received actual training costs up to a given limit. Special MSC field staff would oversee the development of YTS schemes and report to Area Manpower Boards (AMBs) with employer, union and educational representatives. At national level YTS was to be controlled through a similarly-constituted Youth Training Board. The government accepted the *Report* in 1982 and after feverish preparations the first trainees were admitted in September 1983, just as youth unemployment peaked.

This YTS blueprint has been constantly modified to meet continued criticisms of training quality and to reduce the element of state subsidy. A further training White Paper (DE, 1985a) proposed the extension of YTS to two years from 1986 and obliged managing agents to undergo MSC scrutiny for registration as Approved Training Organizations (ATOs). But it argued that the second year should be funded largely by employers from levies for each trainee, collected by managing agents. The separate modes were abolished and funding for disadvantaged young people was reduced to a limited number of premium places. At the same time a new private company, ENTRAIN, was to teach young people the virtues of enterprise and initiative.

Continuing the tradition of voluntarism and market forces in training through YTS

The *Youth Task Group Report* claimed that these proposals were 'a decisive break with the past' (MSC, 1982: para. 3.8). Yet they did not radically depart from 'the pragmatic tradition of voluntarism in state-industry relations' (Sheldrake and Vickerstaff, 1987: 2). Under past voluntarism, governments of all complexions have argued that training is industry's responsibility, to be provided by individual employer initiatives with minimal state intervention. Political mileage has been gained by saving public funds and loading training costs onto firms (Lee, 1983; Taylor, 1982). In turn, non-intervention allowed many employers to use low-paid apprentices and trainees as cheap labour to dilute skilled trades. Between the wars this widespread practice in engineering and elsewhere provoked union bitterness and rigidified their policies on apprenticeships, government training centres, job demarcation and working practices. After failing to get voluntary agreements on higher standards of apprenticeship training they sought to raise youth wages relative to those of adults (Lee, 1979; Ryan, 1986). Governments have been happy to stay out of such arguments if they could.

In their turn employers' well-documented reluctance to pay for training beyond their foreseeable production needs has undermined all post-war attempts to expand Britain's skilled workforce. Both the Training Board system of the 1964 Industrial Training Act and the Unified Vocational Preparation plans of the Labour government met industry's resentment that the costs of 'purely educational objectives' has been shifted onto employers (*Guardian*: 22 December 1981; Finn, 1987: 124). So by the early 1980s some MSC staff were convinced that 'substantial state intervention' was needed (MSC, 1982: para. 1.14).

CBI representatives remained hostile to official intervention, but knew that a more unpalatable alternative to YTS might be imposed if they did not co-operate (Keep, 1986: 8–10). The government's tight money policy, designed to 'slim down' industry, had resulted in a wave of bankruptcies and redundancies and the collapse of apprenticeship and other training (Chapman and Tooze, 1987). YTS cleverly offered employers real benefits from using their existing surplus training capacity, and also a supply of cheap youth trainees. In return for their co-operation, however, employer representatives made it clear that the time and activities of trainees on the job in their work placements should be 'black boxed' under their control, and work experience and skills should only be assessed by 'end objectives', or listings of what competences trainees should have achieved (Keep, 1986: 26).

The result was deep ambiguity concerning the powers of surveillance and control which could be exercised by MSC staff. They had to create and approve the YTS network and to 'work with' employers to ensure their trainees received high-quality training through '*planned* work experience'

(MSC, 1982, emphasis added). Yet although the MSC's planners proposed carefully-shaped 'end objectives' for training, 'black boxing' meant that workplace training could not be independently examined or tested.

The 'quality' objectives of YTS also initially conflicted with the government's urgent need to find a substitute for YOP with enough cheap places to mop up the unemployed. So although YTS was intended to provide training for both employed and unemployed young people, in practice the guarantee of places in a time of high youth unemployment has restricted its cover largely to the jobless. A CBI official with the Youth Task Group concluded that YTS planning showed 'the worrying persistence with which the development of a long-term, strategic national approach to training policy eludes Britain and the comparative ease with which short-term expediency holds sway'. The government's main aim was always to use YTS 'to return responsibility for training activities to the level of the individual firm' (Keep, 1986: 6).

Indeed, more recently the MSC's already limited formal powers have gradually shrunk. When YTS became a two-year scheme in 1986, the managing agents whom the MSC recognized as ATOs became more independent of its surveillance (which was reduced to a mainly accounting exercise focused on those with a high fraction of their profits from YTS) and the number of field staff was cut. The MSC was abolished in 1988, becoming the Training Commission and then the Training Agency of the Department of Employment (DE). Its remaining local functions and staff will pass to employer-dominated Training and Enterprise Councils (TECs).

In fact, over time the tendency has been to neutralize *any* influences not closely connected with employers and the market. A further example was that the move to make skills more transferable by giving off-the-job training leading to a recognized vocational qualification was at first centred on public sector FE, but more and more this has become contracted out to commercial training organizations. Under the National Council for Vocational Qualifications (NCVQ) a new scheme of National Vocational Qualifications (NVQ) is being introduced, supposedly to guarantee the quality and the transferability of YTS training. But the NVQ scheme is intended to make the setting of skill standards more employer-led and the assessment of skills more employer-based. And the last vestiges of the old Industrial Training Board system are to be scrapped by privatizing the remaining ITBs.

Nor does much remain of the early goal of compensation for disadvantage from discrimination or disability. High unemployment, early legislation, and pressures from the EEC regional fund (which partly funded YTS) ensured that YTS always had stated goals of 'equal opportunities' for all trainees. But their only formal acknowledgement was in Mode B schemes, which further subsidized 'compensatory training' for trainees who were disadvantaged or lived in high unemployment areas to enable them to compete in the labour market. Mode B schemes included more 'personal and life skills' training, and most trainees worked mainly in special workshops which were intended to produce and so offset their costs. Any placements were shorter and usually in a variety of work settings. Cost-cutting under YTS 2 has now replaced Mode B by fewer 'premium places' for the disadvantaged, and although 'equality of opportunity' is still a criterion for ATO recognition, enforcement is now left to the ATOs (or former managing agents) themselves.

We can see, then, that far from being a break with the past, YTS has followed the British tradition of voluntarism in training. After a brief excursion into intervention during the youth unemployment crisis which surrounded the birth of YTS, the Thatcher government consistently cut back the role of the MSC in favour of opening up training to market forces, and eventually achieved its earlier objective of abolishing the MSC altogether. Government support has reflected how easily YTS could be developed through market forces, with only a minimal and diminishing role for state intervention and cash. But fashionable free-market theories then claimed this continuation of expediency and non-intervention in training as an 'innovation'.

The weaknesses of 'simple human capital theory': market forces and the precariousness of training

Implicit in ministerial and other official statements about YTS can be found theoretical arguments which may be called the 'simple human capital theory of YTS'. Training is seen as investment which increases productivity, so that individuals gain 'marketable' skills which bring them jobs with higher wages, and society as a whole benefits from their increased output. This approach justifies the reform of training through decentralized voluntary employer-led schemes. Indeed it neatly gives YTS a double role, as a thoroughgoing training reform and as a compensatory programme for jobless and disadvantaged youth which does not involve state handouts.

The basic idea underlying the YTS structure is that employers are the best judges of their own labour needs. Lowering the artificially inflated price of youth labour will induce employers with surplus training facilities to take on unemployed school leavers as trainees for a specified period. In the short run the trainees will be 'additional' to firms' requirements, and the state will pay the trainees an 'allowance' which is in effect an indirect labour subsidy. In the longer run the need for subsidy will be reduced as wage expectations are lowered and the benefits of training and economic revival spread. Through YTS, trainees will supposedly learn skills most in demand throughout the economy, so that after the training they should be able to find jobs either with their original sponsor or with employers who need trained labour but have no facilities to train. Importantly, the skills most in short supply should be 'transferable' between workplaces in contrast to those which are 'specific' to one employer.

This simple human capital theory of YTS emerged piecemeal as a rationale for a structure that was a political compromise between conflicting interests. The theory largely ignored or disowned existing research on how employers make decisions about training. Even within orthodox economics, a strong tradition argues that unrestrained competition gives firms powerful incentives *not* to train (Chapman and Tooze, 1987; Marsden 1986: ch. 1). Training involves high costs before it pays off in production and the break-even point may come only years later. So firms will only spend on training where they can be confident that their trained workers will not leave for the highest bidder. Recession forces many employers to scrap training completely until business revives, but then skilled labour shortages encourage 'poaching' from other employers. Without so-called 'counter-cyclical' intervention by the state or some other agency, too few employers will behave 'altruistically' to offset the pattern. This explains what has happened since the late 1970s with skill shortages alongside a dramatic collapse in numbers of fully-employed apprentices and trainees (MSC, 1988a). So, as the MSC (1980, Appendix 3) itself had pointed out to the government from its own research: 'both theory and experience suggest that left to themselves, individual firms will not undertake enough training fully to meet the needs of the economy for transferable skills'.

Even under traditional in-house apprenticeship, simply leaving training to individual employers put quality at risk. The design and planning of instruction conflicts with short-term financial constraints and the production deadlines of departments providing work experience. So longer-term training goals need to be defended by training officers who are given some *independence* from market forces and the parent firm. In practice, firms vary as to whether training staff can recruit and remove apprentices, control their moves between jobs and determine training off the job (Lee, 1966). Firms which develop a strong training function tend to be large with a long-term organizational and commercial strategy. But they face poaching and many of their managers and employees resent the way regulated training 'interferes' with what they see as their primary task of meeting orders and schedules.

Where (as in YTS) quality is controlled by an external agency with limited powers to intervene, the defence of training from commercial pressures is doubly precarious. The former ITBs tried to raise standards through a system of levies and grants but many firms opted out of training or used their political influence to neutralize the threat. The problems of enforcing standards in smaller organizations in particular brought about the system's demise (Perry, 1976: 273–300).

How real labour markets work: 'segmentation' and the youth labour market

A further difficulty with the simple human capital theory of YTS is that real labour markets are not as uniform and predictable as it assumes. Even fashionable free-market economics accepts that workers do not all compete in the *same* labour market. Differences in aptitude, training and 'productivity' between individuals subdivide the market into non-competing areas or 'segments'; and institutional restrictions on competition make the range of choices open to workers and firms less than perfect. A long tradition of research outside mainstream economics, known as segmentation theory, argues that understanding institutional and cultural factors is essential to explaining how labour markets actually work and that competitive conditions only occur in unusual circumstances which themselves require institutional support (see, for example, Marsden, 1986).

Although segmentation theory remains controversial and underdeveloped we use it because the youth labour market provides many examples of segmentation in action (Ashton and Maguire, 1986). Typically, employers and young people (and employment agencies, educational institutions and families) have preconceptions or prejudices about what is suitable work for various kinds of worker. Gender differences are a major example. Girls work mainly in clerical jobs, retailing, and catering, with few in manufacturing except clothing and footwear. Boys do a wider range of jobs, and dominate craft apprenticeships (Ashton *et al.*, 1990).

It is also important to distinguish what happens as young people apply for jobs, from later processes once they are *in* the labour market. Individuals differ markedly in prospects and earning potential, depending on their family and social backgrounds and also their success in gaining school credentials. To some extent they 'select themselves' for different kinds of work. But employers also employ ethnic, gender and social criteria (such as speech, dress and behaviour) to screen applicants over-cautiously for jobs which are 'better' or in the public eye. For example, employers are reluctant to take a chance on those they see as having failed at school (Roberts *et al.*, 1986b: 523).

Even young people with similar schooling and background are not always treated in the same way after entering the job market. Some jobs give entry to so-called internal labour markets, with privileged training, promotion ladders and better security and pay. These tend to be in large firms, sometimes created to keep trained workers from being poached by other employers. Firms may further try to tie employees down by teaching only skills specific to the firm's own work processes. Internal labour markets also come from union action to control apprenticeship numbers and increase skilled pay, to minimize threats to adult wages and jobs. Workers who fail to enter internal labour markets when they are young are more likely to remain untrained and confined to low-skill and insecure work.

Youth labour markets are also strongly affected by cyclical swings in trade and by political responses to youth unemployment. YTS compares with programmes in a number of European countries which reacted to the depression of the early 1980s by seeking to lower the cost of employing young people. As a result more have been taken on, though often substituting for adults. If cutting youth wages boosts young people's employment, however, the quality of their jobs and long-term prospects may be suspect (Marsden and Ryan, 1986: 96). Young people compete as a group (as well as individually) with certain types of adult worker, especially part-time married women, so they are excluded from many jobs at least until they are older. The industries which took advantage of the new supply of cheaper labour were already using disproportionately large numbers of young people: predominantly service industries where, despite important exceptions, average wages already tend to be low and working conditions and prospects poor (Ashton *et al.*, 1990).

Thus, despite what YTS assumes, training in marketable skills cannot be guaranteed simply by providing the jobless young with unspecified and poorly-controlled work experience. Because the youth labour market is segmented trainees will not necessarily have equal access to placements, nor will they be able to use any training to get jobs. Helping disadvantaged young people through employer-led training depends on how far conventional 'screening' can be broken down and on the types of firm and industry taking trainees.

The concept of the 'surrogate labour market'

To study how YTS worked in practice, we clearly needed an alternative framework which recognized possible market imperfections without prejudging their form and outcomes. We used the concept of a 'surrogate labour market' to cover the common element in various state work-creation and training programmes which have flourished in several countries during the recession of the 1980s. By a 'surrogate labour market' we mean a network of work placements created by administrative intervention to remedy deficiencies in labour demand. Like YTS, programmes of training and work experience for young and adult unemployed set up elsewhere reflect a political preference for so-called workfare, putting the unemployed to work for any state income support. However, each scheme differs in its mix of state subsidy, intervention and market forces. At one extreme lies Sweden, with a centralized system of government and a long tradition of the oversight and extensive funding of work programmes (Burton, 1987). At the other are US programmes of workfare in its original sense, where benefit recipients work for their grants in unpaid jobs. The US programmes are small, decentralized, have a low administrative profile, and are targeted on limited 'problem' groups (Burghes, 1987).

We would argue that in these various surrogate labour markets, the outcome of policy may be explained in terms of different *mixes* of intervention and market forces and the interplay between the two. YTS is one of the largest of such programmes, but it has had a relatively low, ambiguous and declining role for intervention and this allows us to explain and generalize our findings from Southwich to other areas.

A test-bed for YTS: the economy and social structure of Southwich

Because of the recession, *locality* became especially important in segmenting the youth labour market during the 1980s. For example, one study found that 'the chances of the sons of middle-class fathers in Sunderland finding employment were less than those of sons of working-class families in St Albans' (Ashton and Maguire, 1986: 2; see also *Times Educational Supplement*, 29 July 1988; 12 August 1988). It was soon clear that local economic variations could unbalance YTS. Unemployed young people became concentrated in inner cities or depressed regions with high rates of early leaving yet without enough viable industry to provide the employment-based work placements of the YTS blueprint, so that the gap had to be filled by the subsidized Mode B schemes. By contrast, in areas with plenty of employer-led schemes, staying-on rates are higher and jobs buoyant, so that YTS provision becomes restricted to the least 'employable' school leavers. In one example, Chelmsford, the head of the Careers Service 'doubted the need for YTS on the scale proposed' (Roberts *et al.*, 1986a: 262; see also Turbin, 1988: 184, Table 1).

In 1983 Southwich, the town chosen for our study, lay between these extremes. A combination of recession and the local schools had produced large numbers of jobless school leavers who, even in their own eyes, were poorly-qualified and underprepared for work. But the local economy was still buoyant enough to provide Mode A placements for most of them. So it looked as though YTS really could be about training disadvantaged young people in genuine work tasks and not YOP-style job-creation.

The Southwich economy in national and local context

This situation came about because economic conditions are more variable in South-East England than is commonly thought. In the early 1980s, unemployment rates ranged between about 5 per cent in the Home Counties west and north of London to much higher levels elsewhere. Southwich was in one of the few regions to grow both economically and in population during the previous decade. With a population slightly over 145,000, Southwich itself was typical of the country towns which have gained relative to larger and older urban areas. Yet throughout the county there were rural and depressed urban areas where the job structure was unstable or had begun to collapse drastically. The county planners saw further growth in Southwich through new industrial sites and more offices as vital, but although in 1981 employment had grown by 10 per cent on the previous Census, by 1984 it had fallen back, causing doubt about the future.

This local recession reflected the long-term decline of British manufacturing and the growth of service industries. By the 1981 Census the proportion of both sexes employed in Southwich manufacturing firms had fallen to just over a fifth. But the recession accentuated the trend, and the

Census of Employment found that between 1981 and 1984 the proportion in manufacturing fell another 5 per cent, while there was a 5 per cent *rise* in distribution, transport, banking, catering and other services. Current statistics are not available but expansion and optimism undoubtedly returned. The manufacturing decline halted, all but one company reporting full order books, and there was a very visible expansion of small factories, modern distribution outlets, offices and financial services.

The impact of these developments has varied widely. Older male craft workers made redundant, especially from engineering, found it difficult to find new jobs or retrain. New male jobs have gone to young adult migrants into the area, while many of the new service jobs have been filled by part-time female workers and young girls. The published unemployment statistics (albeit subject to changes in definition) show that adult joblessness rose from 9 per cent in 1981 to peak at 12 per cent in 1984 and return to below 8 per cent in 1987.

The social structure of Southwich and the backgrounds of YTS trainees

Like much of South-East England, a distinctive social structure has emerged from Southwich's generally prosperous but rapidly-changing economy. Even in 1981 the Census showed a typical town with many men in 'middle-class' non-manual jobs (Figure 2.1). Being further from London than St Albans or Chelmsford, it had proportionately fewer in managerial, professional and intermediate occupations, yet these still accounted for over a third of all male jobs. With skilled non-manual workers, the 'middle-class' covered nearly half the employed males in the town, and an even higher proportion of employed Southwich women had non-manual jobs, too (64 per cent in 1981), reinforcing the picture of a town with a large middle class.

However, the town is more socially-polarized than the Census shows. Unlike parts of the North and Midlands, it never had, between its middle class and less affluent workers, enough traditional craftsmen to form a 'labour aristocracy' and the recession cut their numbers. Also recent studies (see Chapter 14) show that modern employment patterns, typically with a high proportion of service jobs as in Southwich, are tending to divide working populations into an elite of career professionals, administrators, technicians and managers and a stratum of low-paid, low-skill workers. Social polarization was evident, too, in the physical layout of the town, with a clear division between a west end of mostly private, sometimes very affluent, housing and an east end of older Victorian property and large council housing estates. Interviewing or tracing trainees, we saw large contrasts in lifestyle. Professionals and managers mostly lived to the west and south, sometimes only temporarily located in Southwich's expanding offices, stores and factories. Equally typical of recent affluence were London commuters, and others benefiting from London's demand for workers to fill

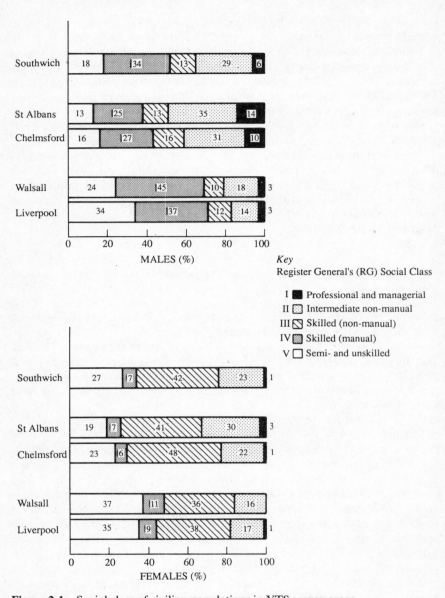

Figure 2.1   Social class of civilian populations in YTS survey areas

Source: Office of Population and Census Surveys, *Census, 1981: Small Area Statistics*, OPCS, London, 1981 and ESRC Data Archive, University of Essex

jobs up the line but nearer home. The local planning office estimates that 20 per cent of the employed population work outside Southwich.

But much of the population was disproportionately affected by changes in the local Southwich economy on which they still depended. Some of these, too, were 'middle-class', including some men and numerous married women in the town's many routine office jobs. And overlapping conventional middle and working classes were the self-employed, a group relatively prominent in South-East England (Central Statistical Office, 1988: 103, Table 9.6). Southwich had a variety of small builders, garage owners, plumbers, small shopkeepers and other trades, many prosperous but others merely 'getting by' during the recession. (According to a local training study, Southwich seems to have an unusually large proportion of small builders.) There were also a few 'skilled manual' households of traditional craft workers living in Victorian terraced houses around the remaining engineering works. But this still left a substantial minority living on the rapidly privatizing east end council estates, where there were more low-wage families. Some, having been hit by unemployment or other traumas, were so untypical of the affluent stereotype of South-East England that they might be described as 'disrupted' working-class.

Sixteen-year-old leavers, mostly with poor academic attainment, are all heavily dependent on their local economy, regardless of background (Ashton and Maguire, 1986). So inevitably, with such a large middle-class population, many lower-achieving middle-class children entered the labour market, and we therefore drew some of our trainees from smart suburbs and commuter villages. However, the overwhelming majority came from the less prestigious and poorer areas of the town.

Youth unemployment in Southwich, and the importance of YTS

As the recession began to bite in the mid-1970s, youth unemployment rose in Southwich, too. Concern first surfaced in 1975 when the Careers Service faced a sharp increase in the number of school leavers seeking jobs. By January 1982 the total of unemployed young people under 18 had risen fivefold, and it peaked even higher in September. By 1986, however, the numbers registered as unemployed were almost back to mid-1970s levels, and throughout the percentage of unemployed school leavers was kept well below the national average. In Great Britain in the mid-1980s about 25 per cent of school leavers became unemployed, but the Southwich rate never rose above 14 per cent, and it has since fallen to 5 per cent. This was partly due to Southwich having relatively more jobs for school leavers. Nationally about 35 per cent of school leavers went into full-time jobs in the mid-1980s (DE, 1987). DES methods of estimation put Southwich at over 40 per cent in 1986 and since then, in line with national trends, this proportion has increased.

Even so, well over half those who left Southwich schools during the early

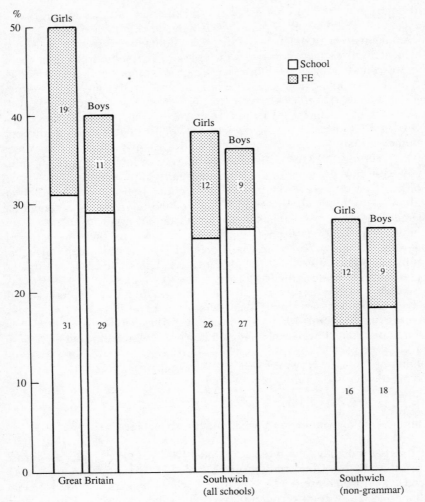

Figure 2.2 Staying-on rates for boys and girls – Great Britain and Southwich, 1984/5

Sources: Great Britain: *Employment Gazette*, September 1987, vol. 96, p. 9, Tables 2 and 3; Southwich: LEA estimates supplied by Southwich Careers Office

period of our research did so without what they would call 'real' jobs and they were absorbed by YTS instead. By comparison with similar areas, Southwich YTS grew disproportionately. The town fell among a group of local education authorities with school staying-on rates and examination pass levels far below what might be expected from their social composition (Gray and Jesson, 1987). When our main study began in 1984, only 37 per cent of Southwich pupils stayed on, a rate which fell to 34 per cent in 1985.

This was below the national average (Figure 2.2) and also that for surrounding areas. Nationally, girls have been more likely than boys to stay in full-time education of all kinds. In 1984–5, about half were in school or FE compared with only two-fifths of all boys. In Southwich, however, the proportions of boys and girls staying on in any kind of full-time education were fairly evenly balanced, because a relatively small percentage of girls joined the sixth form. But even FE enrolment, typically attracting many female vocational students, was down on the national figure.

Moreover, more than the average proportion of young people were leaving Southwich schools underqualified. In England in 1983–4, 22 per cent of 16-year-old school leavers had five or more higher-grade O level or CSE passes, and just over 55 per cent had at least one O level or equivalent (DES, 1986: Table 5). Yet in Southwich we estimated on information from the schools that at most 18 per cent of 1984 school leavers had five or more O levels or the equivalent, and only 48 per cent had at least one O level. These underqualified fifth-formers constituted 95 per cent of the 16-year-old school leavers coming onto the labour market, and they provided about the same proportion of YTS entrants.

Why were Southwich employers more prepared to offer school leavers YTS places than jobs? One possibility was young people's lack of skills. Education's shortcomings provided a major justification for the 'new vocationalism', the shift to work-relevant learning in the 1980s (Ranson, 1984). Employers and politicians have commonly complained about the poor calibre of school leavers, a situation which YTS was meant to remedy. Such criticisms of schools were echoed in Southwich, especially on public occasions such as the annual local industry/education conference. Privately, however, some employers admitted that schools were scapegoats for broader political and social problems.

The organization of schooling in Southwich was probably largely responsible for undereducation among its young people. A high use of private education can depress an LEA's published pass rates by missing many middle-class pupils who stay on, especially if they are educated away from the area (Gray and Jesson, 1987). In Southwich we could not check on the large number of privately-educated pupils, hardly any of whom turned up on YTS. But we suspected that undereducation was chiefly caused by the selective organization of Southwich's maintained secondary schools, which had been in operation throughout our trainees' school careers and which exaggerated the wide social differences between the town's east and west. At the top were two single-sex grammar schools and a more recent coeducational grammar school. This last has only now been absorbed into the nominally 'comprehensive' system which covers remaining Southwich pupils. In the 1960s Southwich Council exacerbated social and educational divisions by developing large one-class council estates (several with reputations for social problems or poverty), and all but one of the east end comprehensive schools were sited on these. The west end schools were surrounded by predominantly private housing.

Overall the 1984 staying-on rate for the three selective schools alone was 77 per cent. But at most only 11 per cent of that age group in Southwich had been offered a selective place, an intake of mainly middle-class children, a proportion of whom came from out of town. All other state secondary pupils attended one of eight large so-called comprehensive schools, whose average staying-on rate in 1984 was only 28 per cent, with a range from 15 to 50 per cent, reflecting the social composition of their catchments. A sensitive reorganization policy might have done something to decrease the educational divide, but the past 20 years have seen almost continuous controversy and resistance in the interests of preserving the top grammar schools. Only falling rolls finally forced rationalization into a sixth-form college, but still without the grammar schools, so keeping the new college relatively small. The old 'comprehensive' schools were drained of many of their best teachers by the new college, but in its favour there has been a leap in the numbers staying on. This now poses a strong threat to YTS (see Chapter 11).

Our postal survey of 1984 school leavers showed strong dissatisfaction with the preparation for work which their schooling had given them. The questionnaire included items from national studies designed to tap attitudes about the decision to leave school, and we also found a high proportion who, though not actively hostile, had merely tolerated secondary education and were now 'fed up with school', especially the classroom. The majority looked forward eagerly, if unrealistically, to *working*, to having a job and some money, and this is why they had left, often with a sense of relative failure which they had first developed at age 11.

Conclusion

This chapter has suggested that supporters of YTS exaggerate how far it represents a real break with the past tradition of leaving training to voluntarism and market forces. But continuity of policy need not necessarily prevent major change happening in practice, and at the beginning of YTS at least there was some extra cash available. Southwich offered an ideal test-bed for YTS's favoured employer-led training. It shared the national manufacturing decline, yet its economy had expanded, reflecting the consumer boom and services revolution of the 1980s. This has meant a generally more middle-class population. However, we found considerable social polarization; Southwich's young people seemed to be underachieving at school and leaving early. Unemployment among school leavers would have been far more serious without the rapid expansion of YTS which we describe in this book.

Chapter 3
YTS and Southwich College

For years, the main alternative for young people who become disenchanted with academic schooling has been full- or part-time vocational FE. The development of YTS, however, has had major consequences for the FE colleges, and Southwich College was no exception. Our research was initially based on the College which (like other FE institutions) expected a key role in the extension of training under YTS. Later, as the free-market element in the Scheme developed, the methods and focus of our enquiries had to change.

'Demand management': the vulnerability of FE to YTS

FE colleges were the acknowledged guardians of the traditions of externally-credentialled vocational education, and YTS could have built its new training on this foundation. However, the campaign to make education more responsive to employers' needs brought pressure on FE. And the reform of training by market forces meant undermining the FE monopoly, to create an employer-led largely private alternative and to force FE into more competitive marketing of its facilities. Even so, FE still provided a bench-mark against which the reforms must prove themselves.

Before the Second World War the colleges remained a neglected and self-contained sector of education, and the percentage who used FE to gain vocational credentials was comparatively small, mostly male and dependent on sponsorship by employers or parents. This underdevelopment of vocational education in England is directly connected with state voluntarism in youth training described in Chapter 2, because governments who viewed training as industry's task were also reluctant to fund technical education, and with a few exceptions industry was also unwilling to pay. After the war, partly under union pressure, a limited number of large firms began to support day release, but smaller manufacturers and much of the service sector remained indifferent (Lee, 1966). There was a modest expansion of technical education in the 1950s and 1960s but the system remained voluntary and fragmented.

As a result, further *education*, as a process with which FE staff could identify, always rested on insecure foundations. Their expertise in the plethora of vocational and technical syllabuses which had grown up over the years, was used to create a demand for credentials from organizations and individuals (Tipton, 1973). This form of 'demand management' arose because official funding was based on a points system which allocated resources on student numbers and especially on the ability of colleges to 'sell' higher-grade courses which would help to sustain a career structure for staff (Gleeson and Mardle, 1980: 175). So Further 'Education' became a label for the very mixed bag of tertiary work in a typical college. Well before YTS, day release, which once gave the FE system a *raison d'être* and sense of identity, had shrunk with the recession and decline in manufacturing. The first MSC programmes for the young unemployed provided some sort of substitute, though they required extensive curriculum initiatives and brought new kinds of students and staff. They also raised many difficult issues about the link between vocational education and social policy. (Lee, 1975; 1983).

With YTS the question of FE's future became critical. At first, when the *New Training Intiative* (MSC 1981a; 1981b) appeared it seemed highly likely that FE would play a major role. The MSC funded the colleges on a voluntary basis to put on 'super-YOP' or New Training Programmes in 1982–3. The colleges found and supervised work placements for un-employed young people, and provided 26 weeks' instruction off the job. This was said to be the prototype for YTS, and colleges were given every reason to believe that their heavy NTP involvement would continue. However, in the longer term FE was never likely to be able to provide enough placements and it was against the spirit of YTS to develop schemes through FE rather than the market. Moreover, the FE habit of associating 'quality' with credentials resulted in a tendency to fit YTS into existing course packages, but the course structures were often unwieldy and complex. This fed accusations that FE lacked flexibility and that syllabuses were out of touch with technical change and the deskilling of traditional craft skills in actual work (Stoney and Lines, 1987: 4–5).

Apart from YTS, FE staff were also anxious about the falling age group and the growth of rival sixth-form colleges. There were other new sources of pressure, too: central government intervention, which resulted in 25 per cent of course-funding being switched from LEA to MSC control; new development plans for individual colleges, jointly negotiated locally with the MSC; financial scrutiny by the National Audit Commission; the National Review of Vocational Qualifications; and the growth of 'open learning' packages which need no institutional base (NATFHE, 1986). Now ET has also appeared.

The colleges had some resources to fight back. Their tradition and participation in earlier programmes brought local knowledge and contacts for a nucleus of YTS work placements. FE remained vital in depressed areas, for disadvantaged young people, and where traditional industrial skills training is still important. But with YTS in full swing there was 'a distinct feeling among lecturers and principals alike that the MSC was making life difficult for colleges, pressurizing them to be accommodating to managing agents and to "sweep up" problem youngsters' (Stoney and Lines, 1987: 14). A widespread feeling developed that FE colleges and staff had been used and misled by MSC and then dropped (FEU, 1985).

YTS at Southwich College: the honeymoon with NTP

In 1983, Southwich College took the NTI very seriously from the outset, because it was faced by a double threat. There had been a decline in traditional day release which was only partly offset by new full-time vocational courses for the growing service sector. Plans for the new sixth-form college also threatened academic GCE work. It looked as though the College could not afford to ignore any new source of business.

In careful early negotiations, it was agreed with the lecturers' union, NATFHE, that no one would be forced to teach NTP trainees or to teach NTP only, so that new staff would be integrated into mainstream college work and there would be less threat of redundancies if NTP slacked off. Nevertheless there was mistrust. New staff would have to work outside the usual college year. Would the influx of the least able, a new kind of student with new problems, divert the College from its traditional role, especially when full YTS arrived? There was also a tinge of political suspicion of the MSC's growing power. But the College could not afford to ignore NTP, which then seemed to promise more jobs and a new relationship with employers.

NTP showed that training would depend on good co-operation between employers, the Careers Service and FE. Early guidance to colleges stressed the need for 'alternance', 'inter-agency negotiation' and establishing 'effective links between training and education on the one hand with the work system on the other' (FEU, 1985: para. 2.1). Except for ITB schemes, the students (not then trainees) were college-based and staff could view their role as integrating training with work experience, finding sponsors, maintaining links, and visiting 'their' students at work. Our early NTP survey of tutors, covering 48 sponsors and 75 trainees, reflects their satisfaction. They had themselves found and vetted the work placements, and predictably rated them favourably. Similarly, the tutors claimed good working relationships with employers, only nine being rated 'fairly reasonable' and two 'poor'. Employers' perceptions of the College and courses were said to be good.

But already there were problems. With MSC encouragement, various private employers (who later became managing agents) developed their own NTP programmes and gave their own trainees preferential treatment over any sponsorship for the College course. Much ambiguity surrounded the role of the Careers Service which, uncertain about its own future, seemed to be developing a role screening the applicants for courses. Careers was accused of trespassing on FE territory and sending the best applicants to private schemes. Difficulties in handling the centralized curricula of the ITB schemes prefigured later problems with MSC 'interference'.

Significantly, the hardest problem was controlling the quality of work experience. Twenty-one employers were using NTP, mostly for service jobs where there was no College tradition of training. This was expansion, but hardly any of it within the College's traditional expertise. Also most sponsoring firms were very small, and none was larger than 750 employees. Some were clearly taking advantage of NTP to substitute trainees for workers, sometimes for adults, but one-day release course was closed when five out of eleven sponsors substituted trainees for apprentices. Further, teachers' control varied even where specific work experience had been agreed. Only four firms accepted agreements about tasks trainees should *not* be given, and there were several reports of over-heavy discipline. Yet failure to integrate off-the-job training and work experience were seen merely as teething trouble which would be overcome in full YTS.

Half way through the year a change of direction by the MSC undermined the early optimism and altruism of FE participants in NTP. In Southwich as elsewhere, Mode A would predominate, and NTP would be run down or classed as Mode B. The College would now have to get most of its YTS work by negotiating with managing agents to provide their Mode A off-the-job training. In answer to our questionnaire, about two-thirds of the NTP staff showed their horror at losing 'their' students and the contact with employers necessary for integrated training. Loss of their key role meant they were faced with difficult negotiations, the rapid reworking of programmes, more disruptive and demotivated students, and competition from private training agencies. College officials saw the need for 'marketing' to protect jobs and possibly the whole institution. Yet later, by 1986 much privatization had occurred, and the College had lost not only newly-developed NTP schemes but also some training which had been the traditional prerogative of FE.

Demand management, 1980s style

YTS brought changed relationships, where tutors found they could only deal with work sponsors through the managing agents who were often newly-established and inexperienced. Some dismissed FE expertise, others recognized the pioneering work in NTP programmes – though in several cases only to 'poach' ideas and sometimes staff for their own competing training packages. Any integrative role was now exercised indirectly by the MSC. The College gradually shifted to overt demand management and marketing, but the value of FE training was openly questioned, and the new 'market' remained highly-fragmented and unstable. NTP experience could not be carried over directly into YTS because funding was changed, the training period was halved, and Southwich FE staff now found that course administration, day length, number and size of groups, blocks, classroom versus workshop and practical content, even the curriculum, were all at issue. These had to be negotiated, approved and set up at breakneck speed for the start of YTS in the autumn of 1983, despite a standstill on MSC decisions during the general election.

To make matters worse, the College became caught in crossfire between the MSC and some of the managing agents, and there were delays in setting up the Area Manpower Boards (AMBs) which had to approve off-the-job training. In interviews staff were sceptical about how far the MSC and the Area Manpower Board controlled the managing agents either then or later. They felt the AMB was too ready to back privatized training outside the College, threatening standard FE courses.

The College's uneasy transition to overt marketing of courses could be seen most clearly in the joint meetings between FE staff, the MSC and the managing agents. Early in YTS these were hosted by the College with the agents invited as junior partners. There was discussion of how the College should adapt the structure of its existing schemes to enable YTS to fit in. But the underlying issue was how far the traditional system, geared to vocational credentials for better-motivated and more able students, could and should be adapted for undermotivated and disadvantaged YTS trainees. Dialogue became bogged down in complex administrative detail; whether the College could produce a modular scheme to fit the varied starting and finishing dates; different occupancy policies and levels; the point at which to introduce off-the-job training and the form it should take; and whether the College could stream trainees by ability to fit courses with different levels of credentials. There is little wonder that the College came to appear inflexible, especially to managing agents with little knowledge of FE.

In further FE interviews in 1985, key YTS staff felt that the College had achieved some standing, the MSC and the AMB did *not* give automatic approval, and the managing agents whose schemes passed most easily were companies with a training tradition linked to FE and an understanding of the College. Staff also felt that the College's efforts under NTP had given credibility to the new non-traditional training. They were drawn into a brief partnership with managing agents who had taken control of 'our' courses, although these managing agents soon began to cut themselves loose.

College staff had built up relationships with MSC field staff during NTP and through the College's remaining Mode B courses, and they felt that through these they could still exercise some indirect control over on the job training, especially during the annual AMB renewal of contracts. The process was indirect and subtle. There were 'certain things you can't say to the managing agent' but instead the tutor would 'provoke questions from an MSC field officer and suggest problems . . . Usually they were dealt with effectively . . .

The MSC's work behind the scenes with managing agents is not apparent except where the problem is solved or the managing agent is withdrawn.'

Tutors felt that encouraging MSC field staff to use them as sources of sensitive and responsible intelligence enhanced the College's role in maintaining training standards. However, they were reluctant to criticize managing agents for fear of worsening the College's longer-term bargaining position. By 1985, staff had come to see integration as 'not my business', and shrugged their shoulders even where intervention might have helped their students. They deeply resented the managing agents' role: 'They stand between us and the sponsors . . . Do we really need them?' They also felt that the managing agents had lost control of training at the placements. Bad placements dropped by one agent would be picked up by newly-arrived schemes competing for sponsors. And tutors felt that schemes nominally in the same occupational area provided work experience of vastly different quality.

Not surprisingly, with three-way leaks of information and rumour about how each agency was performing, mutual suspicion developed and relationships sometimes became very delicate. College staff felt they were used as scapegoats by managing agents and field staff. And in their urgency to expand YTS, field staff and managing agents criticized the College for elitism and being too inflexible to adapt to their less academic and disadvantaged trainees. The changing balance of relationships meant that the College was now discouraged from hosting the meetings of the MSC and the managing agents. Later the College had no representative at the managing agents' meetings. These were now arranged, hosted and chaired by the most successful managing agent on his own premises, where his friendly relationship with the MSC was clear to see. And, in fact, at these meetings without FE staff there was criticism of the College. The MSC encouraged managing agents to hold a separate meeting of work sponsors and FE tutors, but in one instance, out of 30 sponsors invited, 'Five said they would come and one did [and] we heard the College slated'.

The College's contacts with employers began to reflect a hierarchy in its market situation in relation to YTS. Relationships with the larger employers, traditional customers who now had YTS schemes, remained good if sometimes indirect. For ITB schemes, tutors had a list of employers but no guidance on making contact. Smaller schemes sent a few trainees to 'infill' College classes, and tutors were sometimes unsure who the trainees' managing agents and work sponsors were. Managing agents of small-firm schemes were most likely to tell staff that work experience was 'none of your business', and a tutor who visited work placements without telling the managing agent said: 'I got my knuckles rapped'. At first tutors claimed they could learn about placements from the log books filled in by trainees or from trainees themselves: 'We knew they were in bad places'. But later, tutors began to opt out: 'I don't like to ask students: they will hang placements and the College in the same breath'. 'Everyone is afraid of demonstrating what a can of worms the job training is.' So by the beginning of YTS 2, most College staff had stopped trying to exert any control over training at the work placement or its integration with College training.

Tutors and trainees in FE

Lack of integration between FE and work experience became a common problem everywhere, and poor motivation and discipline problems were widespread (Stoney and Lines, 1987). Southwich College's alleged inflexibility and mishandling of trainees gave managing agents, with the connivance of MSC, a rationale for 'breaking loose from the public sector' to develop their own off-the-job training. Independent research from this period tended to see the problems as 'managerial', arising out of poor selection and induction, poor placements and lack of managing agent support, or to lay the blame on the low ability and anti-school ethos of the trainees. Our Southwich study suggest that the underlying problem was the way NTP and YTS took relationships between tutors and trainees out of College control and exposed them to economic pressure.

The role of the Careers Service in selection had always been ambiguous. In 1982 large numbers of unemployed young people had to be processed quickly for NTP but even later, when things settled down, FE tutors and the Careers Service never agreed common criteria for admission. Thus, under YTS, tutors lost any influence over selection to the managing agents, who operated diverse criteria and made varied use of the Careers Service. As a result, one common FE course could serve schemes with trainees of very varied ability and motivation, and in most cases it became impossible to match trainees' needs with an appropriate style and content of teaching. Nor could material be modified much to suit the classroom situation for, as prescribed by the MSC, some courses used syllabuses leading to recognized qualifications and all trainees were supposed to receive classes in social and life skills. So tutors were stuck with a curriculum which could antagonize the trainees by seeming irrelevant. Managing agents complained in turn that the College was not geared to trainees' specific needs.

Classroom observations over two years suggested that tutors' relations with trainees followed the hierarchy of the College's relationships with various schemes. Courses built on traditional skills training went more smoothly, even though some failed to match workplace practice because of the demands of external assessment. The trainees (who were more like students) met with scepticism from employers and supervisors, but, as with traditional day release, 'learning to do things properly at college' was accepted as leading to a marketable qualification. However, where there had previously been little or no training tradition, the College's pioneering attempts were resisted, especially after employer-based YTS replaced college-based NTP. Topic by topic and lesson after lesson, students challenged the lack of fit with their work, and tutors' authority was always precarious. For example, part of a BEC General retailing course was a lesson on sales techniques aimed mainly at budding store managers rather than the shop-floor work done by the trainees. Trainees listened until the tutor introduced a discussion of goods none expected to sell during YTS, when their attention immediately wandered. Even traditional training might be challenged. Motor vehicle trainees complained their workshop tasks at College were not 'real work' and they wanted 'real cars to mend'.

The common element running through bad feeling in the early classes was young people's ambiguous and insecure status. YTS had brought the College not students but 'trainees' who were anxious about their immediate job prospects and confused by the overlapping functions of the College, managing agents, their employers and the Careers Service. Although tutors tried to call them 'students', from the start MSC regulations and the College's administrative divisions highlighted the trainees' invidious status of being neither full-time students nor in work. Even being unemployed was less ambiguous. Because NTP and YTS tried to simulate 'real work', tutors and trainees worked a 48-week year, parts of it when others were on holiday. The College could try to do something about poor canteen facilities and lack of heating. However, they could not combat the trainees' and tutors' sense of stigma, and the otherness of teaching in special huts erected by the MSC. Even a group of conformist clerical trainees whom staff rated 'very nice girls' were upset. Similarly, a group of boys rated 'not a bad lot on the whole, kicked up a fuss when two women administrators regularly interrupted their Friday afternoon class to dole out the small training allowances, often with errors and 'stinginess' in travel expenses and with MSC deductions for bad behaviour or absenteeism. The tutor complained that after these visits the group became uncontrollable 'for at least 20 minutes and sometimes for the whole afternoon'. Resisting the sense of powerlessness by 'mucking about' was one way the trainees could keep their self-respect but it led to their being labelled 'trouble', and tutors' frayed tempers lowered their morale still further.

Trainees' anxieties about jobs were the most important factor outside College control. Traditional FE students also depend on employer sponsorship and worry about work, but the early NTP trainees were very pessimistic about rising *unemployment* and saw training as only a poor alternative to a real job. Their job prospects seemed low and they (rightly, as it turned out) believed many employers had taken them on merely out of altruism 'to give them a start' or as cheap temporary labour. Classes were disrupted by rapid turnover and contact with the College was transient because trainees seized the first job that came along. Those left at College grew more anxious for work and disrupted teaching, taking neither College nor their work placements seriously. Tutors complained that high unemployment lowered morale all round, preventing sustained exam work and undermining any attempt at a year's integrated training with progress in further study.

The NTP philosophy of 'a job at any price' persisted into YTS, but YTS trainees seemed more optimistic about their chances of jobs from their work placements. Possibly employers had changed and begun to use YTS as a 'long interview'; in addition, managing agents pushed the new enterprise philosophy and exhorted trainees to effort and conformity to enable them to 'work themselves into a job'. Yet trainees still puzzled over the link between their placements and the managing agent whom they scarcely saw after the initial interview and whom they associated with the College. And as the most visible symbol of YTS, the College tended to be blamed for any shortcomings in the schemes. The tutor had no carrot in the form of a job to offer the trainees, who strongly identified with their employer against the College, even though their work placement was generally low-skilled and boring. Placements were referred to as 'me job' and College teaching not linked with their limited work experience was 'boring' and 'a waste of time'. These young people had not entered the labour market to be made to sit in classrooms, and the most frequent and damning criticism of College was that it was 'just like school'. In some ways it was worse, 'At least at school you could be out and home by quarter past five. Here it takes ages to get home and you don't leave till seven'. As one trainee put it: 'Work is real, college isn't.'

The College fighting 'with one arm behind our back'

A senior member of staff described the College as 'fighting with one arm behind our back' in its dealings with other agencies, because of the restrictive policies of the local education authority. In December 1982 all LEAs had agreed a national scale of fees for off-the-job training under Mode A YTS. Assuming that YTS would attract large numbers away from conventional FE, authorities planned to subsidize their colleges from this surplus, offering managing agents a third off fees. But this shift failed to happen, and many local authorities came under pressure from government cuts and rate-capping. Only those authorities with too few managing agents still offered generous subsidies, while the rest became less willing or able to do so.

Senior College staff felt Southwich County's withdrawal of subsidy was the cause of a fall in trainees and contact hours (see Table 3.1), as managing agents cut costs by reducing their use of FE or going private altogether. Some began to do their own training, while others bought training below College rates from new private training agencies which sprang up to cater for YTS. Managing agents also tried to cut out the more expensive College workshops, asking instead for simulations. The College tried to respond by shifting resources from regular FE courses to YTS, so as 'not to let the College down' for fear the MSC might complain or managing agents withdraw.

Not understanding LEA financial constraints, MSC field staff and managing agents blamed the College for trying to profiteer from YTS. Yet ironically the LEA's tight budgetary control of the College's work brought fresh problems. Contact hours and 'over-teaching' in regular FE courses

Table 3.1   Number of YTS (NTP) schemes and
trainees, Southwich College, 1983–7

Year	Schemes	Trainees
1983–4	14	630
1984–5	19	642
1985–6	16	585
1986–7	12	372

were cut back. And the fall in income from YTS meant that staff specially employed to cope with new trainees from the College's early success were now underemployed. The resulting budget deficit threatened the whole College. LEA policy had thus driven YTS business away at the same time as it created the need for more College involvement. The College responded by proposing that they or the LEA should become a Mode A managing agent, which would provide a secure source of trainees. But we were told that 'The LEA got cold feet' after 'an over-vigorous marketing stance [*sic*] initially'. Southwich College was not allowed to become its own managing agent, and in fact few FE Colleges have done so (FEU, 1985).

The financial crisis led to further friction between College staff and managing agents who tried to economize by cutting corners in traditional FE practice. Because fees were paid for 'course hours', managing agents tried to cut the time spent in the College, increase group sizes, cut the number of groups, and fill any new vacancies continuously (so-called 'roll-on'). Courses like these under the auspices of BTEC and leading to exams could be defended. But ironically the most vulnerable courses were those first designed by the College for new areas under NTP which were not backed by exams.

Even some FE courses leading to credentials became vulnerable because the vocational exam boards (chiefly the City and Guilds of London and the Royal Society of Arts) had changed their traditional policies and given some larger training agencies the status of accredited centres for the lower levels of their certificates (*Times Educational Supplement*, 20 February 1987). The sudden switch surprised and alarmed College staff because it struck at the heart of FE, the monopoly of exam preparation on which rested the College's expertise. It was also seen as threatening standards, and staff were bitter about the exam boards' financial opportunism: 'FE teachers would be concerned that they don't ask questions as to the quality of teaching staff [in private agencies]; if it means more people taking the exams then the boards say "Whizzo for us!" '

One event was traumatic. A private motor vehicle training association gained accredited status and pulled its trainees out, killing a large course in a traditional FE area. The College complained via the LEA, but felt that the reply from the exam board showed indifference to the educational consequences of private training for its exams. The College claimed that the training association had been too stretched to cover all the practical work and needed to send trainees to FE again for some of their training. Years later, memories of the episode left the College still paranoid about private training.

Conclusion

Part One has outlined the MSC's attempt to make training more efficient by introducing market forces. In practice the attempt to make FE vocational training more responsive to employers' needs caused much bitterness and disillusionment. Some tutors felt the administration had not backed them. Others prejudged the trainees as 'not our kind of student'. A few classes were simply not well run. But primarily the move failed because FE had accumulated from past policies a system of rules and a logic which was quite different from the market. Inflexibility was mainly a result of the external constraints that both LEA and YTS policy put on the College. Ironically the result was to squeeze or even kill off the new low-skill training developed to meet the MSC's plans but which no one outside the College valued. Overall, YTS had weakened the College and offered little in return; a marginal expansion in experimental courses, a role cut back to schemes like traditional FE courses, and filling gaps in the private structure. The best senior YTS staff could hope for was that 'things may settle down and we shall be back to providing traditional FE with two-year YTS'. By the end of YTS 1 in late 1986 the College was discussing with the LEA whether to pull out of YTS altogether. Momentum in youth training had moved outside the FE system, to the managing agents and private trainers whose activities we will now describe.

Part Two
Demand and inequality
in a
surrogate labour market

Chapter 4
MSC intervention and established training

While publicly-funded vocational education in Southwich was under fire, the MSC was urgently opening up training to the impact of market forces by creating YTS schemes and placements, mostly in private firms. Part Two describes the development of YTS in Southwich and explores how the demand for young people's labour was created. In particular, we ask whether the various schemes and placements offered young people equal opportunities of training and jobs.

In Chapter 2 we outlined our concept of the 'surrogate labour market', the network of training and work placements which resulted from the MSC's administrative intervention in the real youth labour market. This chapter begins by describing the administration of the YTS subsidy, through which the MSC intervened to try to change employers' recruitment strategies. We then look at some of the outcomes of YTS nationally and locally, that is, the actual mix of modes and schemes which emerged in the YTS surrogate labour market. The remainder of this chapter and the next will focus on how various types of employer and managing agent used YTS in quite different ways, with very unequal consequences for young people. In Chapter 6 we look at the MSC's problems in controlling training on the job, concluding with a suggested model for understanding segmentation and inequality in the YTS surrogate labour market.

The administrative structure of YTS

MSC intervention was designed to remedy the problem that British training tends to respond only to the short-term demands of production. Also, the recession had greatly reduced apprentice and trainee numbers. So YTS was essentially an attempt to make young people's labour more attractive so as to boost recruitment, especially among the larger firms. The MSC's role was

to fund and monitor a set of 'state franchises' (Chandler and Wallace, 1989).
YTS had to be sold to likely 'work sponsors' who would provide placements
for jobless school leavers. The 'carrot' was the YTS training subsidy together with any production from the trainees' free labour, less any training
costs. In return the MSC wanted some surveillance over the 'black box' of
workplace training and the release of trainees for training off the job.

A variety of employers and organizations came forward or were enlisted
as 'managing agents'; they arranged training both on and off the job in different skill areas. (These skill areas, ranges of occupations which supposedly
had a common core of 'transferable' skills, were initially called 'occupational
training families' (OTFs), but the concept was difficult to sustain and the
MSC later changed the name to training occupational categories or TOCs.)
The range of skill areas and the number and size of schemes within them was
set by the MSC, with the help of predictions from the Careers Service as to
the likely numbers and capacities of young school leavers. These MSC
'quotas' of trainees in different skill areas were intended to cover a dual purpose. *Ideally* they would be fixed to meet estimates of employers' training
needs, but they also had to mop up any unemployed young people. In practice, however, there was no reason why these two estimates should match,
and indeed the gap between them was part of the reason for MSC intervention.

Despite frequent changes in MSC regulations, these quotas remained the
basis of payment on which managing agents tried to recruit enough suitable
trainees to fill their schemes to an economic level. The economic level was
influenced by the changing costs of equipment, tuition and accreditation of
any vocational credentials. But it also depended on whether the managing
agent was an employer using YTS merely to subsidize investment in the
future productivity of the firm's own recruits, or a 'training entrepreneur'
who hoped to make a profit from YTS training grants. The MSC's bargaining position also varied according to whether it faced employers with established facilities and a tradition of training or whether it was setting up YTS
among industries and employers with no tradition, training staff or facilities
to build upon.

The YTS blueprint implied that most schemes would be *employer-led*, run
by larger employers acting as their own managing agents, with training in-
house taking advantage of existing training traditions and facilities. Indeed,
the very largest were given special arrangements to negotiate their quotas of
placements and trainees nationally with MSC's Large Companies Unit
(LCU). These LCU schemes (LCUs) include multi-plant manufacturers,
British Rail, the clearing banks and household-name chain stores. But this
left plenty of large employers still dealing only with local MSC offices. As a
further incentive to big firms, an 'additionality rule' was introduced which
paid training allowances for five trainees for every two young people the employer would normally have recruited. As well as a managing agent's fee and
the benefit of five 'free' trainees, additionality allowed larger employers the
choice of keeping the best trainees at the end of YTS.

Yet not all YTS schemes could be high-skill training with big firms. Some skills (such as hairdressing or building) typically exist mostly in small firms. The government also argued that training *should* be extended to new areas with no training tradition. To bridge these gaps, additional *employment-based* training was organized in 'umbrella' schemes. Here managing agents, not necessarily employers themselves, subcontract 'work providers' or 'sponsors' (mainly smaller firms) to provide the necessary training placements. The agents also arrange for training off the job. As well as local umbrella schemes there are nationally-organized LCU 'multiple' umbrella schemes covering large and small employers in particular industries. Some are run by the remaining ITBs, such as the Hotels and Catering Industry and the Construction Industry Training Boards (HCITB and CITB). There are also large private 'multiples' which cover small employers in, for example, the motor vehicle or hairdressing trades.

Together, these employer-led schemes and employment-based umbrella schemes provided most placements under what used to be called Mode A. However, the extent of the national shortfall of MSC's favoured employer-led schemes is revealed by MSC's own research. In the first year of YTS, 58 per cent of trainees were in subcontracted placements, and even by 1988 barely 20 per cent of trainees were in employer-led schemes; most YTS placements still seem to be in small firms (DE, 1985b: 310; Gray and King, 1986: 9; Deakin and Pratten, 1987; MSC 1989: 14).

Public sector involvement came from large public employers who participated under Mode A, and from the alternative Mode B schemes which subsidized depressed areas and disadvantaged young people. (Mode B schemes were also run by local authorities as well as charities, voluntary organizations or even private trainers.) Although not favoured in the YTS blueprint, local authorities still provide 25 per cent of all YTS placements either in-house or subcontracted.

Southwich surrogate labour market under YTS 1

We will now describe the mix of YTS schemes, managing agents, and Modes which emerged in Southwich's surrogate labour market between 1984 and 1986 under YTS 1. The MSC's ability to shape the distribution of YTS schemes and places was severely constrained. For one thing it lacked the right information, having been criticized at national level for being unable to state precisely what skill training needs exist (National Audit Office, 1985). In Southwich, local staff were no better placed to predict the numbers and the kinds of young workers upon which Southwich's future economic development might depend. Very few local planning statistics were available (see Appendix) and the speed of industrial change made these unreliable. As a result the MSC could divide up its YTS target into quotas for different occupational skills only very crudely on broad regional estimates, mainly using the Careers Service's survey of fifth-form pupils' leaving intentions. Also, the lack of co-ordination between LCU schemes (who negotiate with MSC at national level) and Southwich's local MSC staff, caused further mismatching. It is only recently that the Training Agency (formerly the MSC) in Southwich has begun to develop more sophisticated ways of estimating local labour needs.

Furthermore, despite all the YTS rhetoric of employers' and young people's 'needs', everywhere the early expansion of demand for young trainees was powered by two factors. There was the commercial interest of local employers and managing agents which induced them to participate in YTS. But there was also the government's need to get school leavers off the unemployment register. The national shortfall of large-firm places left the MSC with the urgent problem of expanding YTS to mop up the remaining unemployed. Resources had to be concentrated most on high-unemployment areas to provide more costly Mode B placements. This left only a relatively low level of subsidy for areas like Southwich, where restrictions were placed on Mode B and placements were mostly funded under Mode A (Turbin, 1988: 176).

In 1984 the Southwich MSC staff aimed to recruit trainees for a quota of about 1300 places (the large majority in or near Southwich). By mid-1986 they planned a YTS intake of over 1600. But the surrogate labour market which emerged in Southwich between 1984 and 1986 was even further than nationally from MSC hopes for training with large employers in scarce transferable skills. Although Southwich was enjoying a boom in consumer and financial services it had virtually no big industries (see Chapter 2). As a result, while the town had as high a proportion of employer-led *schemes*, individually these were small and offered few *placements*, only one scheme even reaching 30. Even if we include LCU schemes Southwich had at most 10 per cent of placements in-house with larger employers.

In addition, there were some umbrella schemes, which we will call 'stable-skill', which continued to offer relatively prestigious training in one or at most two skill areas. These stayed about the same size or expanded only slowly. Among the four stable-skill schemes were two of the old ITBs, the CITB and HCITB (recruiting regionally but with probably only about 20 local placements). There was also a private craft federation of hairdressers with about 50 places, and the Chamber of Commerce offered training in the 'quasi-craft' of clerical work, and also retail training, for up to 150 trainees. Together these stable-skill schemes made up around a quarter of local training places.

In contrast, other more 'entrepreneurial' managing agents had taken on a range of fresh skills and expanded remarkably. By 1986 the largest had quotas contracted from the MSC to provide training in a range of skills for well over 400 trainees, and another had a similarly varied quota to train over 200. Altogether, the three biggest entrepreneurial managing agents were contracted to provide almost half the local YTS training places. However, two other entrepreneurial schemes covering a variety of skills, and a church-based care scheme, all with less than 50 places, had struggled and closed by the first full year of YTS 2 in 1987.

Southwich's 20 per cent of Mode B placements was below the national average, but though well below the most depressed regions it was still above prosperous areas where YTS has become peripheral. Also, in Southwich among the Mode A umbrella schemes were two care schemes, run by a church and an entrepreneur, which elsewhere might have been Mode B. This was a result of local restrictions on Mode B. The town lacked a local authority Mode A scheme, and although locally Southwich County's Mode B scheme was relatively large, at around 200 places, its entry was severely restricted. Instead, a 40-place Mode B scheme was being run by an entrepreneur.

Finally, Southwich schemes also contrasted with the national picture because few were under single managing agents. Nationally, early in YTS managing agents tended to run schemes under only one skill label, providing at least some of their own work placements. Only one in three specialized in training, under half commercially (DE, 1985a: 308). In contrast, in Southwich by 1984 most managing agents ran several schemes covering more than one skill label. By the end of 1986 the expansion of the entrepreneurial schemes meant that out of 19 managing agents (excluding LCUs) only eight ran schemes in one skill only and three covered two skills. The rest covered a variety of skill labels, including some multiple schemes with a doubtful common core and a variety of levels from apprenticeship downwards.

We had initially hoped to compare YTS opportunities according to whether they were based on established or new skills. However, although, as we shall see, this distinction is important, in YTS it covered a number of overlapping factors whose effect we have tried to analyse, such as size of firm giving training, the distinction between traditional apprentice crafts and other jobs, and the type of managing agent. Also, traditional skill labels ('engineering', 'clerical', 'retail') were being adopted in a variety of new contexts. There were no fewer than eight schemes with the label 'clerical', six 'retail', four 'engineering', three (and also Mode B) in 'construction' and 'care', two (and also Mode B) in 'catering', and so on. Of the 'engineering' and 'clerical' schemes, several were employer-led, but others were run by entrepreneurs or came under Mode B.

Consequently, the relative value of these various schemes under common skill labels became a further focus of our research. In particular, the large employers and the stable-skill and entrepreneurial managing agents appeared to participate in YTS in quite distinctive ways. In the remainder of this chapter and the next we describe the implications of this pattern of participation for the quality of training and the job prospects offered to trainees under the different types of scheme and skill label.

Restricted recruitment by the larger employers

Large company unit employer-led schemes

Southwich had no really big manufacturing plants belonging to one of the national corporations in the LCU. The local LCU employer-led schemes

were mainly well-known retailing chains or service organizations. Although
LCU schemes make an appreciable national contribution to YTS, local
trainee numbers, as in Southwich, are often small, restricted to twos and
threes to suit recruitment needs assessed at branch level. In some cases
trainees were rather isolated and local management seemed unaware of
YTS requirements, merely slotting trainees into conventional day release
courses at Southwich College. But generally these hand-picked trainees
enjoyed superior prospects and pay. Of ten LCU schemes in Southwich,
nine averaged only three trainees. Only the Post Office had a larger scheme,
and here union pressure had secured employed YTS status and full
probationary pay for all trainee postmen.

Our later research strongly suggested that LCU schemes led by large
employers or ITBs should be clearly distinguished from some of the LCU
'multiple' schemes which are umbrella schemes for small firms (for example,
hairdressers and garages) where there is usually much less commitment to
training and job prospects are poor.

The larger Southwich employers: three engineering firms

Seven larger Southwich employers became 'local' managing agents: three
engineering firms, the headquarters of an insurance company, and three
department stores. For a variety of reasons, almost all had now adopted
limited recruitment strategies.

The three engineering firms used YTS for recruitment, carefully adapting
it to their different market situations. The 'softener' of the YTS subsidy had
been eagerly taken to resuscitate apprenticeship schemes hit by the squeeze.
The managing agents claimed that it did not fully compensate them for the
fact that they invested between £1000 and £5000 per head annually in
apprentices and they all complained of accountants' pressures to economize
on training. YTS was a 'fringe benefit' (unlike the largest entrepreneurial
scheme, Jack's, which one managing agent described as 'running a
business'). The AMB had never insisted they take truly 'additional' trainees:
'They played it flexibly, they evened it across the country.'

Bolts, a small specialist firm with the highest costs, used to train surplus
apprentices and keep the best. Now this seemed a 'luxury . . . all the lads are
taken on against a job'. A few outside trainees were taken on for economies
of scale, but these, too, were sponsored apprentices from close associates.
After delicate negotiations the other two firms, Cutters and Thrusters, had
used YTS to switch from four-year craft apprentices to fewer two-year
technician engineers, resisting union pressures to employ more trainees and
top up YTS pay. The largest firm, Cutters, still also had four-year
apprentices and at first the union insisted they were 'not having it, cheap
labour, short-term apprenticeships'. Eventually, as a compromise, a few
first-year trainees were given employed YTS status after six months. The
unions were told: 'If we don't have YTS . . . we won't have anything.'

For their carefully-targeted trainees the firms aimed to select very carefully: 'We've established over the years what we're looking for. It would be foolish to ignore all that just because you have to take everybody who's warm!' They drew on virtually a common pool of direct applications, some from far afield: 'You're looking at a job and that's a bit of a magnet.' Accordingly, there was agreement not to poach, firms who did being sent the bill for training. The firms mistrusted schools as too academic, even TVEI, but still used the applicants' school *courses* and predicted results to screen for different skill levels, apprentice technicians needing four or five relevant O levels. Careers were expected to refer only O-level applicants (a requirement partly set by FE off-the-job training). Applicants were also aptitude-tested and interviewed for motivation, 'persistence', 'a bit of spark', self-discipline, technical hobbies, family links with engineering, and parental support. Not surprisingly, suitable applicants were said to be scarce, and as a matter of sound business these firms took a close paternal interest in their trainees.

The firms also ran small clerical schemes for which trainees needed O-level English (but not the typing usually taught to lower streams). Cutters used YTS to subsidize its existing two-year secretarial training which gave access to internal jobs, and high staff turnover meant that most trainees were taken on. Again the 'MSC understood' why they took no 'additional' trainees. They would not buy more equipment and, in addition, would not 'go too far down the road of using cheap labour' (and annoying the unions). Cutters had relaxed selection because the MSC was 'adamant that you took a mixed ability proportion', but in fact the firm needed a range of routine clerical workers and still reserved 'the right to refuse any applicant who might not fit'. The other two firms offered fewer internal jobs, but claimed that trainees were certain of work elsewhere.

An insurance company

Endowments, an affluent insurance company, had also taken the YTS subsidy even though 'Within the company [the cost of training] will be buried . . . If we could put a figure on [trainees' production] of course, the company would be quids in . . . I think the company saw YTS as a chance to take school leavers again . . . I suppose we can mould them to our way of operating.' The stream of in-house trainees usually gained internal jobs with employed YTS status and topped-up pay, some within a month and almost all within the first year. There had been no problems with unions: 'They know it won't jeopardize any existing jobs; and of course they see the success, and how most of them get taken on . . . By the time I retire virtually the whole firm will be staffed by YTS!'

To make up a full job for the managing agent (a redeployed executive) the firm had an extra stream of trainees placed out-of-house with small employers. But these were not truly additional: 'I separate the groups from the start . . . The terms and conditions are so different'.

The in-house stream was as highly selected as the engineering trainees. To bypass the complexity of MSC's eligibility rules, the managing agent used the Careers Service to sort out his flood of direct applications and to recruit to his specifications for the out-of-house placements: 'In a sense the Careers Service were doing our advertising for us. Also we're one of the largest employers in the town and if youngsters are thinking of clerical work, they'll think of us.' To match the firm's recruitment criteria and use of FE courses, the in-house trainees were asked for five predicted O-level passes. The MSC's objections had been countered by the logic of the market: 'I know if I take a youngster on with no O levels, if we have vacancy the chances are that the departmental manager won't even interview him.' Even so, these personally- or pre-selected qualified applicants were further screened: 'They've got to be reasonably articulate. Don't look like the back end of a bus, fit in with the company image.' The only trainee from an east end school was last year's head girl.

The out-of-house placements were often in Southwich's top professional and financial offices which some well-qualified trainees preferred. Expanding small firms took on one or even two trainees each year, and job chances (if not promotion) were good. The out-of-house trainees need not necessarily be well-qualified or even very intelligent. Selection was 'more for personality, but articulate'. A local printer had wanted somebody who was 'capable but not clever.' The managing agent said the attractiveness of all his schemes meant he had to be careful to avoid accusations of poaching.

Three retail firms: a prestige department store

Three retail firms illustrate how the same skill label may cover schemes very different in character and prospects. Flourishes, a top department store, was heavily committed to staff training, and initially took 'additional' trainees on the YTS model. However, pressures from both staff and customers soon led to the scheme being cut back. Staff resented the trainees swamping their facilities and the fact that YTS gave better training than they had had. In addition, 'It looked as though the whole store was going to be run by young people!'

The scheme was later reduced to a third because 'we aim to absorb all the people we take on the scheme . . . Our policy is to employ them as soon as possible . . . If they're doing the job they might as well have the proper rate.' Employed YTS status was offered but resisted in favour of an ordinary job by trainees as well as departmental managers. However, opportunities for trainees were becoming scarcer. 'We look carefully before we fill the vacancy with a full-timer, but we have to give leeway because some YTS trainees are so good . . . They've increased the turnover to the point where the concession warrants taking on another person.'

This was another popular scheme which drew many direct applications: 'If they want retail, they either want to go to Marks and Spencers – but they take only three – or us.' The store also sent application forms to the two most middle-class west end comprehensives. The managing agent did a quick preliminary screening of the applications: 'I usually like them to be doing CSE in Maths and English at least, and if they've got a few more O levels, well and good.' Then, in the interviews, 'What I'm looking for is a spark. . .'.

Southwich Co-operative Society

After their involvement with YOP, Southwich Co-operative Society had been wary of YTS. However, 'We've always seen the need to . . . help provide training for the low achievers . . . If anyone was into it we ought to get involved as part of the Labour movement.' With an eye on their union closed shop the Co-op intended to use YTS only to recruit staff, through a hybrid in- and out-of-house scheme which covered its main store and scattered rural branches. Trainees had employed YTS status in the training branch, but were later taken on for specific jobs by individual managers. Costs were subsidized out of the local training budget and by residential courses at the national staff training college.

At first recruitment had suffered. 'The teachers used to say . . . "You can always work at the Co-op or Woolworths!" . . . [Retail] was always a sort of dustbin.' However, 'It's not necessarily the qualifications that you want in retail. It's personality and interest.' The managing agent reluctantly screened by appearance: 'If somebody comes along with long hair and earrings through their nose and ears . . . we've got to live with the public's perception that that's not the right person.' In 1984 the Co-op trainees were noticeably more boisterous than the well-behaved trainees from top schemes. But by 1986 (to the managing agent's discomfort) recruitment policy was tighter because they now used distance learning for training, and they were trying to retain more trainees. Too few applications came directly or from advertising, so the scheme drew on the Careers Service, but the managing agent still refused to select by school courses or to take applicants with poor motivation. He contrasted his behaviour with the entrepreneurs 'whose business is training. They've got to keep bodies on seats . . . But in our case . . . we'd rather have ten who're interested.'

He complained that branch managers resisted YTS and tended to regard trainees as inferior, advising the best to leave and preferring to appoint outside the scheme. So overall, the Co-op scheme's attempt at selectivity clashed with its low pulling power, and its occupancy was restricted to less than half its MSC contracted quota.

A precarious department store

Because of its precarious financial situation, Concessions was the only employer-led scheme taking trainees truly 'additional' to recruitment needs. The store was mostly let to concessionaires, and the managing agent thought the firm's motive for entering YTS had been 'the money!'. Numbers had been set for one full-time supervisor, the scheme did its own off-the-job training and any costs were offset by trainees' work. Even so, the directors 'distinctly [didn't] want to be bothered'. Here, too, there had been staff hostility when their facilities became swamped by trainees. Because this was effectively a sort of 'internal' umbrella scheme for the concessionaires, job prospects were markedly poorer than in other employer-led schemes: 'We do try to recruit through YTS but we recruit older people, part-timers, to keep the balance right . . . Something like 30 per cent will be kept in the store.'

This scheme, too, had received few direct applications, but they had never advertised and found that their visits to schools to try to recruit for YTS were unproductive, so most of their applicants came from the Careers Service. At the interview the managing agent used 'no tests, no school experience. They've got to be physically acceptable to appear in the store . . . And basically they've got to want to come here.' A few trainees had needed remedial education and 'Counselling is very necessary, because they've got an awful lot of personal and domestic problems'. In 1986, first the YTS scheme and then this branch of the store closed. 'Sure [the MSC] were upset . . . They said there was a need for it.'

Restricted recruitment in stable-skill umbrella schemes

The remaining group who appeared to restrict their participation in YTS were four managing agents of umbrella schemes who had kept to the same skills and remained the same size or grown only slowly. There were two Industrial Training Boards, for construction (CITB) and hotels and catering (HCITB), a hairdressers' managing agent and the Chamber of Commerce. Here recruitment was more complex because sometimes the managing agent recruited and screened potential trainees on behalf of the employers who then did a further interview. The managing agents' preliminary screening therefore involved judgements of what sort of trainees employers would accept.

Two Industrial Training Boards: CITB and HCITB

Although the ITBs were organized as LCU 'multiple' umbrella schemes, they had the *statutory* function of upgrading training standards in their industries, backed by a training levy from employers. As the largest national managing agent, the CITB had successfully fought a running battle against the MSC, which wanted other managing agents to run construction apprenticeship schemes with less craft content. So local trainee numbers were kept small, pegged by the national agreement: 'It's all organized for us by God on high somewhere'. In Southwich the CITB scheme was said to be only half the size of those elsewhere because of the many unregistered small builders in the area, and as a result it was heavily oversubscribed.

The CITB sometimes recruited for larger employers, but usually in

Southwich employers or applicants would approach the CITB to accept a placement already fixed up (often with a relative), at which point the managing agent vetted the arrangement. He asked for 'a minimum of three middle-of-the-road CSEs' as a check on basic skills but also to ensure conformity and persistence, and he also applied a simple test of numeracy and spatial relations. This mode of recruitment meant that access to construction apprenticeships was rationed primarily by access to registered employers with placements, rather than by academic selection.

The HCITB had been less able to withstand dilution of its training through the impact of fast-food technology. Hotel or restaurant placements equivalent to apprenticeships were rare and others entailed unskilled work, long and unsocial hours and poor job prospects. Again the scheme recruited partly via applicants bringing their own placements but also via the Careers Service, for a pool of HCITB and other employers. The managing agent took no account of school credentials, concentrating instead on motivation, because 'Catering tends to become your social life . . . You must expect to work when everyone else is at play.' Nevertheless, any better-qualified and motivated trainees were routed into larger hotels with prospects of apprenticeships or management posts, whereas others were sent to low-skill placements in fast-food catering with a high staff turnover.

The hairdressers' scheme

Started by the local Education Secretary of the National Federation of Hairdressers, the hairdressers' scheme had aimed to prevent YTS from swamping the trade and further lowering its already poor training standards. Before YTS, 'Nobody would employ young people any more, they used married ladies. YTS has altered this and there's now more and better training in hairdressing than there's been for a long time . . . YTS has been free, which was an attraction.' Numbers were geared to available jobs, and the second year of apprenticeship made heavy use of the MSC's subsidized programme for 17-year-olds, the New Workers Scheme. The scheme was also limited because the managing agent worked almost alone, and funding did not allow for the extra travel and administration of scattered placements. The managing agent, who had originally taken up YTS 'as a moral or charitable thing', said he found it unexpectedly hard work for little or no return.

Again some of these craft recruits came with placements already fixed up, but there was also a flood of applicants via the Careers Service, mostly from girls with poor school records. The managing agent relied on school reports rather than academic results, but by 1986 he was becoming more selective: 'In the first year we recruited from the debris of school leavers . . . Now . . . we make sure that they're capable of the academics needed on the scheme, not that that's very demanding.' However, there were protests about restricted numbers from both applicants and the MSC: 'They get one parent shrieking at them because their kid's not been given a place and they put on the pressure. We take the kid on and the child is unhappy because they can't cope.' The managing agent now invariably channelled applications via the Careers Service as a filter and a buffer against such pressure. The scheme and its standards were now further threatened by encroachment from a national LCU multiple scheme: 'Their scheme looked wonderful on paper but the training, he claimed, wasn't done at all, it was one big farce.' He had enlisted local MSC help to stop the scheme poaching his placements, but in 1986, the MSC 'phoned up to say they're letting them back in in one area, because of pressure from the parents'.

The Chamber of Commerce

The Chamber of Commerce ran clerical and retail schemes on a non-profit-making basis 'as a service to its members, just like the other services it offers'. Requests for trainees from the Chamber's 700 members were carefully vetted, and the managing agent said the better employers felt obliged to offer jobs: 'You have to persuade them about the training.' Placements were often in small offices or shops where 'additionality' could never have operated, and on the retail scheme: 'With the government changes in retail legislation, it's cheaper for them now to have four part-time women than it is to have a young person.'

The size of the scheme was geared to ensure that they could recruit enough trainees of a suitable standard. Earlier they had once bowed to MSC pressure to expand: 'That's the worst thing we ever did. They didn't want to be on YTS . . . It was such hard work.' Most applicants were attracted by advertising or by recruitment visits to schools, but some of the best then went to Endowments. This caused some bitterness: 'There ought to be some sort of unwritten code of conduct about poaching. It's got to the cattle market stage.' The managing agent disliked filling the scheme through the Careers Service because the officers 'start putting direct suggestions to [young people], and [retail] may not be what they want'. She passed rejected retail applicants to Concessions.

Applicants were given numeracy, literacy and spelling tests, and streamed into clerical or retail work. The managing agent looked at school credentials and those selected almost all had some middle-range CSEs. However, 'They're not the deciding factor, it's to get them to talk . . . We notice how they sit and wait for an interview, the language when they're talking to their friends, even what their friends look like.' One girl was observed chewing gum and swearing as she sat with her friends awaiting interview. She was rejected because an employer 'would just send her back and say, "Haven't you got anything better?" ' In another interview a clearly reluctant boy with spiky hair was grilled about his poor school record:

'Tell me, Tony, what do you think of YTS?'
'Well, it's a handy way for the government to reduce the unemployment figures.'

'If you feel like that, what are you doing here?'
'Well, there's nothing else about, is there?'
'But you're not really bothered are you?'
'Yes, I am . . . [but] under a different government I wouldn't have to do this.'

Afterwards, the managing agent was clearly torn: 'I'm quite tempted to give him a place . . . He's quite bright . . . But . . . he doesn't want to work, so let those who do have the places . . . It's an employer's market now.'

Conclusions

In order to stimulate employers' demand for trainees in particular types of firm and skill area, the MSC had initially negotiated with employers and potential managing agents over quotas for their schemes. However, the YTS subsidy was too low, and the MSC's general bargaining position too weak, to induce larger employers with more costly training to expand their numbers above their immediate needs for recruitment. There was a shift in service firms to substitute younger for older workers. In the interests of good relations with staff, however, the better employers had reservations about taking on trainees to whom they would not be able to offer jobs. In any case, the unions and informal pressures from staff and customers reinforced what their business calculations told them. Rather than take unsuitable trainees, almost all preferred (and could afford) to run below quota.

The managing agents of stable-skill schemes were equally reluctant to bow to MSC pressures to expand too far, because of their formal or informal commitment to maintaining training standards and keeping roughly in line with employer demand. All these schemes attracted enough trainees to be selective and seemed anxious to *exclude* the poorly-motivated or those who would be unacceptable to employers with service jobs. So overall, the MSC remained short of YTS places to mop up the most disadvantaged un-employed young people. The next chapter shows how these places were provided elsewhere in the YTS surrogate labour market where a different financial logic operated.

Chapter 5
Selling YTS: training entrepreneurs and the Careers Service

Faced with the urgent problem of where to find the places guaranteed to disadvantaged and unemployed school leavers, the MSC encouraged the expansion of training in areas of work where it had not previously been established, partly by using trainers with previous experience but mostly by encouraging new trainers and smaller workplaces to enter the surrogate labour market. However, the MSC again lacked control over the pattern of this non-established or 'new' training and over employers' behaviour in hiring young people. Whereas its inability to stimulate extra large-firm placements undermined its training objectives, its weakness in restraining the 'new' training undermined YTS's role in promoting equal opportunities for either the educationally disadvantaged or for young girls.

The MSC's attempts to expand this new training met much greater problems in attracting potential trainees and sponsors. As we saw in Chapter 4, experienced trainers recruited from the better-qualified young people who tended to apply directly, more eagerly and early. They used the Careers Service (if at all) merely to screen and preselect from a surplus of applicants. The new training had to recruit from among school leavers who were less well-motivated, who lacked school credentials and who were more suspicious of YTS. Managing agents who put on the new training had to set about 'selling' YTS to overcome its lack of credibility. They became heavily dependent on the Careers Service, and, with the collapse of the job market, the Careers Service's traditional function of careers guidance was replaced by YTS recruitment and screening.

We suspect that the rhetoric of altruism early in YTS made it difficult for employers or managing agents involved in the new training to admit to benefiting or making a profit, especially when they were complaining of MSC cuts. Also, managing agents had a vested interest in presenting a picture where quality training was actually taking place. The role of the Careers Service was more ambiguous and at the end of the chapter we describe the unease of Careers Service staff in their new role of selling YTS.

The 'enterpreneurial' managing agents

During the first phase of our research between 1984 and 1986, there were five managing agents who could be described as 'training entrepreneurs', although two closed before YTS 2 began. The remaining three – a private motor vehicle training association, and two whom we will call Jack's and Dovers – ran schemes under a wide range of skill labels, and together they accounted for almost half Southwich's quota of placements.

The private motor vehicle training association

Although private, the motor vehicle training association had originally resembled the stable-skill managing agents because it served a pool of employers in the motor vehicle industry and trained for the Road Transport Industry Training Board (RTITB). By 1986, about 40 per cent of its training was done under YTS. 'We do make a profit, make no mistake, but the profits go back. What we get out of YTS is a cash-flow benefit . . . The spin-off from YTS is that when they've finished they come back to do other things.' Profits went to expand training facilities, and the association had recently moved to a smart new training centre.

The RTITB was early in adopting a modular system which permitted shorter training spells well suited to YTS, and the Scheme was enthusiastically adopted by the trade. However, technological changes meant there were many fewer apprenticeships and much garage work had become deskilled and routine, so training and opportunities depended very much on the size and nature of the work sponsors, some of which were family firms.

In response to MSC promptings, the motor vehicle training association had expanded its motor vehicle training, and started a wide range of non-traditional schemes. There was routine clerical work for small garages and other trade employers; construction for small rural builders not registered with the CITB; a retail scheme; and a warehouse scheme for a large customer for whom the association did forklift truck training. In the early days YTS selling had brought competition for placements: 'We went looking, knocking on doors telling them about YTS . . . and often you'd be the third one to ask.' However, after a time the larger schemes had their own clientele of employers, although there were still occasional skirmishes. The pull of London in that area meant that the better employers offered jobs, so that what remained were placements with poorer training and job prospects.

The association used the Careers Service but also advertised prominently, hoping to select academically for its main scheme: 'With MV, I'd say some things were desirable rather than necessary. We like to see some CSEs.' But YTS got left with the least employable: 'You'll find an intelligent lad, offer a place with a good employer, and then . . . he'll ring us up and he's got a job –

as a butcher!' Officially, initial recruitment was non-selective, but informally applicants were still screened for some schemes. One interviewer looked at spelling and family background: 'So many of the kids I've interviewed have divorced or separated parents. I feel sorry for them, but I can't help all of them . . . The employers won't take some of them.' The association used tests to route trainees onto different schemes, and clerical trainees were streamed by previous typing experience. The warehouse scheme recruited low-achieving boys, including school-refusers: 'The jobs are rough and ready. The people they work with, they don't want the academic type . . . We've got them with tattoos and earrings. The main question is, are they prepared to do the job? . . . Careers try very hard on occasion to get us to take someone we're not keen on.' However, the managing agent said it could not always place boys who had been dismissed from other schemes or who were in trouble with the police.

Jack's

The most remarkable expansion had taken place at Jack's, once merely the training centre of a medium-sized engineering firm in a rural area. Running various courses for the MSC's predecessor had led to participation in YTS, which had saved the centre from closure. It also led the MSC to encourage Jack's experienced trainer to run clerical, and craft and design schemes, and (unusually) a small Mode B workshop. They had also begun to undertake induction and computer training for other managing agents. By 1986, training was still on the original rural premises, but activities had expanded to take over a small staff social club, and Jack's planned to move to a redundant workshop in Southwich. Jack's argued that any profits from YTS came only indirectly in the form of training facilities for the host firm and jobs for YTS staff. However, other managing agents saw Jack's as running a YTS 'business' and implied that this would affect training standards.

Freed by MSC funding from a very limited base and situated in an underprovided rural area, Jack's had been transformed, first from a small employer-led to a larger umbrella scheme and then into a training entrepreneur: 'You can't stand still, otherwise somebody will come and take your trainees . . . It was a hard sell at first, to get the companies to take YTS, because at that time YOP had such a bad name.' The engineering scheme had expanded from a small number of skilled apprenticeships to become a much broader industrial production scheme with a range of routine placements.

Recruiting was an uphill struggle against engineering's poor public image among parents and teachers, and the apathy induced among pupils by unemployment. Jack's did not restrict itself to advertising: 'We invite the careers officers into the workshop and show them round . . . Then we go to careers conventions, and we visit schools and we go into fifth years and talk to them.' The range of schemes meant that although they still looked for a small number of applicants qualified for apprenticeships, they now took an unselective entry: 'How can you set a test when there's such variability with placements? We can guarantee a placement at every level . . . *Flexibility*! That's what's paid the dividends.' The trainees had four weeks' varied workshop experience and an aptitude test to select for the different types and levels of outside placement. Jack's own Mode B workshop then took any trainees not placed with employers. With such a broad range of trainees, the managing agent said counselling was very time-consuming: 'You can't help but get involved.' However, there was a conflict between being lenient with difficult individuals and keeping control.

Dovers

In contrast to the two schemes which began from an established craft base, the third entrepreneur was a dynamic businessman with interests in personal services, leisure and catering. His earlier participation in the YOP had brought contact with the MSC, which asked him to run schemes for 120 trainees, and although he began with smaller numbers his schemes later expanded. He, like Jack's, benefited from his underprovided rural location and from economies of growth. He admitted: 'Everybody's in it for profit, obviously, though we still get satisfaction out of doing it.' A rival managing agent suggested that Dovers was already charging sponsors under YTS 1: 'He gets far more money than he admits.' Others were sceptical about his claims for his schemes.

The main schemes had started in routine catering and care work. However, at the MSC's request he later put on a small scheme in health and beauty, to which he later added training for sport and leisure. Apart from the economics of FE training, the size was also geared to available placements rather than job openings. The MSC had turned down Dovers' offer to run a retail scheme. Dovers complained that the care scheme, too, was restricted by the public sector unions, especially NALGO, which kept him out of NHS and local authority work. As a result, placements were mainly private, mostly with elderly people but some with children. Unfortunately, there were very poor job prospects in child care, although this area attracted most of the applicants. Private sector care was reputed to be exploitative, with strong competition from part-timers. However, Dovers pursued these placements with such energy that others complained of poaching: 'Some say, "Dovers is everywhere!" . . . I've got that many places, so many offers of sponsors, because I go out to *sell* the scheme.' The managing agent claimed to reject the worst employers, but later revealed that some inferior placements were kept too long.

Recruitment was virtually unselective: 'We tell them that every person has equal opportunities. I don't think I've got the right to say, "I've got a grant and I'm not going to give it to you".' However, a major reason for such openness was the fact that 'There are so many places, but there aren't the trainees to fill them . . . Careers know we'll take anybody . . . "Oh, we've got somebody we can't get in anywhere. We'll try to get them interested in care or catering".' In interview the scheme was sold hard to these 'applicants': 'After all, it's important to sell yourself.' He stressed 'job opportunities', 'nationally-recognized certificates', and 'learning to relate to elderly members of our community'. Domestic work was described as 'caring for the whole environment of the person cared for'.

Keeping the quota up and the scheme full also meant going to the trouble of devising extra small training programmes to try to make training more credible and to provide for the disadvantaged. Trainees had had 'a bad attitude at school. They were scruffy. Do you know, some of my sponsors put their trainees in the bath.' One trainee was told: ' "You do smell strongly of BO . . . And you've come for the interview in dead scruffy gear, but if you come next week dressed presentably, I'll see what I can do for you." And he did!' However, even Dovers could not find a placement for 'an extra big person, with a totally shaved head on one side and an earring through her nose . . . I told her that I'd consider her if she would come back in a month's time with a crew cut, say.' The managing agent said he found counselling 'the biggest part of YTS'.

Three failed managing agents

The fate of three failed managing agents, all with schemes below 50 places, throws further light on conditions for survival on the fringes of YTS.

A businessman

One was a businessman (formerly a government consultant for small rural employers) whom the MSC had persuaded to develop training in animal care, horticulture and rural crafts. Ideally each craft would have needed a distinct off-the-job training course not available in local FE, but the MSC had not trusted the managing agent to provide his own training so he had continued using expensive but inappropriate FE courses. There had also been insuperable difficulties in matching trainees to placements, and he complained that the MSC's urgency in filling YTS led to a lack of sympathy for trainees: 'It's the numbers game again, you see. They say, "We've got to find a placement. What does he want? Building? Well, we've got this farm and it's outdoor work, so let's put him in that" '. There were also MSC pressures to put trainees in placements with no job prospects. Entry had been unselective and there were counselling problems with the trainees. One had to be bailed out of jail at midnight, and a girl who had been to France in her father's lorry had casually asked: 'What's incest?'

The managing agent said he had pulled out of YTS because of MSC red tape, and money lost through administrative costs and FE fees. However there were rumours that the MSC had closed the scheme. Whatever the truth, there were clearly difficulties in providing coherent schemes for varied small employers on the fringe of YTS, and greater financial problems for small umbrella schemes with scattered employers.

A former local authority scheme

The other failed entrepreneurial scheme had met similar problems. It was run by a former council official in a small town who, when he became redundant, had tried to continue the council's YTS scheme as a business. Hard selling brought a very mixed bag of council and local employers covering no fewer than five different Occupational Training Families often with inferior placements: 'I say to the sponsor . . . "If you can't take 'em on, don't worry. It's not a social contract."' From the beginning the MSC had objected to the range of placements: 'Their policies are designed for, I don't know, Northampton or somewhere where everybody makes things.'

The managing agent had also worked hard to get recruits: 'We would take everybody in a small town, even the tearaways . . . The youngsters we mostly have been getting, I call them "self-motivated underachievers" . . . You sit in school, and the message is, "Don't be outstanding" . . . I say to them . . . "You're on your own, I'm not going to bust my ass if you muck up the place I found you."' His most exotic problem was a trainee who turned bank raider. He had attempted to expand his activities by selling personal and life skills training to other schemes, but then had to close because of MSC funding cuts.

A church care scheme

A church had started a care scheme for philanthropic reasons. It had remained small, partly because it was mainly run by an ex-teacher but also because the MSC had turned down a request to be allowed to provide clerical training to make the scheme more viable. However, the scheme had been allowed to do its own care training for lack of any FE alternative. Placements were mainly in the care of the elderly and the mentally handicapped, with some child care. Again there had been union hostility and 22 placements had been contested. Most care employers would not offer jobs, although some placements gave valuable experience towards nursing which could not otherwise be entered until the age of 18.

The scheme originally aimed to help the disadvantaged, and it had a few very sympathetic sponsors. However, the strain had been too great and 'We decided in the end to take only a percentage'. The scheme became more selective, probing for motivation by holding informal discussions in a room with photographs of care work, and asking for two references, including one from school. But they would still accept girls with poor academic results: 'An awful lot underachieve. They should have done better at school, and we're very glad to get them, to build up their confidence.' Occasionally they picked up a bright non-conformist, such as a girl who had nine O-levels but whose pink hair was judged unacceptable in the sixth form. Among the successes was a former bank trainee with anorexia nervosa who had thrived in a kindergarten placement, and also 'a lot of withdrawn and cussed individuals' who had been made to realize how lucky they were compared with the mentally handicapped people they cared for. However, there were also failures – numerous pregnancies, each year an attempted suicide, some drug addicts, and an arsonist. So counselling problems were still burdensome: 'Either you've got to become involved and risk going under, or you're so detached that you're no use.'

After some hesitation, the scheme was closed by a combination of increasing union hostility, the extra administrative costs borne by umbrella schemes, the MSC's tighter funding and delayed payments, and anticipation that care employers would not pay the YTS 2 levy.

The residual function of Mode B

Even after the energetic efforts of the entrepreneurs and despite their willingness to take disadvantaged trainees, there remained a shortfall of YTS placements to cover the predicted quotas of unemployed young people, so the MSC reluctantly provided these under Mode B. Apart from Jack's small group of workshop trainees, the only other Mode B was a local branch of a larger scheme run by Southwich County. In this bottom layer of the surrogate labour market there was even more difficulty than usual in matching YTS quotas to suitable placements and to the abilities and motivation of potential trainees. The attempted solution was to run schemes in care and various 'multi-skills', where trainees got a range of experience and training in construction, painting and decorating, engineering, motor vehicles, metalwork, reprographics, catering, horticulture, and so on.

These schemes pushed further into areas where there were few placements with real job prospects. The care scheme had gained precarious access to some council placements but only against strong union suspicion: 'What you would do is say to the person in charge of that department, "Are there any union members here? What proportion are they? Do you get any trouble?"' In construction, the trainees either had short placements with employers or they were organized as a task force to do jobs which, supposedly, would otherwise not get done. The managing agent complained of overprovision of YTS schemes in catering, and of difficulties in finding placements in motor vehicle or metalwork: 'Oh yes, there's certainly competition for placements. If employers put up notices, you know, like, "No hawkers, no circulars", I think they'd put up, "No YTS!" At one employer, while my bloke was trying to convert a place to construction, [the motor vehicle association] phoned and they were trying to get them to do clerical.' Understandably, she made no claims that trainees got jobs from YTS: 'You go to these managing agents' meetings and you hear things like, "Ninety per cent of mine get jobs", which to be quite honest I don't believe!

I think if when they leave most of them are more prepared for life, we've had some success.'

Because of its higher subsidy, the Mode B scheme was only allowed to take trainees who had been turned down by two other schemes or who applied very late in the year. They recruited late, exclusively through the Careers Service: 'We pick up everyone no one else wants . . . The MSC are forcing us back into accepting the dregs . . . But MSC don't want to hear about failure, you musn't talk about that on YTS.' About 5 per cent of the trainees were under care orders, and some who had committed offences came as a means of getting a reference for court. Also, 'About 10 per cent are ESN, but it's such a fine line between youngsters from an ESN school and some of the bottom end of the comprehensive school . . . [and] it doesn't prove because you've got no O levels that you're daft.'

In the Mode B schemes were some of the more obvious mismatches between the quotas set by the MSC and the numbers of young people who applied for (or who were pushed into) YTS. The small size and selectivity of the CITB scheme meant a surplus of construction applicants and the Mode B managing agent even set a simple selection test: 'One or two went back to Careers, well, the ones who didn't know how many inches there were in a foot, or millimetres in a centimetre.' So many girls wanted care work (usually with children) that the scheme recruited trainees who were not disadvantaged, including a few who were well qualified, and had resisted pressure from the Careers Service to do office or shop work. Other areas such as horticulture were slow to recruit; and for the catering scheme the managing agent told us: 'This year for the 12 placements I've actually interviewed ten youngsters, but I'll be lucky if I end up with five. Quite a lot of them had interviews at college (for a full-time place), HCITB, or with Dovers . . . There's overprovision in catering in this area.'

With a high proportion of poorly-motivated trainees, discipline had to be tight: 'I dock money when kids are late, and I've been known to sack kids because of their timekeeping . . . [But] it's wrong to expect us to change, in one or two years, what they've become over 11 years at school . . . Basically YTS is in a lot of cases a cosmetic thing, as anyone will admit, and basically you try to do your best with that. It's for the unemployment figures, but . . . If it wasn't for YTS these kids wouldn't get a job anyway, period . . . Lots of the kids we have now, employers wouldn't put up with them, but hopefully we make some impression.'

The range of recruitment was completed by the Mode B2 scheme run by Southwich College. Trainees were selected at 17 from a one-year bridging course after special school, the aim being to find those who might survive in open employment. Placements offered a range of unskilled work like horticulture, institutional cleaning, retail, catering and warehousing, usually where trainees would not have to meet the public. Depending on the trainee, work experience might take up as little as one day a week. But although these trainees were better prepared for low-skill work because of the vocational bias in the schools, they usually had learning difficulties and the chances of jobs from placements were not good.

Small employers in umbrella schemes

In Southwich, the expansion of new training had brought a large number of small employers into YTS umbrella schemes. So in 1987, to gain a fuller picture of recruitment, we interviewed 30 of these employers, selected at random from the placements of trainees whom we had interviewed. Usually we spoke to owners or managers but in slightly larger firms we looked at the workplace and talked to the supervisor.

If these employers had ever been briefed by the managing agents, it had left remarkably little impression and they knew virtually nothing about YTS's training goals. Their attitudes to the purpose and value of YTS as a scheme covered an enormous range. A third were using the Scheme to recruit and felt that 'It's not fair to take [trainees] on when there's no job'. Several of these topped up their trainees' allowances. Others also valued their trainees' labour; one in four felt the YTS allowance was too low, and some said they felt guilty about the way YTS exploited young people.

However, a further one in three thought that YTS was for 'poor young people' whom they were in the Scheme 'to help'. Yet among these were the employers who offered the poorest job prospects, and who most clearly benefited from the trainees' menial labour during anti-social hours. At the bottom of the pile were some very small businesses scarcely viable without their trainees, yet here the employers were most likely to think the YTS allowance too high. Possibly the worst employer, who felt that trainees should work at weekends and without holidays or off-the-job training, suggested that his trainees should pay him! Significantly, his trainees came from three different managing agents who were competing for placements on the low-skill fringe of YTS.

There was little questioning or even awareness of gender stereotyping in recruitment. Nor did employers show much awareness that some schemes were selective. A third who themselves asked for credentials used them to screen for personality rather than ability. A solicitor said this meant he need not 'endlessly sift through the riff-raff'. In contrast, other employers said they deeply mistrusted applicants with credentials as 'generally too soft' or having 'their heads in the clouds'. Yet ironically most of these employers unknowingly recruited from academically-selective schemes.

The employers' attitudes towards the young people who applied for their placements were mostly unsympathetic. Only a handful of employers seemed able to tolerate any evidence of protest or lack of deference. The overwhelming majority seemed preoccupied with getting 'the right attitude' and emphasized appearance and speech. They wanted 'no extremes' – 'we couldn't take a punk'. Almost half complained that their trainees did not meet these standards. Some saw the very fact of being on YTS as evidence that a trainee was 'less able' or from 'the dross' and complained of trainees' poor attitudes and lack of appreciation. Five employers with very poor placements complained bitterly that their 'tolerance' and 'generosity' had been stretched to the limits. One said the managing agent saw him as a 'soft touch' and 'sent him all the thickies'. Several employers ranted at length about the problems of society today, and had seen their offer of a work placement as an opportunity to knock some good old British values into decadent youth. When employers could not get the trainees they wanted, they complained bitterly that they had been sold YTS under false pretences. Managing agents were blamed for being 'too soft' and on the side of 'kids' who 'can up and leave whenever they like'.

Our small survey of employers in umbrella schemes suggested an all too clear vicious circle. The most negative views about young people seemed to come from employers with the most exploitative placements. Yet such placements had been created and continued to be tolerated in YTS because they were needed to mop up disadvantaged young people. In other words, the least responsible and most unsympathetic employers, whose placements carried the most minimal training opportunities and job prospects, were likely to be offered the YTS trainees who were most disadvantaged and worst motivated.

The view from the Careers Office

We look finally at the role of the Southwich Careers Service in recruitment and screening for YTS. The Service gave us regular statistics on recruitment and limited access to managing agents' interviews in the office. In addition, in 1987 we interviewed key members of staff, some of whom revealed considerable uneasiness about the dilemmas posed by their new role in selling YTS.

The ideology of the Careers Service was initially to offer objective and open-minded 'guidance' within a framework of equal opportunities, to enable young people to fulfil as much of their potential and ambitions as possible. Even before YTS the ideology of 'choice' and 'opportunities' had been undermined by evidence of the link between social background and educational achievement, and by the segmentation of the youth labour market which meant that in practice only a limited range of jobs was open to their clients, because employers did not have to notify the Careers Service of vacancies. In times of higher unemployment the role of the Careers Service was restricted to recruiting mostly for unskilled jobs which were harder to fill.

With the collapse of real jobs, the role of the Careers Service became more ambiguous and controversial. Nationally about two-thirds of managing agents found the Careers Service the best source of recruitment, especially for schemes where (in MSC jargon) the Careers Service and the MSC had 'identified a need'. During much of our research, all that

Southwich Careers Service could offer was 'guidance' in choosing between a few hard-to-fill 'real' jobs and the less popular YTS schemes. For the better schemes they were asked by managing agents to send only preselected trainees with academic credentials. Increasingly, in order to perform its role with an easy conscience, the Careers Service had to believe in the value of YTS. Yet, even before overt compulsion arrived under YTS 2, the Careers Service was divided, and some branches or individual officers would not report YTS refusers for docking of their benefit.

YTS meant changed working relationships all round. Formerly, the qualified careers officers had been mainly concerned with schools visits and careers guidance, and employment officers had dealt with office callers and the bulk of YTS work. But as jobs collapsed and YTS expanded, careers officers felt they were being deskilled by spending more and more of their time on routine YTS work: 'We can't do the job we're trained to do.' They felt bombarded by phone calls from employers, school leavers and managing agents. The Job Centre was viewed as an unqualified rival and senior staff argued that all school leavers should be routed into work via the Careers Service and YTS. There was also more tension with the schools who were fighting to keep their dwindling sixth forms, and where there was increasing overlap with poorly-funded careers guidance from teachers. Schools' attitudes to YTS varied, some refusing to allow any discussion of the scheme, others preselecting potential trainees, still others encouraging their most promising school leavers to apply early and directly for YTS and so bypass the Careers Service altogether.

By 1987, the Careers Service's main business was filtering the more able and best-motivated YTS applicants for the top schemes, and 'guiding' as many other unemployed young people as they could into the other very unequal YTS opportunities. Surprisingly, staff often seemed to know relatively little about these. Senior staff claimed: 'All the schemes are good . . . We get a picture. We do phone managing agents sometimes.' 'The opportunities available for a 16-year-old school leaver are phenomenal.' Other Careers Service staff, however, were less confident and more ambivalent. One deplored media hostility and added hesitantly: 'Probably most kids get jobs out of it. Well (*pause*) . . . probably (*pause*) . . . Well (*pause*) . . . most . . . I'm sure it *is* all right. But I'm doubtful . . .' Even employer-led craft training was questioned: 'Managing agents . . . *say* kids get jobs, but . . . how many end up in a factory minding the lathes?' An LCU scheme's placements were described as limited in scope and 'boring', and job prospects in care work were doubted. Another careers officer was also ambivalent: 'It *probably* is a very good scheme – but I'm glad I missed it. *I'd* never go on a scheme, I'd hate it.' A colleague was more openly hostile: 'There's a lot of crap schemes with crap placements . . . and we're faced with selling the scheme to young people who, quite rightly . . . don't see the benefit of the training.' Another thought: 'There's no doubt that YTS has brought wages down. It reduces their expectations and young people are panicked because it's a job.'

Careers officers felt relatively powerless in relation to some managing agents' requests that they should preselect applicants by ability: 'We don't always agree with managing agents' requirements, but . . . there's no point sending a young person for a place you know she won't get. That would only result in their demoralization.' Some officers discouraged trainees from going on the more selective schemes or those with poorer job opportunities. But one member of staff pointed out: 'The trouble is, you all don't like [two entrepreneurial schemes] . . . Yet they do take anyone, anyone at all. You can't have it both ways.'

Similarly, there seemed to be relatively little the Careers Service could do to stimulate boys and girls to apply for jobs which were outside conventional gender stereotypes. Senior members insisted: 'There is no discrimination here. It's just that youngsters don't request it.' But a careers officer burst out: 'All this "equal opportunities" stuff is crap! We can't overcome the system. Employment officers reinforce [bias], employers, managing agents, parents even.'

Gender segregation in the surrogate labour market

Overall, the MSC's lack of power to influence the pattern of schemes in the surrogate labour market and radically to change employers' behaviour in hiring young people could be seen most clearly in the persistence of gender stereotyping in placements. To gain approval by the AMB, managing agents had to say how their schemes satisfied the MSC's equal opportunities policy. But from the documentation which we saw for vetting schemes in the run-up to YTS 2 all that was necessary was a statement that 'all suitable applicants would be considered'.

Like other studies (such as Cockburn, 1987) we found that recruitment and trainee self-selection by gender were all-pervasive. Traditionally male craft skills still attracted and recruited almost exclusively boys. In engineering any girl would have to be 'a bit of a tomboy, somebody with bounce, who's not going to break down and cry if she gets told off on a job'. The only recent female recruit 'comes in on a motor bike with a crash helmet on, and she doesn't cringe if they swear on the shop floor . . .'. Girl trainees moved into sales, laboratory work or instrument-making, and the female clerical trainees 'try not to go down through the factory . . . because they do tend to get wolf whistles'. The motor vehicle scheme only had one girl trainee: 'From a distance you'd have difficulty telling if it was a boy or a girl!' A lack of separate toilet facilities was not the only reason why small garages failed to take on girls. There appeared to be problems on the sales side of the business: 'Parts is a sort of unisex job . . . but we've got difficulty in persuading young ladies to have a go'. Nationally, the CITB was under a cloud for its male bias, but locally it had only two female applicants (less than 1 per cent), both wanting painting and decorating. In addition, it was observed that employers 'quickly come up with a list as long as your arm of problems for girls on sites'. A trainer on the Mode B construction scheme commented: 'If you try to persuade some of these hunky ignorant builders to take a girl . . . even if the girl didn't mind going behind the bushes, it would be unacceptable to me as a responsible trainer.' The other male preserve was sport and leisure where the few women trainees were said to be 'very keen on things that I'm only used to seeing young men keen òn'.

In contrast, girls dominated hairdressing, health and beauty, and clerical and retail work. Even *within* these areas there was gender stereotyping. In clerical schemes girls did secretarial typing or word-processing, or reception work, whereas boys did technical or 'keyboard' work connected with computer programming or finance. At the Chamber of Commerce and motor vehicle association a few boys had wanted to be secretaries but none succeeded, whereas girls were confined to that role: 'It's the employers. There was an advert for an estate agent which showed eight men as salesmen, but we knew that behind those eight men were four of our girls.' Employers also recruited boys for accountants' offices or if they were looking for office managers. Retail work also followed gender stereotypes with girls going into fashion and make-up but boys into menswear, radio and television, and photography: 'It goes by hobbies.' More boys, too, were said to be groomed for management. The three schemes in care work had only ever recruited a handful of male trainees, and one of Dovers' two boys was 'definitely a gay young man with a preference for little boys . . . [but] we put him in an old people's home, and he got on very well there'. The boys who specifically chose care tended to plan nursing careers. Although numbers were small, catering was similar, with boys wanting careers but girls restricted to food preparation, reception, service, or domestic work.

Managing agents were aware of the equal opportunities policy and sometimes tried to educate employers and trainees, but they were locked into the preferences of the trainees and the employers. Even if trainees did try to choose against tradition, they were likely to be regarded as 'effeminate' or 'butch'. In any case, employers had the final say on whom they would employ and where, and their choices were overwhelmingly gender-stereotyped, both between and *within* work skills. The process of multiple-screening in YTS by a number of interviews may even have accentuated the gender selection of girls by their appearance, and the MSC had failed to intervene.

Conclusions

Through the surviving entrepreneurial schemes, the MSC found a flexible means of selling the new training in non-established 'skills' to reluctant employers and the more disadvantaged young people. With MSC encouragement some new training entrepreneurs had expanded from a traditional craft base (which had eased their cash flow), but that expansion had left only a small core of apprenticeships with the bulk of new placements in routine production. Other extra placements were in low-skill service work. All this expansion lacked credibility, because few of the placements seemed to offer either good training or reasonable job prospects. Dovers' efforts in selling YTS were remarkable because they won placements from reluctant employers for the least employable young people, who elsewhere would probably have been subsidized under Mode B. Initially the church-based care scheme had a similar problem, but it was forced to close because it lacked a cash base and it was reluctant to expand and become more entrepreneurial. The two failed entrepreneurial schemes illustrate the greater difficulties of providing youth training on a small scale in more rural areas, without an alternative financial base or permission to provide cheap off-the-job training.

With the collapse of jobs YTS became the main work of the Careers Service, yet at the same time the latter was growing more marginal. Relationships with the Job Centre and schools became strained, and overwork and the changing status of managing agents meant that careers officers had only patchy information or prejudices concerning many of the schemes upon which they were supposed to give guidance. Like the Careers Service nationally, the attitudes of Southwich staff ranged from acceptance of official claims for YTS success, to open scepticism and hostility.

It is an irony imposed by market forces, that a scheme with the formal goal of equal opportunities became a finely-graded sieve for matching young people to placements with very *un*equal job prospects and levels of skills training. Also, boys and girls entered what were virtually *two* surrogate labour markets largely segregated by gender, rather than a common set of opportunities. Although a major goal of YTS was to motivate supposedly undermotivated young people, it was actually *selecting by motivation*. At worst, it was matching the most disadvantaged and least-motivated trainees to the least sympathetic and most expoitative small employers.

Chapter 6
Control of training: explaining segmentation and inequality in YTS

The last two chapters have revealed the weakness of the MSC's attempts to develop YTS along the lines of the official blueprint. The MSC's powers rested only on giving formal approval and funding to schemes, and this left the provision of training places to employer voluntarism. As a result market forces shaped employers' behaviour, and the 'demand' side of the surrogate labour market offered trainees a range of very unequal opportunities. We will conclude this chapter by suggesting a model to describe the pattern of segmentation and inequality in the surrogate labour market. But first we will describe the remaining important dimension of inequality of opportunity in YTS, the MSC's failure to control the quality of training.

Control of training content

The fundamental claim of YTS is that while it does not necessarily guarantee a job, it nevertheless provides 'quality training' which will lead to a job. Yet the deliberate policy decision to open up YTS to market forces undermined external controls over training. We saw in Chapter 2 that the conflict with employers over access to the 'black box' of on-the-job training was only resolved by leaving the MSC without independent powers of assessing the outcomes of training. And early on (see Chapter 3), the MSC scrapped NTP, which had allowed FE staff some scope to vet workplace training.

The MSC's relationships with established and new trainers

In established skills, the MSC was asking for access to monitor an ongoing process, but with the new non-traditional training, there were much more severe problems in ensuring the competence of any new trainers, and in keeping control over smaller employers with fewer facilities and little or no experience.

Having bypassed FE and with the Training Boards reduced in importance, the MSC's controls over training quality on and off the job were exercised initially through selection and surveillance of the managing agents. MSC staff visited the trainees at their work placements and also talked to employers and supervisors. Under YTS 1, the intention was to inspect log-books kept by supervisors and trainees to describe training progress. Trainees' diaries were to be a further check on the variety of work experience. Each trainee received a YTS Certificate profiling the skills attained from training, and it was hoped this would become accepted by employers as a vocational credential.

In Southwich, some YTS trainers (including the Co-op managing agent and two of the entrepreneurs, Jack's and the motor vehicle association) proved to be men with years of ITB experience, who were contemptuous of the Johnny-come-lately MSC: 'I get cynical when I hear them inventing the wheel again . . . Some of the material is the very same [as the old ITBs]. I think most of it must have been chucked away and then different industrial psychologists have looked at the same tasks and invented it again.' The trained staff of one YTS trainer found 'they're coming up against a procession of Job Centre clerks who've been promoted'. However, these established trainers admitted that they had experienced relatively little MSC control: 'We're an established scheme and they know that we want to do it right for ourselves.'

But the rest included two former personnel officers, a redeployed company executive, and others all new to training. Attitudes to the MSC ranged from deference to exasperation. According to Concessions, the 'MSC have always been very helpful, I mean quite genuinely . . . They've always given me ideas, told me about other schemes.' Flourishes said that the 'MSC don't bother us and we don't contact them. I think we must be one of the schemes that doesn't give them much bother.' But others were uncertain or irritated at the MSC's continuous alterations to YTS and at what appeared to be bureaucracy and insensitivity: 'We're trying to put the goals in, but they keep moving the goal posts.' 'I'd say if bullshit is what you want I can give it you in bucket-loads. It's the only way to cope with the stupidity of their ten-page documents.' 'With MSC it's all talk and files. My impression is that they haven't that interest in the youngsters.' The Mode B managing agent contrasted MSC's treatment of Jack's and Dovers with her scheme: 'I think they'd be stuck if they lost the scheme, but . . . they make us do it by the book, and you come to resent that.'

Inside the 'black box': the MSC and workshop training

As a check on training, the log books and diaries proved a failure. Traditional trainers flouted regulations and continued with ITB-style log books. The newer trainers found the format of the log books and the monotony of the diary unworkable, apparently because much of the time the trainees were learning little new that could be recorded. The Chamber of Commerce abandoned daily records after eight weeks but continued written monitoring. Flourishes found the diaries ridiculously overdetailed for retail training. Concessions persisted with diaries as a form of discipline: 'They'll write, "Dusted today", "Dusted today", "Dusted today", but if I saw that I'd say "*What* have you dusted?"' Other managing agents devised informal projects, and 'MSC turned a blind eye to it in the end'. The Mode B managing agent felt lucky if 30 per cent of her trainees wrote anything.

Lacking any valid external check on training quality, the MSC remained (like ourselves) heavily dependent on what managing agents, employers and trainees told them. From what managing agents said, there were wide variations in control of training, chiefly between in-house training in genuine employer-led schemes in large firms, and subcontracted work experience in umbrella schemes. It was difficult to keep an eye on scattered smaller firms, and any attempt to move trainees around to vary training was resisted by sponsors and trainees alike.

In *employer-led schemes* the varied departments of a large firm could offer trainees a programme of different activities under experienced supervision. Yet even here, quality depended on the managing agent's authority over the departmental managers. Even managing agents employed by the parent company to train had met resistance from managers when they tried to ensure that trainees gained a broad training and were not exploited. For example, Southwich's engineering firms had little trouble with their Engineering Industry Training Board model craft training, but all reported that departmental managers lacked patience with inexperienced clerical trainees. Similarly, the Co-op managing agent could control work experience in-house in the main department store. But he had serious problems with managers and trainees in the small and sometimes remote Co-op branches, and he had to use his position of authority in training to insist that 'youngsters are not taken advantage of . . . We guarantee a visit once a fortnight . . . We want to know what the *managers* are doing! Because, let's face it, line management have got a different perspective.' In the smaller branches the trainees' resistance was greater: 'They think . . . if they're moved, out of sight out of mind, which is true of course'.

There were greater problems of control in employer-led schemes where the managing agent had less authority. At Flourishes the managing agent said she got better training from the store's own managers than from concessionaires. At Concessions the trainees 'never want to move, so I say to them, "Give it a fortnight", and then when they've been there a month . . . they've forgotten they were ever anywhere else'. At Endowments there was a contrast between the moves and variety experienced by trainees in- and out-of-house: 'The internals do a fair amount, but [when outside employers] get the youngsters trained up they're loth to have them moved, and the youngsters are the same.' Small employers resisted 'losing' their trainees for training off the job and holidays or sickness: 'At times a sponsor begins to wonder if they'll ever see their trainee again, and the youngsters get nervous . . . If on top of that you tried to move them on . . .'.

Virtually all the managing agents of *umbrella schemes* had found that employers and trainees tended to resist training and trainee moves. However, because they served standards in a particular skill or pools of employers, the managing agents of the *stable-skill* schemes tried harder to control training, though they were not always successful. The CITB had peculiar difficulties: 'In building every job, every site is different . . . You couldn't move [trainees] round.' Trainees in family businesses could not be moved so they had to be carefully vetted: 'We interview both father and son to check, and if we think it's a case of "Little Willie can't get a job", we tell them to forget it. But if they're seriously interested in providing the training, you know they can provide the range of work and will support the College bit . . . good luck to them.' In hairdressing, too, the apprenticeship system tied trainees to one employer: 'They've got to get used to the ways of a particular salon.' As for the employers: 'We've gradually tightened control . . . Well, we have to chase them a bit'. The Chamber of Commerce gave firms 'a full inspection visit . . . to get the feel of the place and to see if the young person will be supervised'. The Chamber itself possibly gave the managing agent influence over members, but tight vetting and control were more difficult in its retail placements. The HCITB also had problems with very varied placements and a high turnover.

In the *entrepreneurial schemes* with expanded traditional and new training, the balance of control shifted towards the employer. The motor vehicle training association seemed reluctant to hear complaints against employers, taking the line that placements were very much what the trainees made of them. Jack's experienced craft trainer felt that, outside a small core of traditional apprenticeships, 'You can *over*train for a job, so when they've been trained enough for what they want, [the employers] tend to take them off YTS because they don't want to lose them'. Trainees who became 'overtrained' tended to get bored and look for other jobs. Jack's found that monitoring-visits to trainees in small firms, were not very effective: 'Sometimes you'll go and see them, and they'll say they're fine, and then a bit later you'll get a phone call. "Oh, I didn't like to tell you when the boss was here but . . ."'

Dovers was short of placements and its rural setting made it difficult to move trainees. But in any case the work differed little in its low skill level: 'As I tell the trainees . . . my basic rule is that caring means to care for all the surroundings of the people you're caring for.' This attempt to present domestic work as 'training' seemed unfortunate given the exploitation in some care work placements, which seem to have been kept far too long. A nursing home 'had them working in their lunch hours, and scrubbing the floors and the toilets . . . I gave them the benefit of every doubt, I tried four different trainees, but in the end I had to take the trainee out.' Similarly, 'In catering they have them cleaning toilets and cookers and cleaning floors, and not even getting the chance of preparing food. As part of a team doing that all right, but not *just* doing that.' There was a battle with some catering employers who tried to make trainees work late, work a six-day week or do shift-work. Other placements offered little training, for example a part-time job in a fish and chip shop converted to YTS. As an alternative to moving the trainees, Dovers sometimes devised individual training programmes which could be specially funded by the MSC. For example, no placement could be found for a deaf black girl, but Dovers arranged two sheltered domestic placements for her, and later persuaded the MSC to pay for driving lessons so that she could help with external catering functions.

One of the failed entrepreneurs said frankly: 'Oh, we had to leave the sponsors to train them themselves . . . With a set-up like this, they were all different, you see.' Here again, routine domestic work could pass for training. A trainee's boss 'asked him to sweep the floor, and when he'd finished he said, "Look you've left several pieces of paper under the chair." And do you know, it turned out that he'd never used a broom before.' After that, sweeping was 'put into the training [schedule]'.

In entrepreneurial new-skill placements, a move was unlikely to bring the trainee extra skills to compensate for any loss of job prospects, and small employers resisted any miminal loss of investment or disturbance. So for the managing agent there was a trade-off between attempting to provide varied training – which might mean finding an extra placement – and upsetting both employer and trainee by forcing a move. A threatened move might force an employer to provide more training. Jack's found that: 'After two or three months you have to go to some firms and say: "There's two choices, either she has to move to get more experience, or you broaden her [training]"'. Alternatively, the threat could be traded against a job offer. In the Chamber of Commerce retail scheme, 'We say, "Well, there are these options. We can move the young person, or it's employed YTS". It's a sort of blackmail, really.' In both instances employers tended to take the trainee off YTS. The motor vehicle association trainer suggested it was often easiest to do nothing: 'There's a chance of a job and they're getting on well. If they've done six months and we want to whip them off somewhere else they're upset, so we often let sleeping dogs lie.'

Unusually, the church scheme had tried to insist that trainees experienced three areas of care work, and found that trainees then often changed from their first choice of care work to become interested in mental handicap. However, 'If the employer says they really need her, and you get the parents coming round and saying, "She's so good, they want her there, can't you, just this once?" I occasionally give in, I'm so glad they've got a job'. In the Mode B scheme, the trade-off was more finely balanced, 'If they come to me and say they've got a job stacking shelves in Tescos, I wouldn't actually discourage them . . . I'd pressure them more strongly if I thought they'd got a lot of potential . . . But if they're not very bright it might be their only chance.'

Small employers' views on training

Our 1987 interviews with 30 small employers from umbrella schemes confirmed managing agents' difficulties in controlling subcontracted training. As we saw earlier (Chapter 5) most of them did not even recognize YTS's training goals and felt rather that they were doing trainees a favour. Only a few genuine traditional craft and clerical placements had any semblance of a supervised training programme, the rest offering only narrowly specific jobs where training was a 'necessary evil' or 'carrying people'. The owner of a one-man company scoffed: 'I can hardly afford to invest in my own future, let alone anyone else's.' Another said: 'They just have to get on with their work just like the rest of us.' The owner of a small wholesale warehouse described his trainee's introduction to work: 'There's the bags, there's the vegetables, there's the scales, there's the lorry, now get on with it.' In a café the employer said the trainee was told: 'You know how to make tea, you know how to butter bread. Just stand there and smile!' Two-thirds described off-the-job training as a nuisance because work was disrupted, calling it a 'privilege', a 'luxury' or a 'holiday' for trainees. They did not see it as their job to police any absenteeism from off-the-job training and would if anything collude with the trainee who stayed away. Yet, illogically, most also claimed they derived no benefit from their trainees.

Nine out of ten employers had scant respect for the YTS certificate, and the remainder thought its only value was to the trainee as a reward for 'perseverance'. A shoe shop manageress said: 'Both my girls say they're a joke. They list all sorts of things the trainees have never done. In my supervisor's view, the certificate is only used to make the [off-the-job] training look better than it is.'

Control over off-the-job training

The other guarantee of quality in YTS was the 13 weeks' off-the-job training. But here Southwich College had been reduced to competing for business with a range of private trainers whom the MSC clearly favoured. Quality control therefore shifted towards the oversight of these trainers' activities by the MSC, but also by the vocational exam boards for whom some were now accredited exam centres. College staff saw this shift as a probable slackening of standards of training and accreditation. However some managing agents disagreed and in turn criticized the College (although perhaps partly in justification of actions taken to cut training costs).

Southwich College's remaining customers

By 1986, for both established and newer courses Southwich College was left with the larger traditional-apprentice craft customers and service employers, plus some residual business from the entrepreneurial schemes. Although, as prominent employers, the engineering firms felt an obligation to support FE, they echoed industry's long-standing criticisms that the College could not finely match their needs for specific skills, and they complained that even with some standard technical syllabuses the College 'didn't think they had the expertise available'. Cutters' dissatisfaction came to a head when all the clerical girls failed their exams: 'I blew up! . . . "That means *you're* not training 'em", I said, "I want additional training."' Cutters then directed which tutor should teach its clerical trainees. Also, 'It's raised the point with us, if we can get the City & Guilds accreditation . . . If we get into distance learning, we don't need the College; all we need is a library. That's the MSC's view.' These managing agents had challenged rising College fees even up to DES level, 'We believe in FE. We want quality through FE, but what beats us is that they're killing it! . . . The potential of us declaring UDI from further education is enormous.'

Other well-established users of FE also sensed their greater power. For example, 'If the CITB says [an item] is necessary, it jolly well is provided'. Endowments' managing agent objected to the rise in College fees: 'We've always put the emphasis on the BECs [but] there could be a point some time when we may start looking after the money.' A major clash (for engineering, too) was that the College's terms did not fit 13 weeks, and forced the uncomfortable choice between day release for two days a week or extra weeks of block training, both unpopular with managers and trainees alike. Flourishes still did its own training, and the managing agent proudly demonstrated from a chart on the wall a complicated distance learning programme. However, it still used the College to put its academically-selective trainees on BEC or GCE courses appropriate to their school records, and they, too, had used their bargaining power: 'We spend a lot of money down there . . . They're better than they were'.

A common grievance was the College's failure to control the trainees. Traditional craft trainers thought that for the new trainees, 'The only approach is some form of discipline'. The CITB's long off-the-job training was before the work placement to avoid a struggle with employers but, 'After a bit you find [trainees] getting twitchy. Then the College find it difficult to keep order.' The hairdressing trainees had resisted the newer parts of YTS, induction and computing: 'The kids were literally jumping out of the windows at the College. The tutor . . . lost them in the first week'. Only Endowments' academically selected in-house trainees accepted College because the courses dovetailed with professional qualifications linked to extra salary and promotion. But the out-of-house trainees became restless if College training did not match their placements. Flourishes' trainees still found College 'very like school', and the training was valued neither by managers nor the trainees, half of whom never completed.

By the end of YTS 1, the entrepreneurs used the College only selectively, either for the residue of skilled craft placements, or where they could not find – or were not allowed to use – cheaper private training. Increasingly,

Jack's used its own centre. Dovers now used the College as little as possible because of cost and because 'they treated young people as if they were children'. The former council official said he turned to private training because of the College's 'profiteering' and its 'dog in a manger' and inflexible 'take it or leave it' attitude. But the MSC had never allowed the businessman to do his own training.

The development of private training

Private training developed out of a mixture of dissatisfaction with FE and an entrepreneurial approach to business opportunities opened up by YTS. Although the motor vehicle association's withdrawal had been traumatic for the College, the managing agent was unrepentant: 'The staff used to treat them like second class citizens, "You're not College students, you're YTS". They were made to bear that cross.' In 1984 the association had gained recognition as an examination centre for City & Guilds and later for RSA, and they had started their own training: 'We couldn't have done it if the exam bodies hadn't changed their style.' The managing agent argued that YTS was putting the clock back: 'When the ITBs came, they took practical into industry and the training into FE. What we've done now is no more than to go back to what they were doing in the early 'fifties.' This was accepted by craft trainees, but he confessed that warehouse trainees were still hostile: 'On Monday morning our phone will be red hot, people with stomach upsets or a broken toe . . . We've tried all sorts. . . . We've broken every rule in the book, but they don't want to know. They just *love being at work*.'

The second defection from the College, by the Chamber of Commerce, had caused less shock because it was not an established high-investment customer and still called on FE in emergencies. The managing agent's complaints were familiar: 'You've got to use different methods. Well, it was abysmal. We didn't really withdraw [trainees], they withdrew themselves . . . The rooms were not organized. They used to go from room to room. The tutors were not turning up. The rooms were unheated. They used to complain they were doing the same subjects [as] they'd done at school, and . . . in exactly the same way.' After buying private training, they, too, recruited their own staff and became an RSA-accredited training centre.

Jack's had never been a large FE customer, and had quickly responded to YTS by becoming an accredited centre and selling services. It started because 'the kids just wouldn't go, we had no end of trouble'. Many FE tutors 'had never been in industry. We'd got a fair idea of what the manufacturers wanted, so we could make the training practical.' At first Jack's bought in private training, but when it easily gained exam accreditation for its training centre it hired its own staff, and began to sell computer training, induction and life skills to other schemes.

To make the transition from FE to their own training, most managing agents used Private Trainers. This organization was a creation of its time. It began as part of a non-profit making correspondence college which offered adult training packages and short courses for the MSC's predecessor, the Training Services Agency. The firm survived precariously on the ever-changing opportunities of government training programmes, and not surprisingly it had received 'horrendous flack' from Southwich College. However, later Private Trainers itself met competition and poaching of staff by managing agents who had learned that the MSC would allow them to provide their own, still cheaper, training. And indeed an experienced member of their staff identified this as part of the commercial logic of YTS, a kind of 'Gresham's law of training' where cheaper and worse training would drive out the good.

The devaluation of credentials: 'City & Guilds with everything'

By 1986, with the approach of YTS 2, managing agents were trying to gear their courses to recognized credentials, but this highlighted the lack of suitable qualifications in the non-established new training areas. At first, the MSC's favoured solution appeared to be 'City & Guilds with everything', as the exam board took every opportunity to expand its activities. The Co-op managing agent commented: 'Let's face it, City & Guilds would validate anything, wouldn't they? . . . But it wouldn't mean anything.' As an alternative, he called on a national Co-op training and a distance learning package which led towards the Retail Industry Capability Certificate and three-year courses run through the Open Tech. However, again 'the weak point is getting people at the place of work keen enough'.

By 1986, Dovers, too, was developing its own training, by recruiting staff from FE and trying to hire the managing agent of the dying church scheme: 'Having seen Jack's . . . I knew I could do it.' Care work was easy: 'This part of City & Guilds is based on a lot of practical work and there won't be problems.' But beauty care was late in gaining cover from City & Guilds, and the main accepted professional qualification was a self-funding two-year course beyond the resources of YTS. Dovers asked one of its work sponsors, a trained beauty technician, to develop a beauty programme: 'And now she's got her own private training school.' After only a little hesitation, City & Guilds had agreed to validate the course. At this point it looked as though sport and leisure could be similarly taken care of, through the services of a former prison officer. Later, there was a hitch and Dovers continued with FE for sport and also for catering.

The managing agent of the church care scheme had energetically set about devising new training, but finding suitable recognized care credentials was impossible because again they required more resources than YTS would afford, and trainees had to have sponsorship by an employer. As an alternative she suggested she should teach O-level, which some trainees needed for entry to nursing: 'But MSC totally rejected it. They said I must not do it, it would go totally beyond the aims of YTS . . . [They] seemed to want to push us in the direction of City & Guilds, but . . . I thought it was superficial . . . I could *kick* MSC!'

Concessions did its own off-the-job training geared towards making the trainees identify with service to the store. We observed the managing agent give the induction: 'Why do we expect you to dress conventionally in this store? . . . If the customers don't like it, what happens?' ('Customer goes somewhere else.') 'If the whole shop goes on strike, what happens?' ('Customer goes somewhere else.') 'The customer is always right . . . What are we all here for?' ('To please the customers.') 'To take their money. It's important that we look at it as our store. If the store goes under, we all go under.' Negotiations for City & Guilds to validate the training were unfinished when the scheme and store closed.

The remaining Mode B scheme had always provided its own training: 'Most kids we get . . . rebelled against school, and see college as the same.' The lengthier training with integrated life skills was more rewarding than some of the narrower Mode A training, and the scheme also retained the residentials which most other schemes had dropped. The managing agent stressed the personal development she saw in young trainees who quite frequently had never been away from home for a night, never been to London and sometimes never even buttered a slice of bread.

Explaining segmentation and inequality in the surrogate labour market

In Part Two we have described how the MSC lacked the necessary powers to guide YTS along the lines of the official blueprint. The play of commercial interests caused the surrogate labour market to behave like a real market and become segmented, with unequal access to schemes and placements which carried very unequal job and training opportunities. A study in the first year of YTS concluded that 'two tiers' were developing (Roberts *et al.*, 1986a: 108), but our research suggests that the picture is more complex than a simple hierarchy. To end Part Two we will discuss the sources of 'segmentation' in the surrogate labour market, and we will then put forward a model to describe its consequences in terms of the unequal opportunities of jobs and training which it offers young people.

Our starting point was the suggestion that although schemes were officially described under a limited number of occupational categories or skill *labels*, we could not take it for granted that training and opportunities would be equally well-regulated in all schemes with identical labels. In Chapters 4 and 5 we discovered marked contrasts between the comparatively few schemes led by the larger employers, a larger group of stable-skill schemes, and the deskilled expansion of the entrepreneurial and Mode B schemes. As a result there were variations of training quality and job opportunities even between similarly-labelled schemes. As a further complication, although the quality of typical placements was linked to individual schemes, some schemes seemed to cover placements of very varied quality.

Drawing on other studies as well as the present research, there are at least four major causes of variation in YTS which overlap but do not altogether coincide. These are: the *gender* connotations of particular occupational skills; the *origin* of schemes; the *recruitment context* of the individual placements; and the *source of control* over the content of training. In relation to gender we have shown how, because of the gender stereotyping of occupational areas by employers and young people alike, boys and girls entered not one but virtually two overlapping labour markets, and in later analysis we will break down our data by gender. We will now discuss in turn the other causes of segmentation and inequality.

The origin of schemes pre- and post-YTS

We saw earlier (Chapter 4) how, throughout YTS, the subsidy determined where placements and viable schemes developed, but with results opposite to those intended. This largely explains the findings of national studies showing a lack of places in shortage skills but too many places in skills 'not in short supply' (Deakin and Pratten, 1987: 495; Ashton *et al.*, 1990). As in Southwich, employers with high training costs have been deterred from providing surplus training places in traditional or established 'real' skills by the low level of the YTS subsidy which reduces it to a 'fringe benefit' (Chapman and Tooze, 1987; Dutton, 1987; Turbin 1988; Ashton *et al.*, 1990). Managing agents such as the ITBs, whose aim was to maintain training standards in a particular established skill or to serve a particular pool of employers, were also likely to resist MSC pressure to expand. As a result, the MSC had to resort to other means of getting enough placements, and YTS provision was determined by whatever 'resources and mechanisms for delivery' of training were available (Turbin, 1988: 194).

These were of three kinds. First, especially where large firms did join in, remnants of training capacity shut by the recession were reopened by the YTS subsidy. Yet there might no longer be any local demand for revived established skills such as engineering. (In Turbin's study the trade-off between subsidy and costs led to *over*provision of these declining transferable skills; see also Dutton, 1987.) Southwich firms revealed examples of reopened facilities being used in a variety of ways, sometimes for genuine apprenticeship, sometimes for training semi-skilled workers along with apprentices. Jack's now turned out a majority of machine operators and was expanding its training into a separate commercial venture.

Secondly, YTS training emerged wherever private trainers and managing agents could gain a commercial benefit from YTS grants, especially if there were economies from running schemes on a large scale. Southwich showed how MSC bargaining with the various managing agents of umbrella schemes was a complicated balance of stimulation, control and containment. But the basic interest of both sides lay in the expansion (and hence overprovision) of low-cost training, and it was only after the Mode A umbrella schemes had achieved what they could that the more expensive Mode B was used to take up the remaining young people. Lastly, if their training costs were low, employers also had an incentive to take on YTS trainees simply for the benefit of their services or output. This added to the overprovision of low-level placements in non-established or non-shortage 'skills'.

The overall result of this pattern of YTS expansion was a mix of schemes whose quality differed radically according to their origins pre- or post-YTS. Pre-YTS schemes were run by established trainers in 'real', that is transferable and marketable, skills. However, post-YTS schemes tended to be of two types. Entrepreneurs (and voluntary and Mode B managing agents) ran expanded and deskilled schemes, either under traditional skill labels or in 'new-skill' areas. In these, skills were not yet established and employers did not even necessarily agree that any training was required.

The recruitment context: a scheme for the unemployed?

Critics of YTS expected it to suffer from problems of credibility because of the MSC's eagerness to mop up unemployment (Ryan, 1984). Results from the Scottish School Leavers Survey suggest that because YTS innovated from the bottom up, a vicious circle developed as it competed with alternative openings for young people at 16. More able young people, in practice the only ones with a realistic choice of options, have seen it as a low-status course and avoided it. In turn, employers have stigmatized it on the grounds that YTS contained few of the kind of young people they wanted to employ (Raffe, 1987)

We have seen that this problem was not shared equally by all schemes. There was a two-way link between the context in which individual managing agents recruited and the relative status and opportunities their schemes offered. Both were determined by employers' expectations, whether these were themselves managing agents or simply offering YTS placements. The more prestigious employer-led schemes and those offering established skill training showed a 'virtuous' circle in which the size or stability of the employer (or the employment) resulted in an excess of applications. The managing agent, often the same as the employer, could then pick and choose, using educational credentials as an indicator not merely of aptitude but of non-academic attributes and motivation. So once the initial *selection* was made, the outcome was relatively predictable and trainees performed as expected.

Outside this small area of YTS the outcome was less certain. Because the likely offer of training was mostly with an unknown or smaller employer, job chances and opportunities were more precarious. (To the extent that the Careers Service became heavily involved in recruiting to these schemes, there was a risk of becoming itself a low-status route into YTS.) The schemes usually ran on an umbrella basis and attracted fewer well-qualified leavers or were undersubscribed. The work provider in turn perceived young people without obvious educational and social status as a poorer risk and put any trainee on *probation*, to 'work themselves into a job', so reinforcing the vicious circle of insecurity for all.

The source of control over training content

As we saw above, the MSC's powers to control training on the job were limited. The original YTS provisions left the MSC's powers of intervention ambiguous, but in any case control of training presented much greater problems in the small scattered subcontracted work experience of the umbrella schemes than it did in employer-led or stable-skill schemes. The latter were also more likely to have established off-the-job training which was taught in FE and guaranteed by externally accredited credentials. In contrast, the training entrepreneurs themselves provided most of their own off-the-job training for their supposedly traditional craft and new-skill schemes. These trainers tended to lack experience, and to suffer from cost-cutting. In addition there was some evidence that in its thirst for business, City & Guilds was prepared to spawn a range of new low-skill credentials of dubious value.

In other words, the quality control of off-the-job training tended to match the distinction we have already drawn between schemes in traditional skills established pre-YTS and the newer schemes in non-established skills started post-YTS.

A model of segmentation and inequality in the surrogate labour market

In this chapter we have considered four principle causes of segmentation (and hence inequality) in YTS. We conclude by combining these into a classification of schemes and placements according to the segment of the surrogate labour market where they usually occur. The classification expands on the work of Raffe (1987) who went beyond the MSC's simple typology of modes and managing agents, classifying *placements* according to their likely job outcomes for trainees. He suggested a hierarchy with a 'sponsorship' sector (where trainees may expect jobs from their placements); a 'credentialling' sector (where trainees may expect their training to be marketable elsewhere, so that they will get jobs in the same skill but with another employer); a 'contest' sector (where trainees may win or create a job in their placement, possibly with luck); and a 'detached' sector (implicitly exploitative, where trainees work with little chance of a job because the placement was created without regard to whether it offered trainees either skills or job prospects). However, this classification looks only at *placements*, and because we did not visit many individual placements

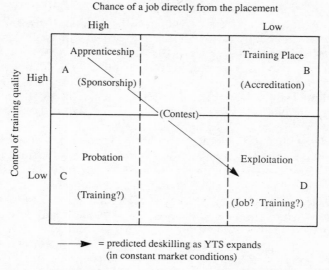

Chance of a job directly from the placement

Figure 6.1   Segmentation and inequality in the surrogate labour market: placements

at this point in our work we had to find an overall classification for *schemes* as well.

Raffe's typology is also essentially concerned with YTS outcomes (or effects), whereas we wanted to point to the *causes* of inequalities in the surrogate labour market. Figure 6.1 applies this strategy to Raffe's typology of placements, which we felt varied according to high or low 'control over content and quality of training' (shown in the rows) and the context which determines the 'chance of a job' from that placement (shown in the columns).

Policy controversies are represented by question marks. For example, in the bottom row (low control), the quality of the training is questioned, and in the second column the prospect of getting a job indirectly from training is doubted.

Taking each box of the diagram in turn, in box A controlled training in a good job context is like an apprenticeship or 'sponsored' traineeship in an established or traditional skill. The employer is using YTS for recruitment, either for normal needs or to substitute for an older worker. Such a placement actually overfulfils the official claim that YTS provides 'quality training' but not necessarily a direct job. Box B shows the additional 'training places' for which the official claim is that they are likely to lead indirectly to a job in the same established skill area but with another employer. Placements in boxes C and D are 'deviant' in relation to the YTS blueprint and therefore more controversial. They show the extension of new training to jobs (typically in non-established skill areas) where there was previously little or none (box C), or to new skill placements where there are no viable jobs (box D), for instance placements in scarcely viable small businesses or recaptured from part-time work. Although low-skill trainees are given extra 'compensatory' tuition in personal and life skills, critics (and trainees, too, as we shall see) doubt the value of such non-established skill training in improving job chances. In box C employers are definitely wanting to recruit, but (usually because few skills are needed for the job) trainees are on probation. They will be weighed up for diffuse qualities of personality or motivation, or possibly family connections. Box D, without controlled training or job prospects, is sheer exploitation.

Compared with Raffe's typology (shown in brackets in Figure 6.1), box A is 'sponsorship', box B is 'credentialling', and box D is 'detached'. But in practice Raffe's 'contest' sector (where trainees compete for possible jobs from placements) pervades much of YTS. Chances of jobs from placements are rarely clear-cut except for employed YTS trainees. The MSC acknowledges this situation in advertisements for employers and trainees as 'a chance to look at the trainee' or 'a chance to show what you can do'. Employers with jobs are invited to take on surplus trainees for a probationary period, to check on their motivation and other qualities before making firm job offers. So, in our typology, the 'contest' sector lies somewhere between boxes A and B, and boxes C and D (within the dotted lines in Figure 6.1).

Figure 6.2 considers how *schemes* may be classified into those giving more or less transferable training and better or worse job prospects. Because we could not visit all the placements, we needed an alternative classification which described how placements with the same skill label differed between different schemes. Here the most important sources of variation are their overall origin (whether they were established pre- or post-YTS) and the typical job opportunities provided by the context or market situation within which they recruit (whether they were run by prestigious employers, and whether recruitment was restricted or expanded). The outcome is a sixfold classification with the rows showing the origin of different types of managing agents in established/traditional craft or non-established 'new-skill' training. The columns show the recruitment context, that is average or perceived job opportunities *for the managing agent's placements as a whole*. The table shows a sixfold hierarchy of schemes described in our fieldwork, with three types of managing agent, training in established or non-established 'new' skills.

Superimposed upon this we should also bear in mind the pervasive dimension of *gender*. For example, fewer girls are recruited to schemes where selection is a form of sponsorship. Girls on YTS also seem to be more likely than boys to be put 'on probation' or not considered material for promotion, on the assumption that their motivation and commitment to work are more suspect.

The diagonal arrows in both diagrams represent our prediction, at the end of YTS 1, of how the Scheme was evolving. They suggest a general tendency for training to be deskilled by pressures to expand YTS through low-skill

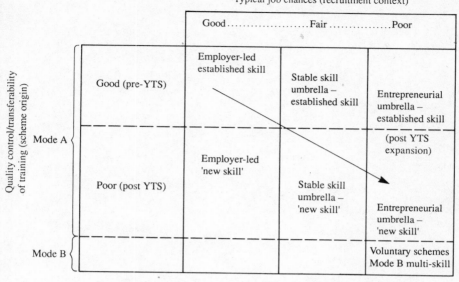

Typical job chances (recruitment context)

| | | Good . . . . Fair . . . . Poor | | |

Figure 6.2   Segmentation and inequality in the surrogate labour market: schemes

placements, whatever the skill *labels* claimed by schemes. Other things being equal, they suggest, too, a progressive reduction in trainees' job chances (although in fact job chances depend above all on opportunities in the external job market, as we show in Part 4).

Raffe observed that he would have liked to provide a rigorous test of his typology rather than construct it after the event. As he pointed out, the 'sectors [in YTS] are likely to be reliably identified only in case studies which investigate a few YTS schemes in depth', yet to test the classification of sectors would require the researcher to 'compare the young people who enter different sectors on the basis of a representative sample of the age group' and make comparisons over time (Raffe, 1987: 22).

Few researchers have the resources for both kinds of work. However, our study of the YTS surrogate labour market has enabled us to use our surveys and interviews with trainees to provide a preliminary test of this classi-fication and to interpret what happened to the surrogate labour market under YTS 2. In parts Three and Four we describe the results.

Part Three
The supply of trainees
and the experience of
YTS 1

Chapter 7
Recruitment and selection

Because of the unemployment situation between 1984 and 1986, the 'supply' of trainees for the surrogate labour market of YTS 1 was drawn from a relatively wide cross-section of Southwich's 16-year-old school leavers. Later, we show that as unemployment fell and YTS became a two-year scheme the intake narrowed. But those who found themselves on YTS 1 without a 'real' job were in a situation not even their parents had, for the most part, experienced or expected. The next three chapters will look at how these young people were recruited to the unequal opportunities of YTS, what they thought of their placements, and what happened to them when they later entered the real labour market. We then outline their attitudes to society, politics and unemployment, and Part Three concludes with a brief account of what had happened to them in the three years after YTS and what they now thought of the Scheme, looking back in 1988.

Our information comes mainly from our postal surveys of school leavers, and from the 'interview sample' of 226 trainees. As we explained in Part One, so broad was the scope of YTS in Southwich in the mid-1980s that we could not compare our trainees with a matched control of young people who did *not* take part in the Scheme. Instead, we carried out a postal survey of all the town's 16-year-old school leavers in 1984 and again in 1985, and we were supplied by the schools with their examination results. (The second time we included sixth-formers, and we also called on a sample of non-respondents, which explains why some tables cover larger numbers (see also Appendix).) This 'leavers survey' gave us a cross-section of simple biographies of 1375 young people for comparison with the national picture. Among them we located 547 YTS trainees, which included our 'interview sample' whom we contacted in early 1985 when they were on the first full year of YTS, and then again a year later in 1985–6 after they had left the Scheme. In 1988 we carried out a final follow-up of the sample by phone and post.

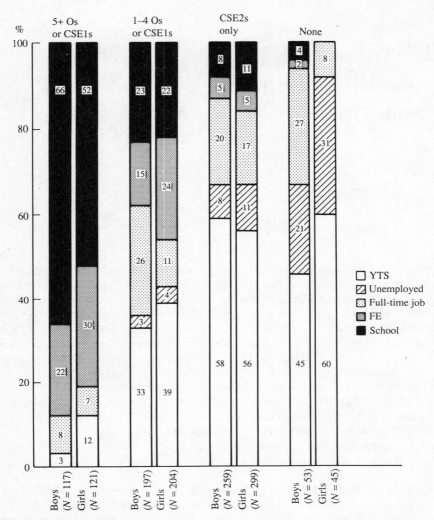

Figure 7.1 Southwich non-grammar school leavers' credentials by gender and post-school leaving destination, 1984

Source: Southwich Cohort Survey. The total number of school leavers in the cohort was 1665, of whom 370 either moved or supplied incomplete data

A comparison of YTS trainees and other school leavers

Advantages of education, gender and social background enabled some young people to 'avoid' YTS (as they mostly saw it). There were hardly any trainees from the grammar schools, but also the non-grammar pupils with the best exam results (five or more O levels) mostly stayed at school or switched to full-time FE (Figures 7.1 and 7.2), while the rest got jobs. Those

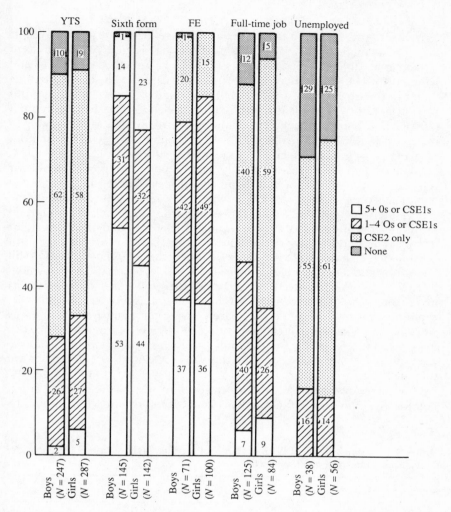

Figure 7.2   Post-school destinations of Southwich non-grammar school leavers by gender and examination achievement, 1984

Source: As Figure 7.1

with a mix of O levels and CSEs were spread evenly between staying on, finding jobs or joining YTS. And those with the poorest exam results were mostly on YTS or unemployed. Clearly, in Southwich YTS lacked credibility among the better-qualified.

The leavers survey also confirmed how the town's low staying-on rate disadvantaged girls more than boys. More boys than girls at every level of attainment went into full-time jobs, even the most poorly-qualified. Yet only two in five leavers known by the Careers Service to have got jobs were girls, and poorly-qualified girls were particularly likely to be unemployed or on YTS. Overall, slightly more girls than boys had joined YTS, whereas in Britain as a whole YTS has always recruited more boys than girls (Gray and King, 1986: 11). This difference was partly because areas less prosperous than Southwich had more Mode B and 'premium' places, which tend to recruit more boys, partly also because Southwich College had pegged the size of some vocational courses popular with girls, so that YTS was able to recruit a few quite well-qualified girls, 12 per cent of those with five or more O levels, or 14 out of 19 such girls who had left education.

Some of the school leavers, mostly the low achievers, proved unable or reluctant to give details of their families and social backgrounds (as in the National Cohort Study; see Courtenay, 1988: 7, Table 4). Even so, the replies showed that those with five or more O levels and continuing in full-time education mostly came from professional and managerial, or white-collar middle-class backgrounds. True, because of the high proportion of such households in Southwich, this creaming-off by education still left a substantial number of middle-class low achievers, about half of whom were on YTS or unemployed. Nevertheless, the social mix of different tracks after school varied considerably. Of the three-quarters of FE students who replied giving their father's job, barely a quarter came from manual or working-class homes. Roughly two-thirds of the replies from those in work who gave fathers' jobs were also middle-class, as well as two-thirds of the unemployed, which suggests that the working-class low achievers were missing.

Our interviews provided the most accurate way of finding the social composition of YTS itself. Only 18 per cent of our boy interviewees on YTS

Table 7.1 Core sample of YTS trainees by gender and by father's occupation/ household composition, 1984

Father's occupation: (RG Social Class)	Boys		Girls	
	N	%	N	%
I Professional and managerial	2	(2)	2	(2)
II Intermediate non-manual	15	(16)	23	(24)
III Skilled non-manual	7	(7)	11	(11)
IV Skilled manual	46	(50)	30	(31)
V Semi- and unskilled manual	12	(13)	11	(11)
No paternal income (father unemployed, absent, disabled, dead)	8	(9)	19	(19)
No answer/refused question	3	(3)	2	(2)
Total:	93		98	

Source: 'Core' sample only – see Appendix

came from middle-class homes as against just over a quarter of the girls (Table 7.1). Just over 70 per cent of both sexes had working-class fathers. But a substantial group of the interviewed trainees (more girls than boys) had unemployed parents or came from broken homes, which may be one reason for the poor response on home background from the leavers survey as a whole. Scarcely any of this group had achieved a single O level.

To sum up, the social character of Southwich had ensured that a fair number of middle-class young people – mostly, but not all, low achievers – had been recruited to YTS. But on the whole trainees were poorly-qualified, and more working-class and socially disadvantaged. YTS had failed to recruit well-qualified and middle-class young people, particularly educationally successful middle-class boys. Southwich girls underachieved relative to boys at every educational and occupational level, which brought the paradox that more low-achieving girls but also more well-qualified middle-class girls had followed the less-favoured route of YTS. Probably low-achieving boys who refused school were also more likely to refuse YTS.

Selection among types of YTS scheme by academic credentials

We compared the academic and social backgrounds of all 547 school leavers in our survey who had entered YTS with our model of the unequal opportunities in different types of scheme in the surrogate labour market (see the end of Chapter 6). These trainees had joined YTS a little too early for their experience to reflect all the entrepreneurial developments which took place up to 1986. Nevertheless, we found that recruitment to the better opportunities in YTS schemes was academically selective, not only between Mode A and Mode B but also *within* Mode A (Table 7.2).

Though numbers are small, the limited recruitment to the employer-led schemes clearly contained more leavers with O levels. Likewise schemes with established (or traditional) labels, whether in large firms or umbrella schemes like the entrepreneurial motor vehicle scheme, tended to recruit better-qualified young people than the new-skill schemes (the exceptions were the stable-skill CITB and hairdressers schemes).

To make any effects of academic selectivity more visible, we added on to our 'core' sample of boys and girls selected at random, an additional over-sample of any trainees with five or more O levels and those with no exam passes at all. This enlarged sample, of 103 boys and 123 girls, was a better guide to *contrasts* in the characteristics of different schemes than proportions. It showed that 59 per cent of boys and 82 per cent of girls in employer-led craft and clerical schemes had at least one O level, compared with 27 per cent of boys and 48 per cent of girls in stable-skill schemes, and 47 per cent of boys and 29 per cent of girls in entrepreneurial schemes. Among the best-qualified trainees (with five or more O levels), ten out of fifteen girls and four out of five boys were on employer-led schemes in-house. The credential difference among our interviewees was wider for girls, partly

Table 7.2 Boys and girls with at least one O level on each type of scheme, 1984–5

Skill label and scheme	Boys			Girls		
	N	(%)	Total (=100%)	N	(%)	Total (=100%)
Mode 'A'						
Established:						
employer-led	14	(67)	21	22	(67)	33
stable skill	10	(23)	43	31	(39)	80
entrepreneurs	15	(36)	42	6	(46)	13
New skill:						
employer-led	5	(33)	15	11	(48)	23
stable	1	(10)	10	9	(22)	41
entrepreneurs	12	(25)	48	8	(20)	40
Mode 'B'*	3	(7)	44	4	(9)	45
Incomplete data	–		34	–		15
Total			257			290

Source: Southwich Leavers Survey: YTS trainees only. The total number of trainees in the Survey was 547 of whom 49 did not disclose their Managing Agent
* The Table and numerical analysis in the text include only Mode B1

because more were better-qualified, but also credentials seemed to be more important in recruiting girls to top clerical schemes.

At the other extreme, 23 trainees had no credentials, but only two were on employer-led and three were on stable-skill schemes, compared with ten on entrepreneurial and eight on Mode B schemes. Only a handful of the 37 Mode B trainees had any O levels (Table 7.2). Interestingly, the differentials in selection widened to three times if they were based on what exam results trainees *said* they had achieved. Boys especially overestimated or underestimated their actual school results and this possibly influenced managing agents during recruitment.

Selectivity, modes of recruitment and sources of advice

At least part of the explanation for selectivity in YTS lay in the way trainees had been advised and put in touch with their schemes. About a third of the trainees in the leavers survey had applied early from school and of these four out of five had O levels. Two-thirds of these better-qualified direct applicants said they got onto their chosen scheme, so bearing out what managing agents told us about self-selection for the better schemes. The invidious position of the Careers Service also came out clearly from the survey. Only one in five school leavers had found real jobs through the Careers Service, but almost two-thirds of YTS trainees joined through that route. Over three times as many boys as girls had originally applied for jobs and been offered YTS places, which reflects the greater availability of 'sponsored' YTS apprenticeships or traineeships for boys. In contrast (although numbers were small) girls were much more likely than boys to have come onto YTS through weekend and part-time jobs being turned into placements.

Predictably, parents were the major source of advice for all our school leavers, especially college students. Also, those who had found real jobs had often been helped through family contacts. In contrast, fewer YTS trainees reported parents as the main source of advice and they were much more likely to have used Careers Service advice. (The unemployed reported getting least help from Careers, possibly not seeing pressure to take a YTS place as 'advice'). Rather than giving positive reasons for joining YTS, a third of the trainees said they needed money, a fifth said they could not get a job, and a tenth said the only alternative was the dole. One in twenty, all girls, said they had been threatened with loss of their social security payments. (This proportion is probably an understatement because young people, especially boys, who have been threatened with loss of benefit are the least likely to reply to surveys.) Only a small minority (one in four girls and one in seven boys) felt they had actually *chosen* YTS. Before YTS, one in four respondents had been unemployed for three months or more, apparently holding out in the hope that a real job would turn up. Only a tenth had had a job before YTS which they had usually left because of bad conditions or being sacked. But a further two-fifths had unsuccessfully tried for work, and a third (mostly girls) had unsuccessfully applied for college. In other words, the trainees overlapped with other school leavers in their initial hopes for jobs or courses.

Nevertheless, compared with other leavers, Southwich YTS trainees were less sceptical and more hopeful about YTS (Table 7.3). True, half believed that YTS would not bring them a job and nearly half agreed that it was cheap labour or a means of keeping down the unemployment figures. Yet almost seven out of eight believed it would help other unemployed people to find work or thought it was a good way to get work experience or training.

Selection among types of YTS scheme by social class

Using our interviews only, we explored whether there was also selection between different types of YTS scheme by social background, but here the picture was more obscure and made difficult by very small numbers. Mode A trainees were more than twice as likely as Mode B (40 per cent against 16 per cent) to come from middle- than from working-class backgrounds. But within Mode A there was no overall difference between the social backgrounds of 'established-skill' and 'new-skill' trainees.

In fact, there were some puzzling patterns. While *established-skill and clerical* girls were slightly more likely to be middle-class (51 per cent

Table 7.3 Attitudes of labour market entrants to YTS

	Percentage of group agreeing with statement:			
	College students (N=152)	Full-time employees (N=177)	Unemployed (N=69)	YTS trainees (N=432)
Do you think:				
YTS helps unemployed people to find jobs	54	68	70	87
YTS schemes are just cheap labour	76	68	72	48
YTS gives people something to do	73	85	84	86
YTS schemes are just to keep the unemployment figures down	67	60	64	49
They are a useful way to get work experience	61	82	54	84

Source: First Postal Survey, December 1984. The percentages are based on the number actually replying to the question on attitudes to YTS

against 43 per cent), established-skill boys were if anything slightly less likely to be middle-class (27 per cent against 34 per cent) than the rest. *Large employers and LCU schemes* had recruited a rather higher than average proportion (38 per cent against 30 per cent) of middle-class boys, but a lower than average proportion (37 per cent against 47 per cent) of middle-class girls. This was especially the case in employer-led clerical schemes for girls (29 per cent as against 51 per cent). Among the small number of *new-skill* trainees in large employer-led and stable skill schemes, the boys were comparatively middle-class (75 per cent and 57 per cent), compared with entrepreneurial schemes (19 per cent), but not particularly well qualified (0 per cent and 14 per cent, as against 24 per cent).

It was easier to see negative social selection by some schemes, that is, the exclusion of trainees from unskilled manual backgrounds. Out of 38 Mode A trainees from unskilled manual backgrounds, only 11 were on established skill schemes, two employer-led and eight stable-skill. In contrast over half, mainly girls, were on entrepreneurial new-skill schemes. The bottom line of recruitment and selection was that on the Mode B scheme almost half the trainees were from unskilled manual backgrounds.

However, lack of a clear statistical relationship did not mean the absence of social influences over YTS recruitment. Rather it revealed the limits of conventional survey analysis. Qualitative material from our interviews with individual trainees showed that cutting across background influences was the complexity of managing agents' screening practices, the influence of family and neighbourhood ties, and contrasting perceptions (by trainees and parents) of the status and respectability of the different skill areas.

Recruitment of boys and girls into different skill areas

The recruitment of boys and girls needs to be discussed separately, because self-selection and the managing agents' and employers' recruitment strategies had ensured that trainees entered virtually two surrogate labour markets, strongly segregated by gender along established lines. Boys dominated established crafts (and low-level multi-skill schemes with craft labels) and also warehousing. There were a few boys in clerical, retail and catering work, but these skill areas mostly recruited girls; hairdressing and carework were almost exclusively female. Mode B was similarly split. Because boys were spread more widely and girls were more clustered, YTS (like the real youth labour market) offered boys a wider range of skill labels than girls.

Boys' skill areas

Engineering with the larger employers
The stringent academic selection for high-cost engineering training meant that the larger employers had recruited from a small group of well-qualified *working-class* boys who left school, rather than stay on. (However, because clerical work was less selective, Bolts' *clerical* scheme had recruited two boys via family contacts within the firm.) Within this highly-selected group, though, subtle grading was in evidence. Mark, from a grammar school, had been able to choose an employed YTS apprenticeship from several offers, whereas Paul, with six O levels from a non-selective school, complained: 'There's [other trainees] all from selective schools got taken on as apprentices, and the rest of us from normal secondary schools are on YTS.' Trainees without O levels (but with equivalent CSEs) were dissatisfied at being put on low-skill assembly work.

'Construction' with the CITB and other managing agents
In contrast, recruitment to construction YTS put a premium on working-class family influence because employers or trainees often came with placements. Over half the trainees' fathers were skilled construction workers. Four had family placements and others were with 'contacts'. Alan, an unusually large and strong boy, said: 'I knew I'd have to go into the family business. It's the state of the country isn't it? You can't find a job.' His job in the firm had been converted to a YTS placement when his parents met one of the entrepreneurial managing agents at a craft exhibition at Southwich College. Even CITB recruitment was partly via placements, although the CITB remained minimally academically selective. The few CITB trainees with O levels had already been turned down for more academically selective

schemes, two for engineering and one for clerical work. However, the only trainee without credentials, a school refuser, had been placed by the Careers Service with the CITB because he already worked for his father who wanted him qualified. On other construction schemes, more boys were without O levels or credentials than in any other established-skill label areas, and Mode A and B multi-skill 'construction' schemes took mainly less-motivated low achievers fed to them via the Careers Service.

The motor vehicle association's craft scheme

Trainees under this established-skill label were recruited partly by academic selection, partly via small family businesses. Almost half had one or more O levels, eight out of eleven had skilled-manual fathers, and over half had worked with cars before their YTS placement. The only middle-class trainee had learned of YTS at the Southwich College craft exhibition, but he was already employed in his father's garage and his YTS traineeship was now 'just working for me dad'. This was a further example of YTS subsidizing young people in small family firms to do jobs they would have done anyway.

Jack's craft and design scheme

Jack's craft and design was a new scheme and it recruited trainees whose school interests had developed patchily to give them one or two O levels in art or photography. Some had found placements through family or personal contacts, which was reflected by the sprinkling of middle-class trainees. For example, Stephen's father was a teacher and his mother a secretary. After he failed to get into art full-time at College, his family had found him what looked like a job, but then 'I got a letter saying there's a [YTS] interview for Jack's and I'd already been to the firm I'm working for now'. Two other O-level holders, Tony and Graham, had failed Chamber of Commerce retail interviews because they did not want a YTS place, but Tony had been pushed onto the Jack's scheme by the Careers Service and his father who 'started to interfere a bit . . . There wasn't much else . . . They'll stop giving you social security.' Graham had spent his school time mostly on art, and he had applied to an advertising agency who took him on through the Jack's scheme. Other trainees with only CSEs had also joined through job applications. Jimmy started at a screen-printers: His employer was very crafty '. . . He'd say, "Come in for two days", and he'd give me £10.00. Then he put me on the YTS.' In our observation of this scheme's training at Southwich College we were struck by trainees' descriptions of poor placements, but also by their individualism and the number who were hoping to 'save towards their own business'. The scheme seemed to serve as an alternative to established crafts for which the trainees lacked credentials or family contacts.

Clerical work (including the Post Office)

Clerical work was not popular with boys, but there were some better-qualified middle- and working-class trainees both in- and out-of-house at

Endowments. Several might have stayed on at schools with better or more stable sixth forms, and Jason described the disruption of sixth-form reorganization, 'The older teachers were leaving 'cos the school was closing down and younger teachers were coming in.' Stephen said: 'I was going to stay on in the sixth form but we were told we weren't going to have one.' The Post Office in-house scheme recruited a less well-qualified group, partly via family contacts. For example, a trainee whose father and brother worked at the Post Office, was an Easter school leaver who had managed to pass the Post Office selection test when he put his mind to it. Possibly the worst example of wasted potential we came across was a working-class boy who got eight O levels despite his east end school. Yet he allowed the sub post-office where he did a paper-round to take him into a Post Office placement, doing counter-work and serving groceries.

Catering with the HCITB
Both our male catering trainees were well qualified and had a strong career orientation and connections with the trade. John explained: 'My sister did a course in hotel management at the College.' He had failed the medical for the army catering corps but the Careers Service steered him onto the HCITB scheme. Danny had not been allowed to do catering at school but, 'When I was in Careers talking, I just said, "Right, this is what I want to do". I'm always doing cooking.' His mate's dad, a chef in London, had told him of the 'wide range' of openings.

Retail work
Retail work seemed to be a fall-back for some of the middle-class under-achieving boys, enabling them to avoid unskilled manual work. (Low-achieving working-class boys were less likely to have the necessary style and in any case usually preferred more 'manly' labouring jobs.) Indeed, some retail schemes recruited more middle- than working-class trainees, almost all with CSEs only. The only boy with O levels had gone against school pressure to stay on because he saw his future as manager and owner of one of his parents' shops. Otherwise, recruits were boys who had really wanted skilled manual or clerical work. Adrian had been 'for about four interviews' but employers 'tend to pick people with about five O levels . . . even for the jobs, you know, work with hands'. But not only the middle class rejected manual work. Philip had been influenced by his father: 'He was a labourer and he didn't want me to do that, says it's a terrible job.' He was underqualified to stay on at school or work in a bank, so at the Careers Service interview at school, 'I had to put "work in a shop" '.

Warehousing
Finally warehousing, the less social and more physical side of distribution, was also distinguished from labouring for some trainees by elements of stock control and goods handling which needed minimal clerical training and included fork-lift truck driving. Again the trainees had not chosen this

scheme and they included only one boy with an O level and one from a middle-class background.

Girls' skill areas

Clerical schemes

It was a mark of girls' relatively limited educational and occupational opportunities and aspirations that almost three-fifths of clerical trainees were middle-class, and a similar proportion had at least one O level (not always the same girls, about one in three from the oversampled high achievers). Middle-class girls had an advantage even when less qualified and half of them lacked O levels (one with no credentials) compared with only one-sixth of working-class girls. There were no clerical recruits from unskilled manual backgrounds.

In addition, high-achieving middle-class girls were most likely to be found in the best employer-led insurance or LCU schemes. Here, the only recruit without O levels was a middle-class girl whose results had not matched school predictions. In contrast, highly qualified working-class girls were more likely to be found in the employer-led engineering firms or as the better-qualified trainees on the Chamber of Commerce scheme. So, in a sense, the latter had 'underachieved' by entering YTS at below the potential of their credentials, in schemes mainly with poorer direct job prospects. Ironically, this was sometimes because *daughters* were using their fathers' engineering contacts, but to get *clerical* jobs. Alison, one of four such girls, had four A- and two B-grade O levels but left school because 'Towards the end you were just treated like young children . . . I could have done [College] but I needed some money . . . My Dad got me a form from here, so I didn't bother about anything else.'

Some middle-class high achievers joined YTS for lack of an alternative. Deborah had taken nine O levels and passed six. She thought of nursing 'but I went off that when I saw this film of what you had to do'. Her parents had suggested a College secretarial course but she had failed English and 'The Careers Office said, "The only thing we can offer you is YTS" '. Claire, with six GCEs, had gone against Careers Service advice to take A levels: 'I suppose I was a bit of a rebel, that's why I went on YTS.' Whereas high-achieving middle-class girls had rejected restrictive west end sixth forms, some east end schools had no sixth-form provision at all to offer working-class high achievers. Kim, with eight O levels, at first wrote to all the banks: 'They said they'd put me name on the files . . . A little while into the YTS the bank wrote to me, but I was too far into YTS.' Rachel would have preferred to take A levels at school where she knew the teachers but she had to leave and for her, too, the offer of a bank job had come too late, after she joined YTS.

Hairdressing

Like some male crafts, entry into hairdressing was often by placement although not through family contacts so much as through previous part-time jobs. Only one trainee had no prior experience and Melinda, a typical trainee, had had her part-time salon job converted to a YTS placement, which was 'the same really 'cos I'd been working there over a year anyway'. Hairdressing was much sought after and the trainees had backgrounds similar to the Chamber of Commerce's clerical trainees.

Catering

In contrast to the boys, only one trainee saw catering as a career, a middle-class girl with O levels and a place at college. The Careers Service had opposed her choice: 'I came out of there with literature on secretarial courses and that'; but she now cooked in an LCU canteen. The other trainees were working-class girls without O levels on Dovers' scheme. None had wanted to go into catering nor did they cook in their placements. Julie's approach was typical. Rejected for retail work, she said she 'didn't really mind what she did as long as it was a job'.

Retail work

Retail work screened for 'personality' and minimal CSEs, which brought some middle-class or better-qualified recruits who clustered in the best schemes. The top scheme, that of Marks and Spencer, had two middle-class trainees with no O levels. Elsewhere only six girls, mostly middle-class, had any O levels, of whom three were at Flourishes, which looked for O levels as well as social polish. A fourth was with an LCU and a fifth now regretted turning down an LCU place, apparently for lack of advice: 'I was going to wait six months and then go to College . . . but I stayed on [YTS]. That was a stupid move as well.' The sixth girl, with only O-level art, was a biker whom the Chamber of Commerce thought unsuitable for clerical work. On the other hand, only three trainees had no qualifications, and the only such trainee at the Chamber was middle-class. She brought her own placement. 'They said they wouldn't take me on full-time. They said, "YTS, that's it." ' Overall, compared with other new-skill schemes, there were relatively few working-class girls.

Care work (Mode A and Mode B)

The three care schemes recruited mainly from the pool of unqualified working-class girls, often taking those from disrupted homes. Out of 20 trainees with no qualifications, 12 were in care work, as were no fewer than 21 out of 39 trainees from homes disrupted by broken marriage, unemployment or a child having been in care. Even so, the three care schemes revealed some variations in selectivity. Not surprisingly, the residual Mode B scheme had recruited two-thirds of the unqualified girls, and over half the care girls (nine out of seventeen) came from disrupted homes. But, less predictably, Dovers' entrepreneurial urge to expand had led it to recruit no fewer than nine out of thirteen trainees with disrupted backgrounds.

In contrast, despite its philanthropic goals, the church scheme had been more selective and only three out of the nine interviewed trainees came from disrupted backgrounds. Also, this scheme picked up some girls who had really wanted nursing or nursery nurse training, and four church trainees, each with at least one O level, had first failed to gain College places. Among them were twin sisters (one with five O levels) from a middle-class home recently disrupted by divorce, and a working-class girl who had left a fee-paying school with two O levels to work first in a cake shop, 'All my mates left, I'd just be stuck with the upper-class lot. I had a good education [but] I must admit I didn't use mine. I thought I'd like to work with children.' Finding the College course full, she drifted into YTS.

The better-qualified girls who wanted care work had to fight parental and Careers Service opposition to their low-status choice. For example, Claire's father, a bank manager, had found her poor CSE results hard to accept: 'I've always hated school . . . My dad . . . kept trying to get me to go on [Endowments' scheme] but I kept telling them I want to do care work.' Linda had two O levels, but the Careers Service 'said they'd only got YTS. What I went for, care, they were trying to put me off.'

Because the low-status care schemes tended to fill up late, they also picked up a few better-qualified but more rebellious pupils who had been delayed by administrative tangles. A 'gothic' punk with black and purple hair and pasty white make-up had left it too late to apply for College: 'I went back to go into the sixth and they wouldn't let me back unless I toned down my appearance . . . [The Careers Service] sent me this letter . . . When I went down there he said, "We don't want to be heavy, but if you refuse, we can cut your benefit down to £9." ' Another reluctant trainee, Michelle, had hated her first (clerical) scheme, but only care work was left so 'I agreed to do child-care as a fill-in until I went to College'.

Boys and girls in Mode B

The restriction on Mode B1 schemes had ensured that they recruited disproportionately trainees who were poorly qualified, lower working-class, and from disrupted homes. Only about one in six had middle-class backgrounds, and indeed about two-thirds of the girls had fathers in unskilled work if they worked at all. Over half the families had experienced disruption, and in nine families there was currently no employed parent. In Mode A only Dovers had a comparable intake.

Lack of credentials had usually followed a disastrous schooling, some-times virtually none during the last two years. Mark said: 'I didn't really worry, I just didn't go. I was in the bottom stream and nobody bothered.' He felt: 'If you get too many [exam passes] you're over-qualified.' David had a similar attitude: 'Well, there's people with exams and they can't find no job can they? I was never there, I skived off . . . They never bothered.' The girls' responses were much the same. Bronwen said: 'I didn't take any exams, I just thought I'd fail.' Lorraine confessed: 'I didn't think exams were that important to me, so I didn't take any.'

Apart from several who had been drawn to construction and care work, these Mode B1 trainees had usually not chosen their skill areas, and they had often reported being compelled to take a YTS place. Six described how they were virtually 'rounded up' and taken off in a lorry at the end of summer. Nigel, a school truant expelled for fighting and hitting a teacher, thought he might get 'put away' but instead 'got told I was on YTS'. He was later kicked off. At least four others had been threatened with dole cuts, and three said they had been referred by social services or probation (although this probably understates the true proportion).

Probably the most disadvantaged trainee we interviewed was Darren, forced onto YTS by the threatened loss of his dole. The unkept gardens and concrete streets of the approach to the house where he lived (on the toughest council estate in Southwich) were littered with rusting cars and bikes, and many windows had broken glass covered with cardboard. The door was opened by Darren's sister, who had been on the Mode B care scheme a year earlier, and now had a baby. Permission for the interview had to be negotiated with Darren's 'guardian', an uncle who was unemployed and remained throughout in another half-furnished room, strumming a guitar amid a crowd of large dogs. The 'guardian' regularly terrorized Darren into giving up most of his already-reduced social security money. We interviewed Darren in the kitchen where the lino was worn through to the boards and there were not enough chairs, so Darren sat on the sink while the microphone rested on the plastic draining rack. Darren's brother was in borstal, and another brother had been excluded from school for violence. During the interview we were joined by other boys playing truant. Darren was quickly thrown off the Mode B scheme for absenteeism.

We also interviewed eight Mode B2 trainees (not included in the interview sample) who were all from lower working-class homes. Only one household had not been disrupted in some way, and in five there was no employed parent and there were often unemployed brothers or sisters as well. As pupils they had been immature rather than actively disruptive, and seemed to appreciate the shelter of school. They were well-motivated towards YTS, which was seen as preferable to a sheltered workshop but less daunting than the attempt to find and keep a full-time job.

Conclusion

Our leavers survey and interviews revealed that academic, gender and social selection determined which school leavers went on YTS 1, what sort of scheme they entered, and who got the better and worse placements in schemes with common skill labels and even *within* schemes. Recruitment of the surrogate labour supply was grafted onto or incorporated into existing practices. Top schemes might be overtly academically and socially selective, but in some craft schemes jobs were gained through family contacts or an early part-time job. Among boys, YTS was helping to transmit small business ownership, occupational status or job contacts from fathers to sons.

The craft and design and retail schemes were absorbing middle-class school leavers who were only patchily qualified or without school credentials.

Girls' schemes were more academically selective but they also revealed pervasive *social* selection. The few anomalies could be explained as mishaps or lack of advice. Even in relatively deskilled catering work or new-skill retail, middle-class and better-qualified girls were in better placements. Care schemes, intended to mop up only the disadvantaged and unqualified, had recruited some of this well-qualified group, too. For these recruits, the normal hierarchy of social and academic status – reinforced by parents, teachers and the Careers Service – was contradicted by the socially constructed 'caring' aspects of girls' femininity. YTS was also negatively selective both academically and socially, as we saw in the low-skill and Mode B schemes. In short, YTS opportunities finely matched rather than radically altered the various advantages or disadvantages which trainees brought from home or school.

Chapter 8
Work placements and training

In this chapter, the trainees from our interview sample talk about the training and job opportunities offered by their varied work placements. We ourselves cannot provide an alternative description because in our research on YTS 1 we visited only a selection of the placements. However, we should not expect a close relationship between objective conditions and trainees 'work satisfaction', because workers' attitudes are coloured by their prior expectations. As we saw in the last chapter, the trainees held high hopes of YTS, and as a result some were disappointed. Most of the trainees gave us convincing descriptions of conditions in their placements, which we have related to our typology of the different 'segments' of the YTS labour market.

Trainees' comments: intrinsic, extrinsic and social satisfactions

Replies to questions about satisfaction or dissatisfaction with YTS depend on how the questions are asked. *Youth Training News* carries regular reports that a majority of trainees are pleased with YTS, based on the MSC's postal follow-up surveys of all trainees. However, the trainees are aware that the MSC runs YTS, the question wordings are somewhat ambiguous and tend towards inviting satisfaction, and over a third of trainees do not respond, probably mostly the low achievers whom we found to be very dissatisfied. In our study, trainees were invited simply to comment freely on their placements, and *most* gave mixed responses which were difficult to interpret as simple approval or disapproval. Also, their attitudes changed both during and after their placements.

We classified all clearly positive or negative comments along three broad dimensions. *Intrinsic* satisfactions included the variety, interest, coherence and relevance of training. *Extrinsic* satisfactions included prospects, security, topped-up pay, physical conditions, hours, travel, the work's value to

Table 8.1   Comments on placements, by gender (interview sample)

Themes	Satisfaction			Dissatisfaction			Total comments		
	Boys	Girls	N	Boys	Girls	N	Boys	Girls	N
Intrinsic	12	29	41	42	57	99	54	86	140
Extrinsic	4	–	4	18	15	33	22	15	37
Social	13	30	43	13	29	42	26	59	85
Totals	29	59	88	73	101	174	102	160	262*

Source: 'Extended' interview sample – see Appendix

* *Note:* Respondents could give more than one reply

the firm, and the employer's compliance with release for off-the-job training. *Social* satisfactions included relationships with the employer, workmates and others. We counted all the unambiguous comments, but included each *type* of comment only once for an individual trainee (Table 8.1).

Even taking into account the fact that some trainees commented on more than one aspect of their placements, over half the trainees expressed some sort of dissatisfaction with YTS, and in total there were twice as many dissatisfied as satisfied comments. Almost half the trainees were dissatisfied with some intrinsic aspect of their placements, as against less than one in five who expressed satisfaction. Equal proportions, but under one in five, showed satisfaction and dissatisfaction with the social aspects of YTS. And a slightly smaller proportion complained about some extrinsic aspect of their placements, with scarcely any commenting favourably.

Trainees' satisfaction related to the skill level of training

Trainees' overall satisfaction with YTS can be understood in relation to its segmentation and the unequal opportunities which we outlined in Part Two. There we argued that regulated ('quality') training was most likely to be found in established skills in large firms and stable skill schemes. However, trainees' satisfaction did not follow a simple pattern. To some extent, their feelings about their work placements reflected their actual situations and training opportunities. But the differences between trainees on established schemes and the rest were not as wide as might be expected. Even on the former there were more expressions of dissatisfaction than satisfaction, while a small but significant proportion of trainees in 'new' skills showed satisfaction (Table 8.2).

Part of the explanation was no doubt that the better-motivated and better-qualified applicants for top schemes had higher expectations and were more critical, whereas recruits to 'new' skill schemes had low expectations which were more easily met. However, as we shall see by

Table 8.2   Comments on placements by skill level

Skill level	Satisfaction	Dissatisfaction	Total	
			Comments	Trainees
Established	51	86	137	106
Non-established	37	88	125	120
Totals	88	174	262	226

Source: 'Extended' interview sample – see Appendix

looking closely at what respondents told us about each type of placement, not all the nominally established skill schemes offered good work conditions and training. In any case trainees were often more interested in job prospects than training in the abstract.

Satisfaction with 'sponsorship' placements in established skills

As we saw in Part Two, the most regulated training, combined with good job opportunities, seemed to be in the 'sponsorship' segment of the surrogate labour market, where YTS incorporated apprenticeships and some trainee-ships. In Southwich such placements were more likely to be found with the engineering employers, the in-house insurance placements, CITB construction, hairdressing, a proportion of the better clerical placements and a residue of craft apprenticeships in the motor vehicle scheme. Not surprisingly, it was the trainees on these schemes who usually showed most satisfaction with their skills training.

One apprentice said: 'It's really good working me way round so I get to know the whole firm. You learn a hell of a lot, watch it, then do it. Your knowledge builds up and up. Virtually, you can do the same job as the standard fitter down there.' Apart from the greater likelihood of topped-up pay, trainees who were manifestly being trained were more likely to accept the training rationale for the low YTS allowance. One girl clerical trainee said: 'I don't expect to be earning the same as the others while I'm still learning'; and another agreed: 'Compared with my pocket money it's a lot, and I'm only training at the moment.'

The failure of 'credentialling' in established-skill placements

However, even among supposedly 'sponsored' trainees there could be dissatisfaction if they worked next to fully-paid apprentices. Furthermore, as we saw in Part Two, employers would not spend time and money on YTS trainees they did not intend to recruit, even though YTS aimed to create placements for 'credentialling' trainees who would not necessarily be taken on. The result was that trainees on schemes with established-skill labels were frequently disappointed and genuine credentialling placements were very restricted (Raffe, 1989). In what they described as 'noddy jobs', trainees felt underoccupied because there was no real work task, sometimes because the placement had been created out of a misguided sense of philanthropy towards unemployed young people. Alternatively, trainees said they were 'dogsbodies' in situations where employers or skilled workers unloaded their trivial or unpleasant work onto them.

There were fewer 'noddy jobs' with the larger employers, partly because their highly-motivated trainees were more likely to complain if placements did not live up to their expectations. One girl placed in-house at Endowments had seven O-levels but at first, 'All I did was to postcode addresses all day. There didn't seem to be any point in it for me, so I made a nuisance of myself until they moved me.' Few trainees were like Susan, who worked in a small shipping office: 'I enjoyed it there in the winter, the ships laid up. There was nothing to do, sitting all day reading a book.' Most felt uncomfortable, like Sarah who was placed in a newspaper office: 'Some days I finish about eleven a.m. because there's not much to do . . . It gives you the wrong idea.' Tracy, a clerical trainee, complained: 'They just like having a YTS in the office. YTS doesn't make you feel like a responsible person. It's not like a real job.'

Situations where the trainee became a 'dogsbody' were more common. Richard, an Endowments out-of-house trainee, was in a small office placement: 'It was a shabby little place . . . They didn't give me much interesting things to do. "You're on the YTS. We can't give you any responsibility, 'cos you're not employed by us." There's hardly any work there, you see, for an extra person, so I had to run around and do bits and pieces that the other people didn't like doing, like running down the road to customers' houses, running to the post office . . . not even a chair to sit on. All I learnt was how to make tea.' Disappointment at being made a dogsbody was most acute in nominally 'established-craft' placements where trainees could see the exercise of the skills they were supposed to be learning. John's motor vehicle placement was in a garage but, 'I have to do the dirty jobs, cleaning and dirty boring jobs . . . I don't get to do any of the mechanical work even though we do it all at College. I keep asking him if he'll teach me but he says he won't. It's not worth it for him as he's not keeping me on at the end.' One Jack's craft and design trainee, Graham, complained: 'I'm a sort of general slave. I make the tea, take piles of stuff to the post office . . . Apart from that, it's sort of like paste-ups, adverts for companies in the newspapers. I'm shoved in the dark room all the time. It's hot and a bit boring.' Another Jack's trainee with a small printer said: 'There was no way he was going to train me . . . Basically, there was nothing much to do. He'd leave me a few jobs and I was teaching myself.'

Although catering was nominally a craft scheme, some of Dovers' girl trainees spent their time skivvying during unsocial hours. One, who worked from 6.30 a.m. to 1.30 p.m. and then from 5.30 p.m. to 9.30 or 10 p.m., complained: 'It was slave labour . . . They gave me all the dirtiest jobs, like you don't normally leave a fridge to get mouldy do you? Then I'd have to clean it all out.' Susan used to have to clean her boss's flat as part of her 'catering' duties: 'She has dogs and that, it was really messy. She took it for granted that [because] I was on the YTS . . . I was just treated like a slave.'

'Noddy'and 'dogsbody' jobs in new-skill placements

There were also complaints that some 'new' skill placements were noddy jobs, lacking content and structure. Typically, these seemed to occur where part-time jobs had been converted into placements. Linda found the casual hours of her private nursing home placement unsettling: 'They used to say, "Just come in when we need you" . . . It's supposed to be proper work, then I should do proper hours.' Mary, a retail trainee, said she did not like taking money she felt she had not worked for. Susan had a placement where she worked as a hotel chambermaid in the morning, 'Then I work [at another job] till two thirty. Then just do odd jobs to help the porter out . . . It's not proper work or nothing.'

However, 'new' skill trainees complained more often of being exploited in placements where the work was sheer drudgery. This could happen on nominally 'white-collar' schemes such as retail work. Anita, at Concessions, complained: 'I was on the china department and there was nothing to do but dust all day long, so I got really bored out of my skull.' Jason was not allowed to do any selling in his electrical appliance shop placement: 'I was given all the dirty work . . . They used to make fun of me. They just saw me as a joke. Most of the time I was in the stock room busting up cardboard boxes.' In Mario's 'retail' placement, 'I used to . . . pick up loads of potatoes and coal and load the lorry. I got all sweaty and dirty and everything. The reason they wanted me was as a sort of dogsbody . . . My job, it was just like labouring really. I had bags of coal chucked at me, one bloke chucked the coal and I had to catch them. I had cuts and bruises all over me.'

Often 'construction' placements meant sweeping and labouring, with long journeys. Adrian said: 'It sounds good, but when you actually do it, it can be very boring . . . It was a long day due to travelling. It was virtually six to six. It's a bit much for YTS.' Steven worked in a paint warehouse: 'They used to tell the people they made the paint themselves but they didn't, they got it from another firm. The last week I was there, I had to rub down 160 paint tins, sand them down, give them two coats of paint and label 'em.' Jason, in horticulture, said: 'All we ever did was pot geraniums. It was so cold where we worked . . . sometimes one hundred geraniums I'd planted the day before would die overnight because of the cold'. One boy in a warehouse 'didn't have no heat at all in the Winter . . . I'd go and sweep some snow . . . just to keep warm.'

Care work in particular was criticized: 'We're just domestics.' 'It wasn't actually looking after the patients. It was domestic work. We'd clean the toilets, the commodes, and sometimes we'd go round and talk to the patients.' 'It was just depressing working there. The old people were all right. It was just what we had to do. We had to get rid of the commodes. I was a bit shocked but you get used to it.' Care trainees, too, sometimes faced long journeys to rural placements. One girl complained of the Home where she worked: 'It's run on YTS people, and it's really hard work and a long way to travel to work every day. I wouldn't mind it, but my sister works less hours and gets more for it. You don't expect it on the YTS.' Another girl was not repaid her travel expenses: 'When I used to work on a Sunday, I used to have to get a taxi in because there were no buses, and I couldn't claim for that. I was supposed to do alternate weekends, but then I'm working every Saturday morning and Sunday afternoon. It's not much is it, £26 for nine days without a day off. I was supposed to get a day off but I'd get a 'phone call from Matron saying come in anyway, and she'd get really nasty if I said no.'

However, caring tasks sometimes brought social satisfaction which boosted satisfaction with placements lacking training. One Mode B care girl said: 'After a while I started getting to know [the old people] and talking with them. I used to like looking at their old photos . . . I got on with all of them . . . really thought it was quite good apart from the money.' Simon had his attitude towards handicap changed through working in his placement: 'I always thought spastics were mental not handicapped. They're more like friends than people you've looked after.'

The trainees' more detailed comments go a long way towards explaining the pattern we found in Tables 8.1 and 8.2, where even some trainees under established-skill labels complained of noddy and dogsbody jobs, but the bulk of exploitation was in non-established skill schemes. However, dissatisfaction with the training content of placements often reflected a deeper dissatisfaction.

Trainees' wish to do a job of work

The MSC intended that most 'training places' should be surplus to employers' requirements. But the trainees wanted to feel they were doing a *real* job of work essential to the firm, and to be accepted as workers and to gain jobs from their placements.

Trainees appreciated being given adult responsibilities, even where these might prove too heavy. At Concessions, Sean had squashed his hand when unloading goods from a lorry but, 'I got experience, it gave me responsibility . . . Some days I'd be running the back door all by myself, well the loading bay, taking invoices, seeing to the goods, helping to load. It was a big job for a 16-year-old.' Diane worked on her own doing office work which piled up during her off-the-job training: 'For someone who didn't know anything, didn't have a lot of qualifications, I was responsible for a lot of jobs that I enjoyed doing . . . I knew they needed me because I took over a complete job. There wasn't enough people.' One girl packing meat in a supermarket commented: 'It makes me feel a lot bigger, grown up. You're with a lot of big adults. It makes you wonder, it makes you think that it's about time you learnt what was going on.' In extreme instances, trainees were running small offices or shops on their own.

In smaller firms, job substitution meant that employers often resented off-the-job training and work piled up when the trainees were away. One boy at a sports centre observed: 'I don't think they like it when I go away to College. They're a bit short of people and they need me.' Sometimes employers bribed trainees to stay at work: 'I used to miss going . . . if we were a bit pushed, and she'd give me a bit extra to make up what I'd lose.' In fact, retail trainers allowed trainees to work through the busiest sale times, and trainees often preferred this.

Trainees' wish to be accepted as workers

The official rationale of YTS is that trainees *should* be treated differently, supervised and regularly counselled. In fact, they wanted to be accepted by their employers and workmates as *workers*. Occasionally trainees reported approvingly that they were treated better than other staff. A construction trainee said: 'My boss was really good to me. He took care of me.' A trainee in a garage said the proprietor 'treats me better than the others. I s'pose he feels he doesn't want me to get hurt or anything while I'm with him.' However, trainees were more likely to value acceptance as workers: 'I was just treated like one of the staff. I really enjoyed it.' 'You were treated as one of the community rather than as a kid and you were actually working.' 'Everyone gets on well. 'Cos you're on YTS, especially the apprentices down there, you'd expect to be treated as the under-dog, but no, you're treated the same as everyone else, as one of the family.'

Insecure trainees, particularly girls whose placements more often involved dealing with people, valued acceptance because any special attention usually marked inferior status: 'Sometimes when we get introduced to visitors, they say, "Oh, and these are the YOPs".' Janet said that at Flourishes, 'We have to wear a badge with "trainee" on it, and everyone knows that means YTS. When I serve people I try to hide it. It's not surprising . . . with that thing pinned on you . . . We had one department manager and she used to say, "YTS girl, could you come here!" I was really annoyed 'cos you don't want everyone to know you're on YTS.' The managing agent said trainees soon 'forgot' to wear badges, and burst into floods of tears when they became employed and could wear staff uniform. Other trainees said they felt excluded when they were not allowed into staff meetings or did not get staff perks.

Where training was good there was sometimes jealousy from older staff, but more often staff behaviour had reinforced trainees' sense of inferiority, at least initially. A retail trainee complained: 'Friendship's really the best thing about work . . . It's hard when they just see you as YTS. At first the staff used to think: "She's a YTS. We'll boss her around a little bit".' 'We weren't exactly "one of the girls". We were YTS to them and that was it.' Some of the trainees reported appreciatively that after a while they had won acceptance, but this did not always happen: 'Some departments, like Planning, they treat you like you're nothing. "Get this! Get that!" Not even a please or thank you or anything.' 'Most of the firm didn't speak to you when you was on the YTS.' 'There are a few who still treat us like YTS. I find that they're the older people who work here. To them we're just kids and we've got to act like kids. They're not treating us as adults.' Such hostility was stronger where older workers saw YTS as job substitution.

A rather different situation was where the more disadvantaged Mode B1 and B2 trainees were in special 'sheltered' placements, such as a mental handicap hospital, a mother and baby home and a day care centre. These protected trainees against the demands of work proper and offered no jobs. Some of the more immature Mode B trainees recognized their limitations, and welcomed supervision and less than a full workload. However, they stood out as exceptions to the general desire to do a job and be accepted as a worker.

The importance of a job: 'sponsorship', 'contest' and 'exploitation'

The trainees' overwhelming wish to do a job and be accepted as workers meant that their overall judgement of YTS rested on whether they knew (or thought they knew) that they would get a job from their placement. This appeared in their different feelings about placements in the 'sponsorship', 'contest' and 'exploitation' segments of YTS. Trainees were most satisfied with training in the 'sponsorship' sector not necessarily because of its quality, but mainly because it carried a job offer which made trainee status acceptable. One apprentice said: 'I know I'm still learning, but it's different when you know you're being kept on. It gives you something to work towards.' Trainees with a job offer and good training were among the few who accepted that training was a compensation for the low YTS allowance, even where they could make direct comparisons with employed apprentices. Peter said: 'I do the same work as the others but I don't get the same money. But on the other hand they've told me they'll keep me.' (The prospect of a job seemed also to erode any larger political criticisms of YTS, a point we return to in Chapter 10.)

Trainees who were in the 'contest' situation of not knowing whether they would get a job, felt less comfortable about YTS, particularly if they recognized that they were substituting for a full-time worker. Amanda, with Endowments but out-of-house, complained: 'That was a proper job, not just training, I felt I was doing someone else's job. They could've employed me.' However, where a job offer was confirmed, even unrewarding work such as labouring became more tolerable. Adrian said: 'I don't mind putting up with it this year, when I know I'll be taken on next year. I wouldn't stand for it otherwise. I'd leave.' Danny had proved himself in an emergency over Christmas and 'They said they'd give me a job at the end of it, so it's not like a YTS now'. A job offer, even if only in the future, narrowed the divide between trainee and worker status.

The greater selectivity and 'sponsorship' on established-skill schemes led to early job offers, but unfortunately small employers on 'new' skill schemes where there was no job would keep trainees guessing in case they tried to move. Jane, a retail trainee, described this uneasy 'contest' phase of YTS: 'It was difficult because we all thought we had to work hard all the time and not make any mistakes in order to get taken on. I feel sorry for the ones who didn't get taken on.' The nervous trainees seldom had enough self-confidence to ask, partly for fear of being turned down, and it was against the managing agents' interest to incur inconvenience and MSC hostility by pushing employers for jobs.

Trainees were most likely to feel exploited where they were substituting for full-time workers or acting as dogsbodies but with no job prospects. Even trainees who liked their placements found it difficult to sustain motivation, and felt devalued because they could easily be replaced. Judith described the bitterness of this realization: 'I get on well with the people there and everything. I love the work, but knowing that the chances are I won't be taken on makes you feel different. You don't feel like a responsible person, not like a real job. If they take on the next YTS, I'm not going to train them up into my job and then have them say, "Goodbye, it's been nice knowing you!".' Graham and another trainee did the dirty jobs but also some of the same work as the firm's apprentices: 'It should be apprentice pay really. I mean we do the same as what the apprentices do. I'd be happier then without the thought of being chucked out at the end. It's slave labour.' Tony would have taken a pride in his menial assembly job but 'When they go to collect their pay packets I get less than half . . . It don't seem right but they say, "That's 'cos you don't work a full week like the others" . . . I wouldn't mind, but now he says he can't keep me on, but I know they have to have someone doing what I do, so I s'pose they'll have to get [another] YTS.'

Exploited trainees spontaneously mentioned their resentment of the YTS allowance. Linda, a clerical trainee complained: 'The YTS pay is terrible. I've never done anything I've enjoyed really . . . but I think the reason I dislike it is the money.' The worse the conditions and harder the work, the more the trainees felt they had room for complaint: 'It's slave labour. You do as much as a full-time and you only get a third of what their wages are.' A retail trainee in a dogsbody job was given 'all the dirty jobs . . . You're working as hard as everyone else but I don't even get half of what they earn.' A building trainee complained: 'They get a man's work for a boy's pay'.

The trainees' views of their off-the-job training

In judging their off-the-job training, the trainees' main interest was again how far the training fitted their work and their image of themselves as workers. Chapter 3 described how young people's ambiguous status as NTP trainees had disastrously affected relationships with tutors at Southwich College. Now again under YTS, trainees' comments followed a familiar pattern. Those on established schemes and training for appropriate (or marketable) credentials were the more satisfied and those on new-skill schemes, which did not provide appropriate training or credentials, relatively less satisfied.

Adam was an engineering trainee who would become an employed apprentice at the end of YTS, and training was 'Like school, but at a higher level and it relates to my work. If I pass all my College exams then they complete my apprenticeship.' He also took an evening class to accompany his day release: 'It's encouraged by my company. I'm taking a fluid power qualification . . . The job I wanted to do, you need training to get into it.' Karen had the O-levels necessary for a college secretarial course, but chose Endowments' YTS scheme because 'I prefer to be working and earning a little bit of money . . . and most of the qualifications are the same'.

Trainees in top schemes still grudgingly accepted the value of training not immediately relevant to their placement, as long as it was clearly valued by employers and marketable. An Endowments trainee, Stephen, was taking BEC General and hadn't 'really learned much at College that concerns me at work. But any new qualifications I get are going to be a help to me. If I do well I'll get a bonus at work.' Occasionally, however, established training could be totally irrelevant. After failing her O-levels, Sarah had been moved out of Endowments to work as a dental nurse but off-the-job training was still BEC General: 'It hasn't got much to do with staring down people's mouths all day', so she would not take the exam. Such mismatches were rarer on established schemes.

The vocational credentials on deskilled entrepreneurial craft schemes were not always so marketable, but training might still be appreciated. Mark, a Jack's craft and design trainee, had found his College photography course useful in his placement with a film processing firm: 'You had quite a bit of training so you're not starting from scratch . . . Obviously we have more advanced machines at work, but the principles are the same.' However, on the most deskilled schemes, the mismatch between off-the-job training and the placements could be stark. Susan, on Dovers' catering course but placed as a chambermaid, found the College catering course irrelevant and did not take the exam: 'I didn't do as well as the others 'cos I didn't do the job as well to go with it.' She also missed the residential: 'They said 'cos I didn't know nothing about it, it wasn't worth me going on it.'

In new-skill schemes credentials were of doubtful value, and trainees valued off-the-job training only if it helped them directly in their placement – for example, till training in shop work, or how to lift patients. But two instances showed how this could mean totally different evaluations of the same training. Andrew, with no CSEs, was put on warehousing against his will. However, the training included forklift truck driving and 'A fork-lift truck driver's just left, and I've passed the test so I've got a chance'. In contrast, another trainee found the same training irrelevant in a smaller warehouse: 'Look at it, you couldn't get a forklift truck in here if you tried.'

Mismatching was most glaring where entrepreneurs or Mode B schemes had been forced to provide a common off-the-job training for a variety of low-skill placements. The limited skill placements negated any attempts to provide a broader training, and there was difficulty in filling the 13 weeks. Terry would only accept a job working in a kennel and found even off-the-job training in 'animal care' not specific enough: 'I expected to learn more about the dogs and things like that, but . . . we learn about different things.' William thought his horticulture course 'a waste of time. It was nothing that concerned the job and what we were doing. We always used to get bored silly so we used to muck about.' Jason had been on three schemes: 'We used to [do] things that you could learn in an hour took us a week there . . . I reckon [everything] I learnt you could get from one day reading a chapter of a book.'

These less academic trainees found that off-the-job training reminded them of the schools they had been only too glad to leave. Michelle, a school refuser, had a playgroup placement: 'I only went [to College] for three weeks, it was too much like school . . . We just talked about children . . . I don't think that was necessary at all.' Andrew, on the warehouse scheme, was a school refuser and apart from the forklift truck driving he had found training 'really agony, boring. You had to sit at a desk all day long.' Theresa had not been to school much in the last year and 'I don't like being in a classroom or anything, it makes me feel uneasy. When we do things in the lessons, I never take much in . . . I just look at them and go blank . . . At work I feel free.'

These trainees were most hostile to the induction: 'Half the time I don't think they really knew what to do with us, we could have done the whole thing in the morning.' They also found that the compensatory personal and life skills training combined what they most hated, similarity to school and lack of relevance or marketability. 'It's just talking.' 'We don't do nothing.' 'It's all writing and talking.' They felt insulted by tasks like 'looking telephone numbers up in a book', 'playing silly games', 'acting plays . . . the sort of thing we should have done at school, not now. The only time I realized I was on a scheme was when we had those courses.' Trainees were criticizing compensatory training because it suggested they were immature and emphasized how YTS was only part-way along the transition from school to being an adult worker. The sole exceptions were the Mode B2 trainees. One had never been able to use a telephone but now 'We have to go into town and then phone [the teacher] up from a call box. It's really useful.' These slow learners liked the continuation of their protected special school environment, and appreciated that they needed extra teaching in literacy, numeracy and personal relations.

Conclusions

The majority of trainees who were critical of YTS provided enough detail to confirm that most placements were unsatisfactory 'noddy' or 'dogsbody' work, because even established-skill employers who were exposed to market forces would not train young people whom they would not recruit as skilled workers. Good high-investment training was restricted to a small 'sponsorship' sector, so that YTS was failing to provide 'credentialling', and many new-skill placements in particular were exploitative temporary unskilled job substitution. Like the small employers, trainees had no respect for dubious non-established credentials or training which did not relate directly to their work. Life skills training was resented because it reminded trainees of their inferior status and marked the way YTS delayed their much-desired transition from school to work. In fact, it was clear that the trainees' hopes clashed fundamentally with the official training rationale of YTS, because basically these young people wanted real jobs rather than placements. The next chapter will describe what happened at the end of their YTS placements when they entered the real job market.

Chapter 9
The trainees enter
the labour market

Government ministers sometimes attribute all trainees' later job success to YTS training, but we should be more sceptical because trainees' employ-ability depends heavily on the buoyancy of the local economy. Also, we have shown that trainees were selected for better and worse schemes on the basis of their initial qualifications, gender, and social background, so YTS training was *mediating* between these initial attributes and employment and served to strengthen or weaken rather than determine young people's chances of a job. Furthermore, sheer luck played a part, whether in the form of low-skill placements which happened to offer a job, or family contacts. In this chapter we will show how we can infer the contribution of YTS from the pattern of trainees' job success. We also seek the views of trainees themselves as to whether they thought YTS had helped.

In December 1985 we repeated our postal survey of school leavers and reinterviewed our sample of trainees, who had now left YTS (see Appendix). Seventy per cent of the young people who had stayed on were still in school or college, and the rest who had left education had virtually all got jobs. Over 90 per cent of those who had gone into full-time jobs in 1984 were still in work (though not necessarily with the same employer). And of the 92 individuals unemployed and not on YTS in December 1984, only a quarter still had no jobs, though an identical number (92) had become unemployed in their turn. (This suggests considerable turnover among the jobless many of whom were perhaps unlucky rather than very different from other less-qualified leavers.) Broadly speaking, then, our findings suggested that the youth labour market had begun to recover, and it was in this economic climate that our YTS trainees were looking for jobs.

Former trainees' job success: the leavers survey

Nationally, job success after YTS placement reflects local conditions, with

Table 9.1 Economic activity of contacted 1984–5 YTS trainees, as at December 1985 (per cent)

Economic activity	Boys (N = 195)	Girls (N = 232)	Total (N = 427)
Full-time job	76	63	69
YWS	6	10	7
Part-time job	–	3	2
Still on YTS	2	–	1
Full-time FE	1	2	1
Unemployed	14	21	18
Other	1	1	1

Source: Southwich Cohort Survey, December, 1985 – see Appendix

low success in areas of high unemployment. MSC research (with a 60 per cent response rate) suggests that in the buoyant South-East of England 70 per cent of trainees get jobs (Youthaid, 1986). Using all sources, we contacted about 75 per cent of the 547 known YTS trainees in the first shot of our leavers survey. This showed virtually the same success rate for Southwich as did the MSC, although the boys did markedly better than the girls (Table 9.1).

Almost a third of the trainees had already left YTS by April 1985 (three months after the latest starting date). Of those employed in December 1985, almost a quarter of the boys and almost a third of the girls already had jobs in the previous April, while among the December unemployed just over a third of the boys and a quarter of the girls had already become unemployed by April. (Of course, we cannot assume that their labour market position had been stable in between.)

Only a third of the trainees were still in their placements, although a further fifth said they owed their job to a *contact* made through YTS (that is, not necessarily the training), such as moving within the firm or meeting another employer (Table 9.2).

About 60 per cent of the boys' jobs and 70 per cent of the girls' jobs appeared to involve progression from a YTS placement, while a third were doing jobs not apparently linked to their YTS training. On an optimistic view, about half the boys were practising some established technical or craft skills, but the rest of the boys were in unskilled jobs. The girls were overwhelmingly in low-skill jobs. Only a third of both boys and girls rated their prospects good.

Taken separately, as the MSC found nationally, the success rates for Mode A trainees was much higher than for Mode B trainees, about half of whom had left or been thrown off YTS by April 1985. By December, out of 50 boys only 21 were known to have jobs and three were on YWS. Only seven were still at their placements and three more said they owed their jobs to YTS contacts. Eleven were unemployed, as were probably most of the 13

Table 9.2   Sources of work of employed former trainees, by gender (per cent)

Source of work	Boys (N = 145)	Girls (N = 144)	Total (N = 289)
YTS placement	35	32	34
YTS contact (not placement)	22	20	21
Advert	6	9	8
JobCentre/Careers Service	14	14	14
Relative/friend	17	15	16
Other	4	7	6
No data	1	2	1

Source: As Table 9.1

non-respondents. The girls did worse, and out of 29 only seven were known to have jobs, two from placements and two from YTS contacts.

YTS schemes and trainees' later job success

To help us to separate out the influence of training in different schemes, we divided the careers of the trainees whom we interviewed according to our typology of YTS opportunities (Chapter 6) and the source of any job (Table 9.3) – that is, from the YTS placement, in the same skill training area (which implies that YTS training has served as a credential), or in a different skill area (where any contribution from training must be non-specific). Numbers are again small, but they indicate that trainees' job success varied considerably in different schemes. The high percentage obtaining jobs from employer-led and established placements confirms that larger employers and some smaller craft employers were using YTS mainly for recruitment. Compared with Mode B, Mode A trainees were considerably more likely to be employed in their placement (an average for boys and girls of 40 per cent against 8 per cent). Opportunities from placements were also good (58 per cent) for *boys* in the entrepreneurial motor vehicle and craft and design schemes, where labour was scarce and some trainees brought their own placements. In contrast, *none* of the girls from entrepreneurial schemes was employed in a placement. Altogether, of the trainees who got jobs, half had been employed in their placements, and arguably employers' use of the YTS surrogate labour market to recruit, not YTS training *per se*, was the reason for trainees' job success.

What of the trainees no longer in their established-skill placements? The boys were just as likely to be in a different skill area or unemployed as carrying on their YTS skill. The girls from established skill schemes, however, were much more likely to find jobs in their YTS training skill area, although this mostly meant clerical work which was booming in Southwich.

Table 9.3   Type of post-YTS employment, by scheme and gender, December 1985 (percentage of interview sample)

		YTS placement		Same skill area		Different skill area		Unemployed*	
		Boys	*(Girls)*	*Boys*	*(Girls)*	*Boys*	*(Girls)*	*Boys*	*(Girls)*
Mode A schemes									
Established	(N = 100%)								
Employer-led	(N = 17(17))	65	(53)	12	(35)	12	(12)	12	(6)
Stable-skill	(N = 15(31))	40	(42)	40	(35)	7	(10)	13	(13)
Entrepreneurial	(N = 19(7))	58	(—)	—	(43)	16	(14)	26	(43)
All established	(N = 51(55))	55	(40)	16	(36)	12	(9)	18	(15)
New skill									
Employer-led	(N = 4(11))	100	(73)	—	(18)	—	(—)	—	(22)
Stable-skill	(N = 7(17))	14	(24)	—	(35)	43	(12)	43	(29)
Entrepreneurial	(N = 21(23))	38	(—)	5	(4)	38	(26)	19	(70)
All new skill	(N = 32(51))	41	(24)	3	(18)	34	(16)	22	(43)
All Mode A	(N = 83(106))	49	(32)	11	(27)	20	(12)	20	(28)
Mode B	(N = 20(17))	5	(12)	5	(—)	30	(6)	60	(71)
All trainees	(N = 103(123))	41	(29)	10	(23)	22	(11)	27	(36)

Source: 'Extended' interview sample – see Appendix

* The large majority unemployed but including several part-time jobs

The contribution to job success from 'new skill' training appeared even more ambiguous. Almost all the remaining Mode A boys not employed in their routine machining, warehouse or labouring placements had switched areas or become unemployed. The girl trainees of the stable retail schemes had usually found other retail jobs, but again we should remember that retail jobs, too, were plentiful. (In contrast, the few boy retail trainees had either switched areas or were unemployed.) The lack of jobs from placements in Mode B meant that even the boys were now mostly unemployed. Similarly, hardly any of the girls from the Mode B and entrepreneurial Mode A care and catering schemes had got jobs from placements or were in the same skill area, no doubt reflecting the way catering and care placements had been created from part-time jobs with no real job prospects.

Thus, the main contribution of YTS 1 to trainees' later job success, despite the recovering labour market, seemed to be through job opportunities in placements, and the value of even established training seemed at best ambiguous or at least not proven. At worst some Mode A entrepreneurial and Mode B schemes showed no positive effect on trainees' chances of jobs at all.

The persisting influence of trainees' academic attainment

The 'mediating' rather than determining role of YTS is also shown in the clear relationship between the trainees' credentials and their later job

Table 9.4 Trainees' school attainment and post-YTS employment by source and gender

Credential level	Percentage employed full-time in							
	placement		training skill		other job		(N = 100%)	
	Boys	(Girls)	Boys	(Girls)	Boys	(Girls)	Boys	(Girls)
Five O levels*	60	(47)	—	(19)	20	(14)	5	(15)
One O level	52	(35)	16	(33)	24	(15)	25	(29)
CSEs only	38	(32)	9	(21)	24	(10)	55	(60)
No exams	33	(12)	7	(12)	20	(11)	15	(17)
Not known							3	(2)
All	33	(30)	9	(24)	23	(11)	103	(123)

Source: As Table 9.3

* Excludes trainees who returned to college for full-time courses

success. The academic selectivity of schemes with in-house job opportunities had led to more of the better-qualified trainees being kept on in their placements (Table 9.4). This was particularly true of the boys, reflecting the pattern of apprentice recruitment, and almost all the boys with O levels were employed. Girls with O levels apparently did less well from placements although, as we show later, many girls employed in their clerical placements later found alternative jobs. Even here, however, employers might have valued the girls' O-levels rather than their YTS training.

Boys and girls with CSEs only did markedly less well out of their placements and very few got jobs in the training skill area. However, even the unqualified boys got jobs somewhere, which again implies that their job success came from available jobs rather than YTS training. In contrast, unqualified girls were conspicuously unsuccessful, only one in eight being kept on in their placements and similar low proportions finding jobs in or outside their training area. This reflects at once the heavy recruitment of unqualified girls into dead-end care or catering schemes, and their unacceptability to employers in other personally-orientated service jobs like retailing.

If we look at the nominal skill level of the trainees' work, an even more striking pattern emerges (Table 9.5). Trainees with at least one O level (particularly girls) were three times as likely as the rest of the sample to be doing work which was at least nominally skilled. The bulk of the trainees with CSEs or no credentials were doing unskilled work or unemployed. Girls in clerical jobs with O levels were in large company secretarial or clerical work, the rest were doing filing or routine office jobs in small firms. Boys with O levels working in established crafts were more likely to be taken on as apprentices by the second year than those with fewer qualifications. So again we see selectivity between and within schemes at the same skill level.

Table 9.5   Nominal skill* of trainees' employment by credential level (per cent)

Credential level	Skill level of current job*			Totals (N = 100%)
	Skilled	Unskilled	All	
One or more O levels	72	14	85	(74)
CSEs	24	43	67	(115)
None	14	33	47	(32)
No data				(5)
Total (%)	39	31	70	(226)

Source: As Table 9.3

* This is, of course, only the most general indication of actual skill

The emerging influence of social background in job success

In Chapter 7 we showed how social class influences in recruitment were contradictory, with working-class boys having an advantage in craft placements through their family contacts. This was reflected in the roughly equal numbers from middle- and working-class backgrounds who later got jobs in their placements. However, after YTS experience the influence of social class emerged more strongly in the careers of the rest of the trainees. Middle-class girls were generally more successful in finding jobs (both in and outside the training skill area), so that after YTS training 80 per cent were employed compared with only 56 per cent of working-class girls. We also found that (against the trend of recruitment onto schemes) middle-class boys were slightly more likely to be in their placements or to find work in the training area.

It was difficult to separate out the influence of social class from that of credentials, but among those without credentials middle-class trainees were almost all employed, half in skilled work, whereas only a quarter of the unqualified had found even unskilled jobs. These findings are in line with our earlier evidence that employers were selecting by social class as well as credentials for the better placements *within* skill areas and schemes. Also, as we show later in this chapter, middle-class trainees had been better at salvaging false starts on poor YTS schemes.

The trainees' wage expectations

Critics' fears that the YTS allowance would lower wage aspirations seem well-founded. Boys, who were more often in established craft routes, had higher expectations than girls. However, trainees were worried mainly about getting a job – 'I just hope I'll be working that's all' – and some said they would work for only a little more than the allowance or the same amount. Their first wages after completing YTS confirmed that almost one

Table 9.6   Trainees' first net earnings after YTS (per cent)

Earnings range per week (£)	Boys (N = 103)	Girls (N = 123)	Total (N = 226)
40 or less	6	11	9
41–50	17	17	17
51–60	19	22	21
61–70	12	11	11
Over 70	13	4	8
No data/moved	33	35	34

Source: As Table 9.3

in ten had started work at £40 per week or less, several for only £30, which must have left them little better or even worse off than during YTS training (Table 9.6). Some of the boys with high earnings were working long hours and travelling large distances on labouring jobs. The modal wage was near that set at the time by the YWS subsidy for 17-year-olds. Yet most respondents were satisfied, only about one in ten feeling they got less than they expected and a similar proportion feeling they got more.

Views on the value of YTS: trainees in established skills

As we might expect, trainees' views on whether YTS had helped them find jobs or in their work reflected the pattern of job success described above. Those who had been happy in 'sponsored' career placements were satisfied a year later, and the boys seemed likely to see themselves as continuing to acquire skills and possibly move to gain promotion. Paul, working for a screen printer, said he had learnt a lot and planned to 'learn all there is to know and then move on'. Similarly Dominic was still satisfied in his engineering job: 'I'll finish my apprenticeship just before I start looking around.' But also lurking at the back of their minds was the possibility of future self-employment, or dropping out to travel. Girls in clerical jobs were less likely to have well-defined career and training routes, although a few of the best-qualified and most highly-motivated had achieved what looked like good positions. For example,when Debra threatened to leave, her solicitor employer took her off YTS and made her principal secretary. She then hoped to start studying law.

However, other trainees still employed in their established-skill placements were disappointed that their jobs were now less skilled than YTS training had prepared them for. Rachel was bored typing all day from tapes: 'You get to expect you're being trained for something better somehow.' Christopher had enthused about his placement in the accounts department of a bakery, but when we saw him again his interest had flagged: 'I haven't been taught anything new now I know the whole job . . . I preferred the job last year. At least it seemed I was getting somewhere.'

About one in ten trainees, mostly girls, had been employed in their established-skill placements but then moved elsewhere. They had usually moved from choice to better jobs, and a few who had complained that their training was inappropriate for their placement later became more satisfied when the training proved useful in another job. Stephen complained about his training with Endowments, but in his new job he had continued his BEC National on day release: 'In two and a half years a chap is leaving . . . If I'm still here I've got a good chance.' Because Angela was on Flourishes' retail scheme, she had found her BEC course (to match her O levels) too skilled, but by the second interview her move to a part-time job in a record shop had paid off and 'They're considering me for assistant manager now . . . I'm the only one who knows anything about some things like bookkeeping.' In retrospect she felt she had been trained in 'thorough methods, even if you don't use them you know how things should be done'. The few girls who moved out of established or clerical skills usually chose to retrain in what they felt were more secure or interesting careers, three as nurses and one as a hairdresser. Significantly, however, our only girl engineering trainee had been forced to take a counter job with a parts supplier. Dovers' catering training also proved non-transferable. Debbie had found a job in a Wimpy Bar: 'When I got me certificates through I took them in to show 'em. They said: "What are we supposed to do with them?" But I hung them up on the wall anyway.' In any case her ambition was to look after the children's parties. Other trainees had moved out of catering, one to pick mushrooms part-time for her brother-in-law, another to work at Tescos with her mother and sister. (In contrast, two male catering trainees had not found HCITB training useful, but discovered that their City & Guilds qualifications gained them entry to hotel jobs even though, as John said, 'You don't really need anything for what I do. It's mainly preparing vegetables.')

Boys not taken on at established-skill placements usually had difficulty finding similar work. Of two engineering trainees, one entered printing through family contacts, and the other, who was black, went to London and became a motorbike messenger. All the construction trainees not employed in their placements switched to different work, except for one who found a building job through a family contact. Of four motor vehicle trainees, one pursued an earlier ambition to join the Navy and the others took low-skill jobs, one stacking supermarket shelves on the night shift, another as a kitchen porter and the third on routine assembly work in a clock factory. The boy from the inferior sub-post office scheme entered printing through church contacts, and a craft and design trainee worked in a fashion shop.

Trainees' disillusionment with non-established training

Trainees in 'new skill' schemes were less likely to be employed in their placements, unless their scheme had been employer-led. One well-qualified girl had been placed in a small LCU branch and became the manageress: 'I have thought of my own business, especially if I was unemployed. That's what the unemployed should do . . . I'd like power and responsibility.' These trainees employed in their placements emphasized not the training but the importance of being in the job and catching the boss's eye, saying that YTS 'gave me the chance to show what I could do'. About the only instance where new low-skill training *per se* had clearly made a difference was Andrew's forklift truck training, mentioned earlier.

Failing a job from their placements, most boys and girls from new-skill schemes had either moved to different work or become unemployed. Only one care trainee, middle-class and well-qualified, had found a care job outside her placement but that was through her sister. Two others had also found jobs through personal contacts, but one was in a factory and another in a supermarket, while a third well-qualified girl was working as a waitress until she could use her O levels to get into nursing. Care trainees who had wanted child care jobs were especially disheartened. Ann had failed to get a place on the College full-time nursery nurse course but YTS had seemed a second chance and she had followed her employer's advice to study part-time for a Montessori qualification. Later, however, she convincingly described how the employer had trumped up a pretext to replace her with another trainee, and she found that she needed primary school teaching or a nursery nurse qualification to work in a day nursery: 'I just don't know what I need any more.' Lorraine, too, felt frustrated after a YTS care scheme: 'I'm glad because at least I didn't go straight on the dole . . . [But] I wish now I'd worked in a shop or something different than what I did.' Gina explained the catch-22 situation in care work: 'I wouldn't go on it again. It was a waste of time. They don't take on people till they're 18. Then it's too late 'cos you've left and when you go back they've got a new YTS.'

Beauty work, another popular choice, also proved a blind alley because of the problem of credentials. Siân could not afford the private beauty course so she had accepted a YTS place: 'It sounded a really nice course but when you actually get on it you realize that they've told you a load of rubbish. They told me we'd be doing exams here, not only in manicuring but in health and beauty work, and there was a couple of others. We ended up just manicuring.' A year later she was unemployed but still hoping to be able to afford a proper beauty course one day.

The lack of marketability of YTS experience

Part of the argument for YTS is that, regardless of skill training, it improves motivation and instils good work habits which make trainees more employable. In fact, among our trainees there was *no* evidence that this had ever occurred. As we saw in the previous two chapters, most trainees began by wanting a job and resenting YTS. They could be won over mainly if YTS offered a job, but if they were not taken on in their placements their motivation was likely to be *damaged* because they had experienced a 'double failure', first on leaving school and then after going through YTS.

Employers' low regard for YTS was symbolized by the way they had neither asked about the YTS certificate or experience, nor seemed to acknowledge it when choosing among applicants for jobs. As for the trainees, they often had to think hard about whether they had received the certificate; it had usually arrived very late, even up to a year after the scheme had finished. Indeed, in job interviews trainees tended to conceal that they had been on YTS, feeling their training was irrelevant and YTS itself was stigmatized. Rather than receiving any indirect benefit from YTS training, former trainees were more likely to find work through two other more visible processes.

Firstly, the improving job situation had enabled some of the better-qualified trainees to overcome a false start on YTS, using their O levels and family support to shop around for better opportunities. For example, Rachel had failed all her RSA exams on a YTS clerical scheme, but with six O levels she first got a job in a bank and then switched to a higher-paying job with British Telecom. After six months' unemployment John used his O levels to enter the Civil Service (commenting that YTS had been useful in showing him what *not* to do). Tracy, a personable middle-class care trainee, was singled out for a job in the records office of the hospital where there were otherwise no jobs from placements.

Secondly, family or other personal contacts had boosted the apparent job success of former trainees in various other ways. Placements initially gained through these contacts had made post-YTS employment more likely. No fewer than nine boys and eleven girls were now employed in jobs from such placements, and more had used them to move on to other jobs. For example, Linda's part-time job in her mother's shop had been turned into a placement, and she had continued to work there when the shop changed hands. After 'dead end' YTS placements, families and friends had found jobs for other former trainees, including work with British Rail and jobs in factories, a café, a cinema, industrial cleaning and labouring. Altogether, no fewer than 47 of the trainees, 25 girls and 22 boys, were in employment after YTS which had in some way been dependent on contacts made through family or friends. A few more trainees, six girls and three boys, had found jobs through contacts on the scheme but in skill areas quite different from their YTS placements.

These alternative routes into work which do not depend on YTS mean that in Southwich the effectiveness of YTS training is lower by at least one-third than the bare figures of job success suggest. Employers' reliance on credentials had helped the better-qualified trainees to salvage false starts, inflating their already high success from recruitment to better placements. But the safety net provided by family and friends helped particularly those trainees who were less attractive to employers. Without this second safety net YTS's bias towards better-qualified or middle-class trainees would have been much more pronounced.

The social situation of the unemployed

Boys who were unqualified or from unskilled working-class backgrounds could still get labouring jobs from placements or outside, and we noticed that unemployed boys were often physically immature or small. Girls with similar social or educational disadvantages seemed more likely to become unemployed, because equivalent low-skill service jobs for girls asked for a minimum of style and polish in personal relationships. In addition, the importance of social contacts in finding jobs means that the unemployed were also more likely to come from families disrupted by unemployment, marital breakdown or some other problem, although in any case YTS recruitment already ensured that most of these trainees were recruited to dead-end schemes. Just over half the unemployed trainees had neither parent nor step-parent employed, and some also had unemployed siblings.

The former trainees without jobs at our second interview had not all been consistently unemployed since YTS, but in their unstable careers on the fringe of the labour market they tended to meet more irresponsible employers and unsavoury jobs. Two had been made redundant from placements, Andrew when his roofing firm went bankrupt and Angela from a part-time job in a sports shop. Seven had been sacked, mostly at the end of a period on YWS or when their eighteenth birthday would have meant a pay rise. One girl with five O levels was sacked because her keenness had caused resentment among older workers. Jason had found a fencing job after a year's unemployment but was sacked because he was 'too weedy'. Three girls left jobs because of pregnancy. A boy in a small bakery was sacked when he injured himself by slipping on the greasy stairs, and another was sacked when he got flu. (There were other instances where young people had fallen ill and been sacked at a moment's notice because small employers needed to fill their jobs.) Three had held temporary jobs, two over the Christmas period and another as a bus cleaner: 'It was really hard work and dirty . . . I'd had enough of it after a week.' In all this, the former trainees' keenness to work shows up remarkably in how seldom they seem to have left jobs of their own accord. Indeed, only one trainee said she had 'deliberately' left a job, but she complained of sexual harassment.

Continued unemployment was not a result of young people clinging onto unrealistic ideals. The few better-qualified unemployed former trainees from established-skill schemes were less likely to lower their aspirations for non-manual work, and support from parents enabled them to wait and apply for good openings. But only a few of the poorly-qualified retained impractical ideals. Two girls felt that they would soon become famous models, and Siân still cherished the hope of becoming a beautician. David (whose father had made him take the dirty bus-cleaning job) was looking for picture-framing work and felt he should still have some choice: 'There's everyday boring jobs, but I think some people have a pride in what they do.' Sadly, two girls who wanted child-care work were still studying the Montessori correspondence course which they now knew would get them no jobs. The only former trainees whose lack of a regular full-time job could in any sense be counted 'voluntary' were two boys earning more money doing casual building work than they could have got from regular labouring and a girl clerical trainee earning more money part-time in a bar than she could have got full-time in an office. Boys were more likely to have access to the black economy of odd jobs and labouring on building sites or vehicle repairs, although only three openly admitted such work. Girls seemed more restricted to babysitting or domestic or cleaning work.

Over time, as they had learned how few jobs were available, the unemployed had written off their original ambitions and said they 'would take anything now'. Looking for jobs was soul-destroying, especially the ritual at the Job Centre: 'It's boring. I hate it. You stop looking for jobs eventually 'cos you know it's not going to be any good.' 'I hate going to the Job Centre, it's so depressing and I can't afford to pay the bus fares.' 'People think you're lazy, but you get turned down all the time. It puts you off.' 'After a while you lose all motivation to apply for anything.' Linda and Lorraine from care schemes had reluctantly reduced their ambitions to getting part-time cleaning jobs through the help of friends: 'She's put my name down so I'm just waiting for them to ring me.' 'If I work really hard, I might be able to go full-time there. It's a way in. I know some people there.' Denise's YTS placement had been in an old people's home, but now she felt cleaning was the only job she might ever get: 'You see I never went to school for the last three years, so . . . I wouldn't be able to work in a shop.'

Unemployment was unexpected, and young people found the experience very depressing. Even those with jobs said overwhelmingly that what they missed most about YTS was their mates, and the main complaint of the unemployed was isolation through lack of work contacts and cash. Those near the town centre returned to the truanting lifestyle of their late schooldays: 'I just mooch around town with me mates, sit in the Wimpy, play a game of pool.' But many lived too far from town. Sean said of YTS: 'I didn't like it when I was there, but I miss all me mates . . . Now I can go all day without seeing a soul.' Another boy said his main companion was the budgie. Girls in any case seemed to spend less time outside the home, but for those far from town the problems worsened. Lorraine paid her unemployed parents for her keep: 'I only have £6.50 left when I've paid for my clothes and bus fares . . . I can't go out at all or even go into the town to the Job Centre. I don't really see anybody.' The unemployed now looked back nostalgically on their YTS placement as a happier and more hopeful time: 'There was something to get up for when you were on YTS. Now there isn't anything.' But one thought: 'YTS is better than the dole, but then when you're back on it, it makes it worse than if you'd never worked at all'.

Unemployment created strains at home: 'Bad it is. Mum nags all the time.' Nichola's parents 'get onto me about it. Me Dad still blames me for not doing well at school . . . I'd leave [home] now if I could.' Karen *had* left because her relationship with her father worsened when she dropped out of YTS: 'Dad says I'm a lazy little git . . . Mum says, "Go and look for a job, Karen!" But *she* wanna look. I say, "There's nothing out there, Mum!"'

Domesticity, babies and leaving home

Even a year after their YTS experience, boys found the idea of settling down decidedly premature, but while they were still trainees most girls anticipated that marriage and children would probably interrupt full-time work, at least until the children went to school, and a year after YTS marriage prospects and children loomed distinctly larger. Karen would marry in June: 'And if [my boyfriend] wants to move I'll be going with him so I might not work then, I expect I'll go part-time.' For girls like Elizabeth, an unqualified retail trainee, marriage plans postponed what were probably unrealistic work ambitions: 'Eventually, I'd like to go into nursing, go to evening classes when I've actually got the money to pay for them or hairdressing.' And even for a trainee like Lisa, who had said earlier that children would not interrupt the career she planned after YTS, a steady boyfriend meant she was prepared to think of giving up work. Marriage and children often seemed an attractive alternative to the kinds of work girls were likely to get after YTS.

Lacking opportunities of part-time work in the black economy, in various ways unemployed girls seemed to retreat into the domestic role. Karen said: 'My friend, Sue, and I look after the baby. Then I look after my little brother and sister and my sister's little boy.' Angela's YTS experience had consisted of dusting crockery at Concessions, so she found domesticity more rewarding: 'It's given me a chance to help my mum since I've been unemployed . . . I do more around the house then I did on YTS. There's more variety and the money's not much different.' Julie took over the domestic chores for her parents who both worked, and they bought her clothing. Marriage or relationships also seemed an attractive alternative to unemployment. Nichola had an employed boyfriend: 'I'd like to have a house, a nice house, and some children, and a car. Of course, it depends on how much he earns by then.' Gina was on the point of moving in with her employed boyfriend, her only hope of leaving home. Bronwen was engaged and busily planning marriage. Five of the unemployed girls already had babies and two were pregnant. Only two, both better-qualified girls, had ever worked, one part-time, and all now lived on social security. But they still maintained an ideal of future domestic happiness. A former care trainee living temporarily with her YTS boyfriend in one room wanted 'a few more children' with 'a house in the country with a big garden for them'.

The unemployed seemed more likely to have left home, eight boys and three girls, compared with only two girls who had left for jobs and two boys who had gone into the armed forces. Three mothers could not tell us where their daughters were living, and worried about their way of life: 'Well you can't say a lot when they're that age. She moved in with this feller but we don't have a lot of say in her life.' When we eventually managed to trace Darren (whose 'guardian' took all his money), he was living rough. His social security stopped, he was in trouble with the police.

Conclusion

The major contribution of YTS to trainees' later job success came from employers' use of the Scheme to recruit from placements. Beyond this any independent contribution of YTS training was difficult to establish, because if they were not employed in their placements, only clerical and some former retail trainees seemed likely to get jobs in their YTS training area, and these were in any case the most flourishing parts of the Southwich economy. Otherwise, young people were likely to switch or become unemployed, and there was no evidence that either they or employers saw any value in 'new skill' training. Education and social background had played a part in recruitment and emerged even more clearly in the pattern of later job success. The apparent effectiveness of YTS training was also boosted greatly by the way trainees with O levels were able to retrieve false starts in YTS. Without the safety net of jobs gained by less-qualified trainees through family or personal contacts, the inequalities of opportunity in YTS would be much more dramatically exposed.

Chapter 10
'Moral rescue': views about society, unemployment and YTS

This chapter describes how the trainees' more general attitudes matched up to Mrs Thatcher's 'enterprise culture'. In 1984–5 during their YTS training, and again one year after, we asked the interview sample their opinions about society, politics, unemployment and YTS. Then, three years later in 1988, we followed them up by phone and post to find out what they were doing and what they now thought of their YTS experience. In fact it was doubtful – at least on the basis of trainees' responses to our questions – whether as 16- and 17-year-olds they yet had 'attitudes' which were at all coherent, well thought-out and consistent. Nor is it possible to say what their YTS experiences alone contributed towards trainees' more general views. They were maturing rapidly under a range of influences, and arguably their general outlook owed much to their parents' lifestyle and the 'local labour-market culture', that is, the way attitudes seem to be linked to local wage levels, employment rates and peoples' experiences in seeking jobs (Ashton and Maguire, 1986).

In Southwich, trainees seemed to embark on YTS training heavily influenced by an individualism linked to the incipient boom in South-East England, which is based on non-unionized service and distributive jobs and where much of the population is, at least nominally, middle-class. This individualism was revealed in our leavers survey in responses to a list of standard questions to tap commitment to work. In other studies, responses from unemployed young people suggest that they share the work ethic of the employed and long to be in normal jobs (Banks and Ullah, 1989). Even early in their YTS training, our trainees matched this pattern. Over three-quarters agreed with the statement, 'Even if I won a lot of money I would still want a job', and 70 per cent agreed that 'Almost any job is better than being unemployed'. In contrast, 90 per cent denied that 'Unemployment is usually better than having to go to work' and barely 20 per cent thought that 'Success is a matter of luck rather than hard work'. Overall their attitude responses were the same as those of young people who *had* found jobs or gone to college.

There is room for scepticism, though, about the validity of such formal attitude 'measurement' in isolation from other methods. Also, the distribution of our respondents was skewed towards middle-class school leavers. Significantly, many of them wrote extra comments, albeit mostly on the value of self-help and hard work. Our trainee interviews allowed us to explore these attitudes in more depth.

The trainees rejection of the idea of 'social class'

The sociological literature suggests that individualism varies according to whether or not people acknowledge the existence of social class. So in both the interview and follow-up we asked young people whether they 'thought there were social classes in society these days', and whether they themselves belonged to any particular social class. We also asked them to choose from a list including 'middle class' and 'working class'. Over three-quarters resisted the concept of 'social class', some flatly refusing to respond because the idea smacked of snobbery, divisiveness and unequal worth. A clerical trainee from a professional background said: 'There aren't any classes nowadays, I can't think why they ask such silly questions.' Nigel, a craft trainee from a manual background, replied: 'Everyone's the same nowadays, nobody's better than anyone else'. Alan, a Post Office trainee from an evangelical and manual background said: 'I'm just a person . . . That's how everyone should be . . . It's how people respect each other.'

The most common voluntary self-definition was 'middle class', by which trainees seemed to mean the bulk of ordinary people who lay between a small and remote upper class and a disreputable but diminishing lower class. A male retail trainee from a clerical background remarked: 'There's only a few of the upper class left. The rest, the lower class has almost disappeared.' Some trainees acknowledged there might still be a small and remote upper class 'like the Royal Family and that'. A few like Stephen, an engineering trainee, saw business owners as a separate group: 'The upper class are people who own all the factories and shops and restaurants.' Karen cited as upper class, 'The bloke who owns the company, he's very well off. He's got a Ferrari, and he's got a bathroom in his office and shower.' But such detail was rare. Similarly, people below the 'middle class' were described, if at all, in very stereotyped terms. Ann said: 'There's middle class and there's dustbin men.' Debra, from a 'respectable' manual background, worked in a solicitor's office and thought: 'The working class are the people I deal with at work who live in terrible houses and get beaten up . . . They've no money and huge debts.'

The trainees were aware of the inequalities between people, which they usually described in material or monetary terms. But on the whole such differences were not seen as 'class' differences or social barriers because they were thought to match the efforts which people had put into work. Damien, a building trainee, said: 'There is still an upper class, but there's no such thing as working class and middle class because everyone's able to work hard and get some money.' Tracy, a care trainee, felt that 'Everyone's the same really, it's just whether you're prepared to work at it'. Business ownership was not thought socially divisive because self-employment was commonly seen, especially by male trainees, as a desirable and attainable goal.

On the whole, this individualistic picture of society seemed undisturbed by any personal experiences of differences of living standards, housing, culture or schooling. It was therefore striking when a few trainees either identified themselves initially as working class or later chose the label from our list. This minority were also among the few trainees who were likely to see trade unions as necessary and useful. Characteristically, these more 'class-conscious' trainees tended to come from the small number of families where parents worked in traditional manufacturing or craft-based industries, although the most militant trainee worked with his father and brother in the heavily-unionized Post Office.

Lack of alternative identification with youth subcultures

Few Southwich young people identified strongly with any other social groupings such as particular youth subcultures. Identification might be expressed in styles of dress, hair and make-up, but (as we saw in Part Two) mainstream YTS rejected (or repelled) those young people who looked more unconventional. In fact the few who were punks or who adopted other conspicuous styles were later either unemployed or in marginal jobs. April had been put in a sheltered placement with no job prospects because 'There were a lot who were smooth and because I didn't wear the same kind of clothes I stuck out like a sore thumb . . . It's not so much clothes, but the music you like. Then your clothes fit in with that.' Occasionally unemployment had stimulated former trainees to exaggerate their style: 'People think we're posers. I suppose we are a bit. We just like dressing up and going out.' However, this required cash, and a rurally isolated unemployed girl complained: 'I used to be a "casual", but round here no one bothers much and I can't afford the bus fares into town. I'm nothing much now.'

Most former trainees preferred to distance themselves from any identification with particular subcultures. One employed girl said: 'There's down and outs, people who don't want to work, punks, vandals, robbers and trouble-makers, and there's normal people who want to work.' Similarly, an employed boy remarked: 'There's trouble-makers who don't work, and ordinary people.' This identification with the 'ordinary' seemed to fit very closely the conventional work-orientated individualism described above.

Attitudes towards government and politics

When we asked about politics, even the most informed or articulate
respondents tended to switch off, taking the instrumental view that there
was nothing in politics for them personally: 'I don't think I'd ever vote. It
doesn't interest me at all, unless there was something that actually involved
me.' 'I don't believe in voting if there's nothing you think is worth voting
for.' 'I don't think I'd ever vote unless there was something that I was
interested in doing something about.' 'I'm not interested in stuff like that. I
don't read the newspaper. I don't know what's going on about – who is it in
now? I don't know. I s'pose we should have had more at school to explain it.'
'I don't know what the parties are, so I wouldn't know who I was voting for
anyway.' 'I switch off when that comes on.'

Our survey coincided with a surge in Alliance support which may explain
the surprisingly low proportion (only one in eight) who said they would vote
Conservative. But only a fifth said they would vote Alliance or Labour. In
addition there were three National Front supporters and a few others who
could not state or remember their preference, making up just over half the
sample who would vote at all. The small Conservative support went across
class lines, although the Conservative 'working-class' fathers were noticeably affluent, a majority living in detached rural private houses. Parental
influence seemed important: 'Me Dad says the Tories look after the country
for us', and, 'I've been told the other parties wouldn't do any better'. Yet
even among young people who were Conservative supporters there was
some hostility towards Margaret Thatcher.

In contrast, a majority of Alliance supporters were girls from middle-class
backgrounds, with over half from professional or managerial families. The
Alliance vote expressed a vast dislike of the present government and Mrs
Thatcher personally, for failing to solve manifest social problems: 'We need
someone civilized. I don't think she's fit to run the country.' 'Since Maggie
Thatcher's been in, there's been more unemployment . . . I blame her for
everything.'

The association between voting intention and social background looked
strongest among young Labour supporters. Only four fathers had middle-
class jobs and most were working-class Labour voters living in the
traditional pockets of Labour support (although seven fathers were out of
work and three families had only one parent). As one trainee said: 'I
suppose I'd vote Labour so's not to get left out in this house.' Rachel, a
clerical trainee, said: 'With the Conservative government they're more an
upper-class sort of government, so they perhaps wouldn't think so much
about [unemployment]. With Labour or a working-class sort of government,
perhaps they'd think more about the working-class sort of people and try to
help them get a job.' Steven, an engineering apprentice, said: 'All this
government's trying to do is to make the rich richer and the poor poorer. I
vote Labour 'cos they care more about the working classes.' However, we
should not exaggerate such class-consciousness, and even among Labour

supporters only a minority specifically linked voting and class interests. Labour support was as likely to be expressed as a personalized hostility: 'Maggie Thatcher ain't done a lot for me.'

The small support for trade unions was also to be found almost entirely among these prospective Labour voters. Peter was in a unionized firm: 'I believe in trade unions and I think the Labour government are for the workers really. The Tories are trying to smash the unions . . . I prefer Labour 'cos they're mainly the working people and deal mainly with unemployment. I'm also against having all these Royals.' However, while taking part in YTS the large majority of trainees (who tended to be in service jobs in small firms) had been against trade unions, and after YTS only 33 were in unions, some under compulsion. Adrian, an engineering apprentice, did not value union membership: 'I joined 'cos I had to, that's all. I'm an individual meself. I don't want to cause no trouble.' Adam worked in a shop: 'You don't need unions apart from in factories and things like that. You don't need them in a shop.' Sue, also a retail trainee, associated unions mainly with conflict: 'I couldn't stand it, I don't like working in an atmosphere. I like it to be friendly where I work.' In fact union membership was often discouraged by service employers. Debbie worked in a fast food restaurant: 'We're not allowed to be in [a union] . . . They say if I tell anyone about anything that happens at work then I'm out . . . They threatens you. That's not right, is it?' A few of those in the more exploitative jobs could see the need for a union, but their jobs were not unionized.

The transition to adulthood and work: workers versus the unemployed

Questions about their feelings about the family, courtship, and the possibility of leaving home and setting up their own households, showed that most of these young people felt in a marginal or transitional situation, no longer children yet hardly financially independent, and still to some extent under parental surveillance if not actual control. As a result, although a few of the more reflective trainees perceived that their parents had a particular status in society, they felt unable or unwilling to claim that status for themselves. For example, Sean's father, originally a manual worker, had recently been promoted to an administrative post, but Sean did not feel part of this mobility: 'My parents, they're middle class, I suppose, but I'm just starting out so I suppose I'm lower class at the moment.'

Few had yet developed a strong identification with a particular kind of work or clear plans for a work career. We recall that girls anticipated that work would probably be interrupted by marriage, and even skilled craft apprentices surprisingly often had ambitions or fantasies of moving on, self-employment or dropping out to travel. In any case, most had not chosen YTS and the most salient factor shaping their attitudes was not so much the kind of work they did but whether they had a job at all.

Occasionally they made explicit their sense of the gulf between work and unemployment as the lowest layer in society. Simon said: 'The lower class are people who can't find jobs.' Jonathan classified himself as 'an ordinary worker' but thought that after the upper class and 'your middle class, your managers . . . you've got your unemployed these days'. For those with family or personal experience of unemployment, this model was more deeply felt. Martin, unemployed and rating himself lower class, said: 'The upper class is people with office jobs [and] decent houses and [who] have worked hard at school. The middle class is just your average person who goes out, works quite hard, and gets just enough money to pay off everything. The lower class live on social security.'

At worst some unemployed trainees had come to see society in terms of a core of those settled in permanent jobs with the unemployed on the margins. Tony, black and unemployed after a Mode B scheme, said: 'There's only two classes left, the working and the unemployed.' Lorraine said: 'The upper class people are well-off people with permanent jobs and then there's the unemployed like me.' Another trainee divided society into 'People who've got jobs and those who never had'. Marianne saw work as necessary for social participation: 'There's the ones who have money to spend because they've got jobs. Over time they begin to keep to themselves, because they make friends at work and they do more.' Bernadette, also jobless, felt that 'In a way the upper class are getting more separate from the rest of us because they're getting more, they've got more to spend'. Unemployed young people resented what they saw as their 'exclusion' from work, as if the first rungs had been removed from the ladder of opportunity. Alan said of white-collar workers: 'Half of them do nothing useful to make all their money. All they do is sit behind a desk all day.' Andrew was more explicit: 'There's definitely the top lot, high-up office workers that can't be bothered to give the younger kids the jobs. They just think about themselves and just trying to get to the top. There's the middle-sort-of-range ones. They'd be sort of like factory workers, shop workers, and at the bottom you get the kids that are on the dole and that.' Sometimes hostility focused on particular groups. Debbie, a retail trainee, said: 'I think they should bring the retirement age down to, say, 50 . . . I think they should retire and let the younger people find a job.' Teresa said: 'I think 45 is long enough to be working, and married women, they don't need the money, should move over and let us have a chance.'

Although in Southwich there were scarcely any workers from ethnic minorities, a few of the most disadvantaged trainees blamed their own unemployment on immigrants or 'the blacks'. Darren, who was living rough, was prepared to admit he had little to offer any employer but even so felt that 'There's not enough jobs for whites any more. There's more coloured people getting the jobs in Southwich than elsewhere, all the Chinese and Indians.' However, Maria, a care trainee, had changed her views as a result of off-the-job training: 'Before I would have said unemployment was caused by all the foreigners coming in taking our jobs, but I've been told different. This tutor put us right.'

Only a fairly small minority of young people explicitly pictured society with a distinct underclass of the unemployed, or as a clash between workers and workless. Yet this was symptomatic of the divisiveness of unemployment, and its potential for forming young people's identity along other than traditional 'middle-' and 'working-class' lines.

The lack of economic or structural explanations of unemployment

The divisiveness of unemployment and its role in identity formation were clearer to see in young people's comments on unemployment and the unemployed. We asked general questions about whether they thought there was a problem locally and nationally, and if so what they thought caused it and could anything be done about it. We also asked who were the unemployed. Three out of five trainees agreed there was an unemployment problem in Southwich and, although it was difficult to get them to think more widely, a further third thought there was a problem elsewhere. However, a third could offer no cause, and of the remaining two-thirds, remarkably few felt able to offer even the simplest structural or economic explanation, or even to see unemployment as a policy issue.

Despite the training rationale of YTS, very few mentioned lack of skills as a cause of unemployment and those who did were likely to be receiving skilled training. An engineering trainee explained succinctly: 'Employers just don't want to train people any more . . . Everyone expects someone else to do the training, so it doesn't happen.' A few trainees felt the blame lay with employers who were unnecessarily choosy: 'Not everybody's got six O levels. Well, I haven't, for instance.' 'Employers say they want experience, but with school leavers you can't be experienced.'

On the whole, any broader 'economic analysis' was crude and fatalistic: 'There's no money left so the jobs have to go.' A sport and leisure trainee said: 'Well, it happened in the 1920s and it's come back again. I don't think it's going to get better this time'. As a woodwork trainee, Andrew had thought unemployment would 'settle down', but a year later working part-time night shifts in a supermarket he had changed his mind: 'It's all gone too far now. We're just going down fast. It's getting worse, rising costs and everything. The rest of the country is as bad. It's just the way it's always been.' Robert, an engineering apprentice, said: 'It's just a stage the country's going through. I don't think anyone's to blame.' Mark, a retail trainee, said: 'If they stopped all these imports coming in and everyone bought British, then we'd not be in such a mess.' Several trainees mentioned cuts in public sector jobs, but did not link them with government policy.

Indeed, most young people felt that any government was powerless: 'I don't think it's fair blaming the government all the time. There's nothing they can do. They're just doing a job the same as everyone else.' An employed middle-class girl said: 'Even if we had a different government, I don't suppose it would change things. I don't know, but I don't think this one does anything.' And even a trainee who felt that 'Something ought to be done about unemployment', said cynically: 'I'd never vote. Well, none of them know what they're doing. They're all old people in the Houses of Parliament, with Victorian values.' A trainee who was highly critical of YTS as 'cheap labour' also said: 'I wouldn't [vote]. It's nothing to do with me. None of them know what they're up to in my view.' Another thought: 'Politicians just make it worse. They argue all the time. It just comes down to who's got the biggest head.'

'Blaming the victim'

Press coverage and government policies on unemployment have played down economic or structural explanations and the role of policy, and instead have 'blamed the victim'. Similarly, although most former trainees had taken YTS places after failing to find jobs and the majority recognized an unemployment problem, they still held the view that unemployed individuals were lazy, not looking for work or too choosy. The following comments were typical: 'The unemployed are the lazy ones' 'I don't think people try, because there's quite a few jobs about if you want to work.' 'There are lots of jobs in the Job Centre. They don't want to know. I could have picked one up, why can't they.' 'If you're not too snobby there isn't much trouble in finding a job.' 'A lot of people are layabouts, go into the Job Centre once a week and say, "No, too boring, not enough money, too far to go". They just put the card back and go to bed.' 'The unemployed are too choosy, they want too much money. There's always hundreds of jobs in the Job Centre, and loads in the paper.' 'They leave school thinking they only want to do one particular thing and they won't try their hand at anything else.' 'They do college courses and expect to get a good job in what they're trained in'.

Personal experience of unemployment after YTS training or occasionally the unemployment of a friend, could modify this harsh view. David, now an engineering apprentice, said: 'My mate has been laid off twice this year. I've been with him when he's gone up the Job Centre but there's nothing there. They all want experience, but how are you supposed to get it?' Another apprentice, Mark, said: 'I've got a couple of mates who just can't get jobs and they've tried . . . There's just more people than jobs.' Both were left-wing and more generally sympathetic towards the unemployed.

However, the belief that jobs were available could survive even personal experience of unemployment. Lisa took a YTS place because 'you can't find a job. I've tried and tried.' But later she said 'if you look hard enough . . . you'll find one' and claimed that 'people on social security just hang around'. Janice, an unemployed former retail trainee, said: 'People don't look hard enough to find jobs. They think there's not enough.' However, 'There's no job for me at the moment. Well, not round here anyway.' Before his present job, Andrew had been unemployed and 'looking for a job and I couldn't find anything', but now in work he said, 'People can't be bothered . . . they're bone idle', and he still felt there was no unemployment problem: 'For me, yes, but I 'spose there isn't really, not around here.' Alan, unemployed for six months after Mode B, also showed ambivalence: 'There's enough jobs . . . but you can't find them anywhere, can you'.

YTS and 'moral rescue'

The resilience of negative views among the unemployed came partly from YTS itself, which had ensured that so far most young people had not suffered the frustrations of the job search for very long. Even YTS was of higher status than unemployment and seemed to provide a platform from which trainees felt able to distance themselves from the jobless by blaming them for their lack of effort. YTS thus provided trainees with a sense of what might be called 'moral rescue' from the evil of unemployment, a successful outcome being a sign of YTS's grace toward the deserving. George, a former school truant and now a construction trainee, said: 'At least I did something . . . but the others, you saw them at school, just lazy.' Others spoke of their gratitude to YTS and how it 'worked for me'.

It was in this way that YTS helped to sustain an individualistic and divisive work ethic. Stigma isolated the unemployed, and their social and emotional distance allowed hostile stereotypes to flourish: 'People I went to school with never went to lessons, hanging around . . . They never really bothered about finding a job, they were quite happy to go straight on the dole.' Some became quite heated: 'He's just a lazy little toad. He's found jobs but he can't be bothered to keep them. He expects his parents to support him . . . He scrounges off them.' It made little difference if placements or jobs had come from family contacts. One boy thought: 'There shouldn't be any unemployment . . . I've never had any trouble, often I've had too many opportunities.' And another said: 'There are jobs if you want to work hard enough at finding them. I kept pestering and eventually I found them.' Yet both had found their jobs through their families. A third trainee who worked in the family business said he kept telling his unemployed mates 'to keep on trying. Some just sit around. You have to go out and give your name and address, it's no good just waiting.'

The existence of YTS or other government schemes had become evidence that 'jobs' were available. 'Most of my mates who've just left school, they've all got jobs on YTS.' 'My boyfriend, he was unemployed for a while, but I got him to look for a job and he's now working on the railway' (actually on a Community Programme). Similarly, turning down *YTS* was used as evidence of people's negative attitudes towards finding *work*, sometimes regardless of trainees' own views of the defects of the Scheme. As a result (and perhaps because trainees did not see why others should escape what they themselves had had to undergo), even a majority of those who criticized YTS were in favour of social security being withdrawn from YTS refusers. For example, Melinda, a hairdressing apprentice, thought there were 'not enough jobs to go round' and that YTS was 'slave labour', but she backed withdrawal of benefits: 'Otherwise it encourages them to be on the dole'.

Only a few former trainees specifically blamed YTS for their own or others' unemployment: 'If the firms keep taking people on [YTS], then the next year take someone else on, then the real jobs get less and less.' 'I think if there was less YTS schemes there'd be more jobs about. At the moment a lot of shops take them on just to use them. They'd rather have YTS than pay out for a wage.' Those who blamed YTS did not necessarily blame the government, although some did: 'The government could do something if they stopped running schemes and put more money into the jobs them-selves.' The most critical had had poor experiences on YTS or later. Susan, a former catering trainee, had been dismissed from placements which she considered exploitative, and she had spent six months unemployed before getting a job through her mother: 'The government, they're not prepared to spend more money and create more jobs and put more money into jobs. They've done this YTS, but it doesn't help any more.' By the second interview a third of the young Labour supporters were unemployed and this had sharpened their hostility to YTS and the government.

A postscript to YTS 1: the trainees look back three years later

To discover young people's final verdict on their 'moral rescue' by YTS, we followed them up three years later. We gained replies (or information from relatives) for just over half our interview sample (57 per cent of Mode A). Although a majority still showed mixed feelings, time had simplified and polarized their judgements. Only two out of five now approved of YTS *as a scheme*, and while one in six among the remainder felt uneasily that they had been 'lucky' as individuals, the majority were hostile or even bitter and abusive about YTS. If anything, this probably *over*represents favourable views of YTS, because while our respondents were surprisingly evenly spread across managing agents, there were more from established-skill schemes and with jobs from placements. We failed to contact some of the more disadvantaged, including four-fifths of the former Mode B trainees, most of whom were without phones, widely scattered and did not answer letters.

Though overall dissatisfaction had increased in the three years since YTS there were differences by gender and type of scheme. Among established-skills trainees, those 'sponsored' as apprentices remained relatively satisfied but virtually all the young men who had entered expanded entrepreneurial 'craft' schemes had become especially disillusioned and dissatisfied. Indeed, dissatisfaction with entrepreneurial schemes of all kinds was widespread. Among the young women the bulk of places had been in non-established skill areas and two thirds now criticized their YTS.

Over half the 'satisfied' former trainees were still working either at their placement or with the same employer, and a further quarter had had jobs from placements but had moved on. Among the most enthusiastic were young women still working for larger employers: 'I couldn't type when I left school. YTS is the best thing that ever happened.' 'When I first left school there were two things I didn't want to do, YTS or office work. Now look. It proves you don't know what you want.' Also still very positive were some former apprentices. A hairdresser now managed, and would soon own, the shop where she did her placement: 'I'm eternally grateful to YTS. It's got me where I am today.' There were also satisfied former trainees from new-skill schemes including young men with jobs from placements in large shops, warehouses and a sports centre and women mostly employed in smaller shops and offices. All said they were still 'grateful to YTS because it gave me a job' or 'a chance'.

Their satisfaction was only partly explained by pay. Average earnings for young men were £115 a week, but the difference between those who approved of YTS and those who did not was only £123 as against £110 per week, and was largely due to a few high earners, most of them self-employed former construction trainees, earning over £250 per week. But the 'satisfied' young men who remained in their placements earned on average only £88 per week, the engineering firms being relatively poor payers at under £100 a week. The contrast between young women who approved and disapproved of YTS was more striking – £100 against only £66 per week. But again the 'satisfied' who had stayed in their placements earned relatively little more than dissatisfied former trainees, only £80 per week on average, and the contrast was largely accounted for by five young women (all but one from middle-class backgrounds) who had left low-paid placements in Southwich and now earned between £125 and £200 per week working in London. Yet these former trainees, too, were inclined to say, 'YTS made me', attributing their success solely to the Scheme.

There were some extremely low weekly earnings throughout the group, with three young men at £70, £75 and £80 per week (and four more below £100), and among young women, three at £50, three at £70 and one at £80. Among young women not in their placements one earned only £50 and another £70 per week, and other low earners were some who had left YTS to retrain as nurses. These pay rates lend some support to the argument that YTS helps to depress wage expectations, although it seems from the pattern of dissatisfaction that while former trainees may be prepared to work for relatively low pay they do not necessarily value the YTS scheme which left them ill-equipped to do anything else.

Increased dissatisfaction after YTS came when sought-after placements (mostly in entrepreneurial schemes) did not materialize, proved exploitative or disappeared altogether. Such a change was less common among young men, because it had usually become clear before the end of YTS that the promise of 'traditional craft' skill training would not be fulfilled. One said: 'They didn't give me a job and nobody cared.' In all, three young men reported jobs from placements which had later failed, and a printing trainee who could not get a union card had had to take a factory job. Beginning more hopefully, young women seemed more likely to suffer disappointment because they met more barriers to skilled jobs, and secure well-paid retail or care work was rare. A former clerical trainee from an engineering firm was extremely bitter: 'They make you feel *they're* doing *you* a favour! But you flippin' well slog your guts out for them for no money at all. People were trained before YTS – trained and *paid* a proper wage!' Another was equally bitter: 'I feel really betrayed by YTS . . . You're only of interest while they can make a profit out of you.' Others too felt their 'skilled' training had been specific to one particular firm. Three whose YTS careers had seemed success stories – one aiming to train in law, an LCU branch manageress, and one with a dream job as a beautician – were all disappointed three years on, and we found at least ten such instances of disappointment.

The dissatisfied former entrepreneurial 'craft' and 'new skill' trainees were now further along the unsettled work careers which we described earlier. One-tenth of the young men were currently unemployed and two more trainees had been out of work in the past. In addition over one in three had changed jobs a number of times, and half those from the more dubious schemes now worked in jobs different from their training skill area. For example, former entrepreneurial 'craft' trainees had jobs as shop assistant, clerk, factory hand, postman, forecourt attendant or labourer. So it was not surprising that entrepreneurial craft trainees who *were* still in their placements or the same skill area were more cynical about YTS and tended to say, 'It was all right for me, but I was lucky', or to feel (like those working in family businesses or low skill areas) that YTS merely 'suited me dad' and 'you didn't need YTS'. Others said more bitterly that YTS was 'slave labour' or 'a load of rubbish'. The most they would concede was that it was 'better than the dole, I suppose' although one commented that YTS had made things worse because 'employers won't look at you'.

The outlook for some young women had become even more depressing. One in seven of those we contacted were currently unemployed, but we learned of others who had escaped unemployment only by marrying and leaving the area (one commenting that 'YTS abused my rights'). The only young woman to improve her opinion after YTS participation was a former clerical trainee, who had earlier been extremely bitter after the collapse of her placement was followed by spells of unemployment and part-time work. She had been 'rescued' by a clerical opportunity and now felt 'really grateful' to YTS. Most of the less-skilled had been forced to switch from their training 'skill' by poor pay and conditions and insecure work. Among 19 former trainees from care schemes, the only two who approved of YTS were a middle-class young woman who had got all her care jobs via relatives, and another who was now a care monitor for Dovers and saw YTS as 'a marvellous opportunity for young people'. But another former Dovers' trainee complained that YTS 'leaves you unemployable, not good enough to get a proper job'. Another said: 'YTS is a con. They ought to *have* to give you a job.' The most anyone would concede was: 'It's good for hairdressing and clerical work, but too many employers use you.'

Overall, there was a remarkable polarization in the experiences of our former trainees. Those from some of the better schemes (and with favoured backgrounds or good school records) were now becoming established in well-paid work with good prospects, some moving to London and already buying flats and living with their partners. In contrast, the life chances of most former trainees on inferior schemes seemed to have been unaffected or even made worse by the further disillusionment of YTS. One young woman said: 'I thought it would help me to escape the label of "thicky" at school. It didn't, though.' Sadly, she longed for a baby to fill up her days. Over half the former care trainees (themselves from single parent families or disrupted backgrounds) were now unmarried mothers, but unfortunately babies did not necessarily offer a solution to their isolation. A mother of two, still living at home with her parents, was one of several former care trainees who now looked back on YTS nostalgically, 'I wish I was still on it . . . I'll never work again.'

Conclusion to Part Three

In Part Three we have looked at the 'supply' side of the surrogate labour market, the trainee recruits, and how their varied backgrounds interacted with the 'demand' side described in Part Two. Our findings reinforce and extend the model of unequal opportunities which we outlined on the basis of information from the managing agents. The most able trainees ended up in the most prestigious schemes where employers restricted YTS to future recruits. The more disadvantaged the trainee, the more insecure the skills training and the worse the job prospects became. Young people's current and later satisfaction with YTS followed this pattern, but revealed that some training under established-skill labels (even in employer-led schemes) offered only limited non-transferable skills and relatively poor job prospects. The various new-skill training places offered few workplace skills, and trainees rejected any alternative compensatory social skills training off-the-job as irrelevant to the poor job opportunities in their work placements.

While they were on YTS many trainees were able to sustain a view of themselves as workers in an open 'enterprise' society which rewarded effort financially, and although there was much dissatisfaction with YTS, they nevertheless criticized the unemployed for laziness. However, even during YTS training, disappointment set in when promised skill-training failed to materialize, and young people became even more disillusioned after YTS, especially low-achieving girls whose access to service jobs was restricted by the scarcity of full-time work and their lack of social polish.

By 1986, having completed our research on YTS 1, we felt able to make some predictions as to how the newly-announced YTS 2 would work out in Southwich. We expected that competition among schemes in the surrogate labour market would get worse, increasing the deskilling and devaluation of training standards. Training quality was further threatened by the expansion of the role of managing agents at the expense of the MSC. In addition, charging employers for trainees would increase their power to dictate their terms of recruitment or training in YTS. However, at the same time, the supply of trainees to YTS was shrinking because of the reviving job market, improvements in sixth-form facilities, and the shrinking number of young people. We reported a crisis of confidence in the viability of YTS among local managing agents who had been the Scheme's greatest advocates and we expected it to worsen (Lee *et al.*, 1986). Meanwhile, our trainees had indicated that YTS could never compete with opportunities from full-time education and *real* work.

Part Four
Loss of control
and deskilling in
YTS 2

Chapter 11
Boom conditions with falling numbers

By 1986, as we concluded our fieldwork on YTS 1, the government had 'moved the goalposts' again. We already knew that MSC plans and documentation were far advanced for another scheme, Training for Skills (TFS). But Lord Young blocked the change as one of his last moves at the DE. Instead of TFS, a refurbished and reflagged two-year YTS scheme (YTS 2) was launched and claimed as a major upgrading to meet changing conditions such as those in Southwich (DE, 1985a). However, South-East England had begun to boom, and Southwich's young people were soon to have better educational opportunities in a new Sixth-Form College, partly as a result of a rationalization of schools forced upon the town by the imminent fall in the size of the age group.

Part Four will show how our predictions for YTS 2 were borne out. This chapter describes what happened to the surrogate labour market, and Chapter 12 examines training in the more vulnerable schemes. Chapter 13 looks at how market forces came even more to the fore as direct control of training passed from the MSC to the managing agents and employers, and the major guarantee of training quality became the new credentials of the National Council of Vocational Qualifications, NCVQ.

The aims and administrative structure of YTS 2

Despite the attempt to create a new image, YTS 2 still had to mop up unemployment, so training was extended to two years even in non-traditional skill areas and places were offered to all 16- and 17-year-olds. By 1988 the withdrawal of social security rights made the scheme in effect compulsory, although the change was delayed and carefully packaged in terms of 'options' and 'choice'. Lord Young claimed: 'Each and every

Table 11.1 Destinations of young people reaching the statutory school leaving age, by year* (per cent)

Destination	Year				
	1984–5	1985–6	1986–7	1987–8	1988–9
YTS	25	29	29	20	18
Sixth form	24	24	21	37	36
FE college	11	10	15	10	8
Employment	14	16	19	20	26
Unemployed	9	7	6	5	4
Others/unknown	16	14	10	9	8
Total fifth-year pupils $N=100\%$	(2416)	(2191)	(2591)	(2527)	(2389)

* Careers Service October estimates. Because Careers Service figures are collected early, pupils may later do something different. Also, although cover has improved, 'unknowns' affect the proportions in different destinations

unemployed young person under 18 is now guaranteed high quality training . . . and anyone under that who remains unemployed will have chosen to remain unemployed' (*Guardian*, 29 January 1987; 7 September 1988).

There were further cuts in funding and moves towards market forces. Neither the trainees' allowances nor managing agents' fees were raised in line with inflation, leaving some costs to be recouped from a levy on employers for each trainee. Mode B schemes were replaced by fewer individual 'premium' places. Second-year training now covered skills specific to particular jobs, with only half as much off-the-job training. Even personal and life skills training had now to encourage initiative and enterprise, stimulated by ENTRAIN, a private company set up by the MSC. YTS 2 also meant a reduced role for the MSC and external controls. Managing agents were to become Approved Training Organizations (ATOs) after MSC scrutiny and staff training at MSC's Accredited Training Centre, and these ATOs would then take over the MSC's function of monitoring training. Meanwhile union representation on the AMBs was reduced.

However, any suggestion of exploitation by employers was to be countered by stressing the quality of training. Each trainee would receive from the managing agent a signed agreement specifying the training and skill 'competences' to be gained from the work placements. Quality and marketability were to be enhanced by linking YTS training to 'recognized credentials', which would increasingly be 'preferred' schemes rationalized into a system of national credentialling by the newly established NCVQ. There was to be a drive to expand employed YTS status to make YTS a more attractive route compared with jobs and extended education.

The impact of YTS 2 on the Southwich youth labour market

In Southwich, the uncertainties of school reorganization first led potential sixth-formers to switch into FE. But in 1987 huge numbers of pupils stayed on in the newly-opened Sixth-Form College and FE fell back to its original share of the age group (Table 11.1). Later this surge abated but by then there was a marked trend for non-academically inclined school leavers to get jobs again. Registered unemployment shrank.

It is evident from Table 11.1 that YTS 2 was failing to compete with education and jobs; Southwich was joining towns where there is virtually no room for YTS except for apprentices and the hard to employ. It was also a *two-year* scheme for relatively few. Nationally, the latest available MSC estimates suggest that nearly a half of trainees stay only for the first year. In Southwich, with few premium places, this proportion of short-stay trainees, though hard to estimate exactly, was undoubtedly higher.

YTS 2 and Southwich College

In 1986, a gloomy Southwich College had considered pulling out of YTS, but by 1988 there was more optimism not only about YTS but also about the College's other work. A-level numbers had held up, and the local boom had brought growth in full-time vocational studies, and also in day release which some employers found cheaper than giving employed YTS status. YTS was said to be 'buoyant'. Compared with 1986–7 when there were 372 mainstream YTS trainees (see Table 3.1) plus 125 'infill' trainees, by 1987–8 the mainstream intake was 409 and still rising. First-year infill numbers were incomplete (104), but the College now also had 211 (plus 28 infill) second-year trainees.

Fees had not been raised, so FE was currently more competitive with private trainers. Staff also felt their closer knowledge of employers' needs and better marketing were beginning to pay off (HM Inspectorate has commented that nationally FE has superior labour-market intelligence; see *Times Educational Supplement*, 22 April 1987). Relatively little new business came from the second year of YTS 2, because apprenticeships or the better traineeships already used FE for second-year day release. However, this meant that, compared with other trainers, FE kept more second-year trainees. The College savoured the moment when the motor vehicle training association had to ask for help with more specialised YTS 2 training. Other managing agents also continued to need FE for specialized training or for lack of cheaper alternatives. Also, FE courses were infilled by trainees on schemes which fell below strength (such as the LCU schemes), so the College reaped advantages of scale from its pivotal role in local training.

Other potential or actual new custom was more dubious, and the contracts from managing agents were sometimes slow to firm up. Deregulation of Southwich buses had led to negotiations about possible trainees. The

College was proud of picking up an LCU multiple scheme in car body work, and it had also been approached by another in hairdressing. However, these multiples were mistrusted by the local MSC as inferior, so ironically although Southwich College was poised in its turn to undercut training entrepreneurs who had earlier taken away its business, it could only do so by colluding in a further potential reduction of training standards.

In 1988, the College expected it might gain work as a result of the withdrawal of benefit from YTS refusers, although the prospect was not welcome. In the event, we were told late in 1988 that the expected number of refusers had not materialized, partly because they had got jobs and partly because they continued to refuse to participate in YTS. In any case, these young people told the Careers Service that an educational institution like the College was the last place they wanted to train in.

Nevertheless, although Southwich College was temporarily buoyant, FE remained vulnerable because any changes in funding might tilt the balance back towards private training or away from YTS altogether. The effect of the switch to NCVQ credentials remained to be seen. All the new custom came from economic and demographic developments or policies whose effects were outside the College's control and difficult to predict. Indeed, in 1989 FE suffered a fresh blow with the news that much of their work would shortly come under the control of local employer-led training councils (TECs, see Chapter 14) and that a quarter of all staff would be cut (*Guardian*, 13 April, 1989).

The pattern of YTS 2 in 1988

We reinterviewed our managing agents in mid-1988, including now the main tutors on the schemes and, looking for examples of the best new-skills training, we also included two LCU retail schemes. By then market and other forces had led to the closure of five of the schemes described in our earlier research. Mostly they were small. Five – two smaller entrepreneurs, the church-based scheme, Concessions and Flourishes – each had less than 50 placements, with Flourishes having only a dozen. Although the local authority scheme lost its overall Mode B subsidy, it stayed open.

As yet, the overall *target* quotas for trainees in established and new-skill areas had not changed much from the peak of 1986–7, beyond the addition of an estimate for the proportion of trainees who would stop on for the second year of YTS 2. Because of the falling number of potential recruits, the trainee quotas for some schemes had become meaningless. Particularly in new skills and entrepreneurial schemes, recruitment was spasmodic and turnover was high and fluctuating, which made it difficult to work out occupancy or stopping-on rates. Occupancy varied quite considerably, with the top schemes probably managing around 80 per cent (with one or two small schemes full), the bulk of schemes at 70 per cent or below, and a number of smaller schemes with as little as 30 per cent.

Employer-led schemes

The engineering firms

The established craft trainers, mostly very experienced, were quietly triumphant that YTS 2 had come into line with ITB apprenticeships, yet at the same time they were extremely sceptical and wary of the detailed training agreements: 'The writing, putting words on paper, puts the onus on me to make it happen, and I get anxious . . . that their "hit" team, or whatever you call it, will find us out. Why not *trust* us? We don't *start out* trying to abuse the system.' The fate of YTS closely mirrored the economic fortunes of the three engineering firms. Thrusters had expanded and asked for a larger trainee quota; Bolts was consolidating and had virtually cut out its external trainees; Cutters, was shrinking because of rationalization and new technology and had reduced its quota. Although the two more successful and expanding firms now offered employed YTS status and grooming for specific jobs ('As far as they're concerned they're not YTS'), they still ran below quota but would not lower their selection criteria. Instead, Bolts had started a routine production scheme. Cutters would afford neither employed YTS status nor job guarantees. It had stopped its careful selection but still ran below half-full.

Neither Bolts nor Thrusters could get enough clerical trainees, although their schemes offered the possibility of nine or ten credentials. Bolts, with a full quota, gave employed YTS status, but had encountered jealousy among older workers and pressure to stop training as soon as trainees were employed. In any case these clerical trainees easily found jobs elsewhere after their first year. If the subsidy was cut, this clerical scheme would close and the firm's production training would end because 'It doesn't need a scheme to do that'. The firms would still recruit a minimum of apprentices, although the trainer at the largest firm said sourly: 'Let's say that at the moment [YTS] helps to offset the costs but it's becoming a pain in the rear.'

Endowments

Endowments' managing agent said that as the MSC reduced his trainee quota, 'It will be the external placements that will go. We don't need them.' They still had enough recruits, although they lost one or two in-house trainees to banks and more of those out-of-house left for jobs. The company now took its employed trainees off YTS so, ironically, from the MSC's viewpoint this quality scheme had few second-year trainees, no employed YTS status, and trainees appeared to leave without credentials (although they later completed the two-year BEC National course on day release).

With a lower subsidy, the company would still recruit school leavers for data processing, but the managing agent would switch to other activities.

Retail schemes

The closure of Flourishes' scheme

Flourishes decided that the small number of its trainees did not justify the extra administration under YTS 2 so asked the Chamber of Commerce to feed it well-qualified trainees from whom it further selected (often, however, losing trainees through delays). The managing agent felt that YTS had been 'ruined' by an unnecessary second year: 'I'm disgusted . . . Why prolong the agony?'

The Co-operative Society

The only remaining local employer-led retail scheme, the Co-op, still used YTS to recruit. It now selected more carefully for its distance-learning training, although the managing agent insisted: 'Most of it's just personality.' The quota of two dozen was almost full in the first year and about half full in the second year: 'But if we don't recruit it's not too hard, we're not financially dependent on YTS.' This experienced trainer was sceptical of YTS 2: 'One year is enough for retail proficiency, two years is difficult to prove it's necessary.' There remained the problem that once trainees (who already had employed YTS status from the training section) were given jobs, managers and trainees tried to stop training, and to keep up standards: 'The managers themselves need training.' The managing agent strongly opposed 'starving out' young people, and said of adult training: 'It would just be cheap labour. OK if you've got an underutilized training facility like Jack's.' He expected employer-led YTS to continue but 'If the government pulled the plug on finance, the industry won't support it'.

The LCU mother and baby store

At one of the LCU schemes, a mother and baby store, the managing agent claimed to be 'on the A team or something so [the MSC doesn't] bother us . . . Our training has a really good reputation. They'd be well set up to get a job anywhere in the high street.' It recruited other school leavers but only trainees were considered for promotion: 'They know it's linked to them going further in the company.' However, the scheme attracted mainly girls who were more interested in babies than careers and 'Those who won't make junior management don't want training, you can't blame them'. Trainees were not employed until after their YTS training, and only 30 per cent were eventually recruited. The Southwich work supervisor thought one year of training long enough: 'They've then got the intelligence and the capability, more so than an 18-year-old without the training . . . It's important to reach maturity, but [two years] is a lot of training.'

The LCU grocers

The Southwich branch of the other LCU scheme, a grocery, was the training centre for the county. The head of personnel chose trainees on personality, and the successful were employed after a year, although boys had better prospects. She enthused over how training gave confidence but later admitted: 'Quite honestly, I think [the second year] is a damn con . . . They really know the workings of the entire store by the end of the first year. There's a limit to what can be learnt . . . You're doing the job then probably better than the rest of the staff.' Shortly after our research, the store pulled out of YTS 2 and returned to more limited training.

Stable skill umbrella schemes

The impact of YTS 2 and changing market forces brought pressure on the stable-skill schemes to become more entrepreneurial. Those offering schemes under traditional craft labels with apprenticeships and FE training offered their trainees more incentive to stay for two years. Others (including the hairdressers who still used FE) had a higher turnover, and withdrawal of the money for any places 'vacated' by trainees cut their profit margins. As a result, they now had to recruit continuously, which disrupted training and provided a further incentive to use their own tutors rather than the more inflexible FE. They also had to hang onto trainees with poor attendance, which undermined discipline and their control of training standards. By 1988, the three craft schemes which we had earlier described as stable were keeping control, but lacking a craft base the Chamber of Commerce had been badly hit by competition. On the other hand, the motor vehicle association had cut its YTS activities to return to its RTITB craft origins and become less entrepreneurial.

CITB and HCITB

The CITB managing agent said that fitting YTS 2 into the construction apprenticeship was 'almost a foregone conclusion'. Sponsors were invited to register their second-year trainees as apprentices: 'And we say to them, "If you do, the CITB will give you a jolly good grant". Therefore about 90 per cent of them do.' Apprenticeships were then back-dated six months to the beginning of work experience and trainees were given employed YTS status. Numbers were up because 'Ours is tied to a definite industry'. In line with the building boom in South-East England, the CITB's quota was set to double.

The HCITB was in a less secure position in relation to its parent industry, although the move to YTS 2 and HCITB's prominence in the new NCVQ scheme (see Chapter 13) could strengthen its bid to gain a dominance comparable with that of the CITB. However, current proposals to privatize the ITBs will strike at the financial roots of the CITB and HCITB apprentice-training monopolies.

The hairdressers

The hairdressers' private craft scheme seemed more vulnerable. The managing agent had considered starting his own training centre but hitherto he had needed FE for assessment, and also 'You get no directions from MSC, they're not reliable enough'. He had had to call on local MSC help to fight off an encroaching LCU multiple which was undercutting his scheme and training standards: 'I took over some of their placements and [the employers] were all nudging and winking and saying, "They [trainees] don't have to do their off-the-job training, do they?". They've in a sense corrupted the employers.' The scheme had doubled in size and become more selective: 'We get less very low achievers or top achievers.' Salons now used the scheme rather than take girls from Saturday jobs: 'Several people have said they've never had such good girls.'

Half the trainees went into a second year but this created problems: 'The older stylists are getting asked questions by the trainees that they can't answer.' The lack of trained hairdressers (a legacy from before YTS) meant trainees were poached by employers who did not train: 'One girl is going round to the highest bidder.' However, rural employers could not fight back by giving employed YTS status because employed trainees would lose travel expenses of up to £20 a week. The managing agent complained: 'YTS . . . wasn't exactly a "moral crusade" but near it . . . Now we've been put in the position of competing for business . . . Now it's more of a case of keeping people on the scheme, before it was finding them jobs . . . We're almost on the point of balance to handing over to employers . . . At the moment they put up with losing them for the training because of the money, but . . . now they've done away with the wages council, the employers can do away with YTS. They can offer a trainee £10 for the first year and £15 for the second year and their *own* training.'

The motor vehicle training association

In 1986 the motor vehicle training association (backed by its parent national group) had unsuccessfully fought the MSC over extending two-year training throughout YTS. 'The local [MSC] field staff, in private they were absolutely in agreement . . . We're not prepared to put things on paper and specify spurious criteria . . . Many *are* inventing schemes, writing fancy programmes, but we can't see any merit in it, because with the tighter guidelines . . . we're constrained to deliver.' The managing agent had offered the MSC only an upgraded one-year retail scheme and refused even to submit his warehouse scheme: 'You can fill it up with various types of nonsense, but we're not into that. The problem is a warehouse has a very limited number of skills to learn.' He felt that YTS 2 was 'less to do with training and more to get the unemployed off the register . . . "Here's twenty weeks. How can we fill it?".' The funding squeeze was an attempt to hand training costs back to larger employers, but it betrayed the private trainers: 'We're a nuisance, people like us . . . If it's company-based . . . YTS money will just be another bit of money that goes into the large training bucket . . . The government has said, "Industry will pay".' The association had 'flirted with' the new adult training, but nationally the group associations were suspicious and the managing agent mistrusted the local set-up: 'It all seemed too risky.'

The association had cut back its schemes to motor vehicle repairs, parts and clerical work, 'To be able to concentrate better on what we could do'. It, too, had needed local MSC help to restrict the incursions of an LCU multiple with a bodywork repair scheme. Employer demand had merited a larger scheme quota, but trainees were in short supply: 'We don't usually get what we want . . . We'll take grade 19 [CSE] if we have to! . . . If compulsion brings us another crop of trainees who we'd normally not consider we might have a look at them.' Only half the trainees now went into the second year (compared with three-quarters in YTS 2's opening year), with a few employers paying for separate FE training. The local boom had eroded the clerical scheme, and the small parts scheme was below half strength despite its good job prospects. By 1988 the managing agent felt that 'YTS has slipped down the ladder politically . . . We're bound to see YTS phasing out. It just seems to prove the point that it was an unemployment measure, and people will think back to YTS as a stale period in history.'

The Chamber of Commerce

With severe competition from both clerical and retail jobs, the Chamber of Commerce's schemes showed clearly the peak and decline of YTS 2. At first, with excess recruits and a 60 per cent carry-over (even in retail), it could offer eight possible credentials: 'The greater the numbers, the more staff we have and the more qualifications we can offer . . . and the more they'll stay on.' But 'It's a vicious circle', and first-year occupancy had dropped below two-thirds, of whom only a third stayed on. Virtually none were retail trainees, as the managing agent had foreseen: 'Two-year retail is a joke!' Falling numbers brought staff redundancies and demoralization. Cynically, the managing agent felt that a visit from ENTRAIN had merely fostered staff dissatisfaction and brought no extra resources. Any increase in charges would make YTS 2 'just not worth it for employers. They'll just employ direct.' She would never take YTS refusers: 'We aren't that sort of scheme'. However, the Chamber had become the region's major adult training agent, although she insisted this was not an entrepreneurial move, 'We want to offer a service [to our members]. That's all we've ever wanted to do.'

Entrepreneurial umbrella schemes

In 1986, the entrepreneurial and fringe managing agents feared that charges would deter employers from providing placements, especially for disadvantaged trainees. A contributory factor in the death of the church-based care scheme was that 'the NHS and personal social services, none of them have got any spare cash to spend', and along with others the church managing agent correctly anticipated that charging employers would undermine training standards: 'The sponsors will call the tune . . . We have enough problems at the moment prizing [trainees] out of the work placements for training, and once [employers] start paying, they'll resent any external interference, I should think, even monitoring . . . The special training relationship's . . . changed, they really are workers.' By 1988, the effects of financial pressures could be clearly seen among Southwich's few surviving entrepreneurs. There remained only Jack's and Dovers, but they had been joined by the local authority scheme which had lost its Mode B status and was forced to become more entrepreneurial to survive.

Jack's

Jack's had moved from its second home in a small disused factory into a modern warehouse with specially converted facilities. It still had double the trainee quota of any other managing agent, but occupancy had never reached the peak targets of 1986–7, and substantial cuts were due. The only skilled trainees were their apprentice engineers, about 15 per cent of their total, whose employers tended to pay for FE training unconnected with the training centre. The smaller number of craft and design trainees also went to Southwich College. The bulk of training was the 'multi-skill' scheme where, along with the skilled trainees, only the minority premium trainees were likely to stay for the second year. A tutor told us how the MSC's eagerness to keep the course full had brought criticism when he tried to move trainees from employers who offered poor training or prospects: 'They complain to MSC and MSC come back on me, "That's not your job. Your job is to train." ' Clerical trainees also often left or were taken off after one year. However Jack's did not welcome compulsion: 'You get the hard-core compulsory group who are a nuisance and no good for the group, then our disciplinary procedures would have to terminate them.' Searching for alternatives to YTS, it ran a Job Club, had held (but lost) the MSC's large adult training contract, and provided electrical training for adult workers. However, 'If [numbers] drop any more we're going to be out of business . . . There's too many managing agents with too many places.'

Dovers

Reflecting its smaller resources, Dovers' training centre was a converted house with net curtains, the lounge as the office and the bedrooms used as training rooms. In 1986 Dovers was the only managing agent to express no doubts about extending non-traditional training to two years: 'I've been told by MSC that I should just get approval with no problems.' But in 1988 a reliable internal source gave a more sceptical view of Dovers' training: 'How can we do a development plan (for the MSC)? . . . If we'd submitted a plan last year, for instance, look how out we are in numbers, £400 down! . . . Somebody will have to go.' Employers were clamouring for trainees, but it had recruited below 70 per cent of its quota. Dovers had been encouraged by the MSC to resuscitate the motor vehicle association's warehouse scheme (for which, according to their submission to the AMB, the Careers Service had established a 'need'). Dovers' manager admitted: 'It's very much at the experimental stage. We've never run it before, so there's bound to be some teething problems.'

The manager said motivation was a problem, especially in care training: 'We can just about stretch out the first year but by the second year it's inevitably very repetitive . . . Several of them say to me . . . "I've done this at school and I've done this at home for years, what's the point?" And I'm not sure really.' In the second year of catering, 'Many of them know the job already and they've no more to learn'. He now spent most of his time chasing up trainees: 'Some don't bother at their work placements, only go in when it suits them and don't turn up here. When they do, we fine them, sometimes considerable sums, but with wages of £70 a week some of them can afford to say, "Stuff your training" . . . We need agreement from the MSC to get rid of someone, because of trouble with numbers . . . The daft thing is that then we have to chase them up and virtually beg them to stay on the scheme.' He thought compulsion 'will cause chaos. The tutors don't want it. It won't help the existing trainees, and at the same time MSC is trying to upgrade the image of YTS! . . . It's a farce . . . Long-term projections are hopeless.'

The local authority (former Mode B) scheme

The local authority scheme still took the hard-to-place, and up to half its trainees had premiums. However, the managing agent felt that, compared with the entrepreneurs, she had suffered MSC discrimination. The MSC had picked holes in her detailed ATO submission. ATO recognition had been long delayed, the scheme had been given no transitional funding, and it had been forced to lay off experienced staff. 'We seem to be constantly penalized because we're a council scheme . . . Careers seem to have a special arrangement with one or two schemes, because at one stage for one particular scheme we weren't getting any at all and when I went to Careers there were all these names. I said "What are all those names in this list?" Last year competition got quite nasty. One scheme, I won't say which, was deliberately telling [trainees] no other schemes existed.' Careers officers seemed reluctant to label any trainee premium and 'Schools are becoming increasingly difficult to get into. Even Careers find it difficult.'

The scheme still offered a range of low-skill flexible training, but most boys wanted construction (often for lack of CITB placements), and girls wanted care work. A handful did FE horticulture or printing courses. At the MSC's request it had added motor cycle maintenance: 'But it was difficult to get the placements and if they're working with motor cycles every day they cover the off-the-job syllabus too quickly.' The job boom and staff cuts meant that more trainees were in work placements rather than workshops, but if they got jobs they were taken off the scheme: 'To be honest, those we have left (in the second year) are those who the employer is keeping on and wants to continue their training and those [about 20 per cent] who we have a real problem with . . . We don't put them in training at the end, so they're not aware of being left.' The managing agent was against compulsion but for compassionate reasons: 'If someone's being a real pain, then we can't tell them to go away any more because they'll lose their money. You get to know their family and commitments and we couldn't do that to them.' She was also sceptical of ENTRAIN for which the scheme had been a pilot: 'It seems as if anytime a youngster says "I want to . . .", however ridiculous, they say, "Go out there and do it!" . . . I went to their conference recently, lovely hotel, lovely people, but no content whatsoever.' She apologized for seeming cynical: 'I've seen these ideas come and go, change this way and that. I'm afraid I'm not so idealistic about all this any more, not like a newcomer would be.'

The Careers Service and YTS 2

Pressures to fill YTS 2 also now affected the Careers Service. A careers officer complained about poorer co-operation from managing agents and the lack of access and follow-up: 'We've been told the priority is [recruitment] . . . It's frustrating having good jobs on the books and kids on YTS . . . We used to send out a letter to all young people going on YTS, a letter stating, "Don't give up hope of a 'normal' job" . . . Now we can't approach them and tell them. It's seen as unsettling.'

It was taboo at the Careers Office to talk about 'compulsion'. The official line was that 'The usual reason for refusal – "cheap labour" or "I want a job" – I think more often than not it's from a misunderstanding of what YTS can do'. Withdrawing social security rights 'could be very helpful because of the added incentive to the young person . . . We could contact the [Un-employment Review Officer] and say, "Would you like to have a chat with them in order to give them a bit of encouragement?".' But a colleague complained: 'It makes us look like we're policing the scheme, makes it really difficult with the kids.' YTS refusers did not lack motivation and reporting them would not help. Instead the Careers Service would lose the trust of young people, who would now avoid making contact.

Conclusions

Thus our latest survey of Southwich YTS schemes largely confirmed our earlier predictions. Admittedly, charging employers for trainees had not yet created a shortage of placements. But, especially for the entrepreneurial managing agents, there was greater competition for fewer, more unwilling trainees. There was also even greater difficulty controlling their training. Without a large enough craft base or alternative funding, agents' staff were being cut, standards reduced, and schemes either faced collapse or were diversifying.

Overall, as job and education opportunities improved and the number of potential trainees fell, employers with high-cost craft training employed fewer, carefully selected trainees and training was more job-specific. YTS 2 was also losing ground in non-traditional areas, with employers preferring to take trainees off the scheme early or trainees finding jobs. Second-year YTS was thus polarized between better-qualified trainees receiving good training with actual or potential jobs and the disadvantaged on inferior schemes where there was less prospect of work. The net result of opening up YTS 2 to market forces and competition had been to make the segmentation and inequality which we described in Part One more pronounced.

Chapter 12
Vulnerable training

It was unnecessary to look again at the whole range of recruitment and training in Southwich YTS. Our interviews with managing agents confirmed what we already knew, that standards were least susceptible to the short-run commercial pressures in the 'sponsorship' areas of YTS linked to large firms and established training. But these were a relatively small, possibly shrinking, part of the total and the claim that YTS 2 would upgrade quality depended on what happened in the new-skill areas where there were more trainees yet quality appeared most vulnerable (even under YTS 1) to cost-cutting and to the loss of FE and MSC control. The managing agents themselves expressed most scepticism about the second year of training in 'new' skills. The schemes run by the entrepreneurs under traditional craft labels also seemed vulnerable.

We therefore adopted an in-depth method, selecting randomly a small number of second-year trainees from each of these more vulnerable schemes. We interviewed them and at the same time interviewed their tutors and observed second-year off-the-job training. We also visited their placements and talked to their supervisors or employers. This chapter describes our findings, which relate to 29 girls and 26 boys, seen from the varied perspectives of all those involved (Table 12.1). Though small, we believe this sample provides a reasonably representative picture of the general quality of training on these schemes.

As we note below, our attempts to observe training and hold interviews met many difficulties. Funding cuts meant that conditions on some schemes were cramped, so rooms for private interviews with trainees were rare. 'Out in the field' took on a new meaning when unsuitable footwear sank ankle-deep in the quagmire of a building site, or a 'streetwise' interview was interrupted by a reversing lorry. We failed to obtain interviews from some evasive employers with little commitment to training. We gleaned what we could from others who were 'too busy', with their heads under car hoods or

Table 12.1   Second-year trainee interviews, by type of scheme

Employer-led (new skill)	retail	(2*)
Stable-skill umbrella (new skill)	retail	(7)
Entrepreneurial umbrella		
Established skill labels:	motor vehicle	5
	craft and design	3
	clerical (2 schemes)	5
	catering	4
		(17)
Multi-skill:†	'engineering'/	4
	'construction'	5
	'welding'/mv/metal	5
		(14)
New skills:	care (2 schemes)	10
	warehouse*	5
		(15)
Total		(55)

* One retail and all warehouse trainees were in their first year in new schemes
† Under YTS 2 this term was increasingly used for broadly based schemes
outside apprenticeships still using the labels of established crafts

rounding up disorientated old ladies, cooking batches of scones, or (once) sacking a trainee. The trainee's 'workplace' could be a leaking wooden shack in the middle of a field at the end of a dirt track. These difficulties sometimes told us far more than any interview about the quality of YTS 2 training.

Entrepreneurial schemes with traditional craft labels

Motor vehicle maintenance

The motor vehicle association's new training centre looked orderly and efficient, with all the tutors neatly dressed in smart suits and company ties, yet we were refused permission to observe second-year training. Someone confessed: 'We do have terrible problems with discipline, especially in the first year', and some second-year trainees were 'almost illiterate'. He volunteered the opinion that employers were too busy to train any but the most able trainees: 'A young person with a bit of initiative and mechanical know-how is going to get on. Without that you can't blame them for putting a broom in their hands.'

We visited five of the scheme's placements. The most regulated training was at a large garage, part of a chain, which offered the trainee an apprenticeship with employed YTS status. The manager said, 'He's doing the same kind of work as everyone else but under continued supervision', which the trainee confirmed. The manager and the other mechanics showed an interest in his off-the-job training, but the manager complained that YTS training was 'watered down' and 'You don't get the same commitment. He's easily led by the others.' The firm would probably pay for further FE training but 'He's there as our representative. I've told him he won't go if he's not good enough.'

Unusually, another garage had selected a promising girl trainee: 'They took all the pictures down and tidied up the garage specially.' Her early training had been well supervised. She said: 'If he knows we've, say, done gear boxes, he'll let me have a bash at work.' Another garage owner (who had turned his hobby of racing cars into a business) had two trainees doing small jobs unsupervised: 'If we were paying out good money, then you'd expect more . . . If they do it wrong I give them a clip round the ear . . . We treat them like kids really, that's what they are, isn't it?' His lack of formal training made him sceptical: 'At college they learn one way to do things . . . Then they learn how we do things here.' He would not pay for further training after YTS: 'It depends really what the boys value most, a wage or training.'

The remaining trainee was unqualified but was employed in his father's garage where he had worked since the age of eleven: 'I was doing a hell of a lot of it even before I left school.' His father (who had learned from *his* father) complained: 'They're telling him how to do things by the book he's been doing here for years . . . But you have to do it to get the money.' The son did not expect to pass the next exam because 'you have to write for that' (unlike first-level multiple choice). After completing YTS training 'Dad would just give me a spanner and tell me to get on with it'.

Jack's craft and design scheme

Most of Jack's craft and design students went to Southwich College, but for a specially-sponsored course which the managing agent said some employers found unsatisfactory: 'Like the printers, they don't even have a design room so they can't see the point of it.' A few were sent to FE courses as far afield as London: 'If the employers want something more specific . . . There's two sorts of trainees really, and the system doesn't take account of that.' Our three trainees confirmed that they and their employers found Jack's FE course too low-level and general: 'They treat them like sub-standard students.' However these continuing second-year trainees now had employed YTS status and two employers, an architect and a printer, paid extra for standard FE courses while the third, with a design office, would soon follow suit.

The design trainee was proud that he now did 'everything in the production of artwork from start to finish'. Only a girl trainee in the architect's office said she was still supervised but resented it: 'I'd prefer to have more [responsibility] but they don't seem to trust me.' Nevertheless her employer said 'We hope she'll go further', and she herself aimed to become a technician after five years and now liked FE training: 'It helps you at work.

You can see it happening on site.' The printing employer said bluntly: 'There's no training as such, just watching . . . YTS just have to get on with their work, you can't carry people in a company of this size.' The trainee valued his specialized FE course because it was 'what I'm doing every day', and he felt an asset to the firm: 'I'm the most qualified person [the employer's] got, I'm a good advert for him really.' His employer, however, grumbled that College was 'a blooming nuisance, you can't run a small company with people popping off here and there', and might stop the training because he felt YTS costs were almost as high as a wage.

Clerical schemes

The motor vehicle association

The motor vehicle association's clerical tutor felt that the course compared well with her FE experience because classes were small and used equipment from the training centre (which also put on evening classes). However, although trainees did two courses, restrictions on YTS funding meant they were only allowed to sit one exam, and they were then encouraged to take further training and more exams part-time through the centre. Two of the three clerical trainees resented this, but they were considering evening classes. The third, a boy, did not need typing in his work for an estate agent. His boss was typical in his view of off-the-job training: 'It's not really convenient but it's part and parcel of [YTS]'. In a buoyant market, the trainees were now employed and they felt they had been trained while doing 'a real job'. However their employers were vague about training. The estate agent said: 'For the first three months they're supervised constantly, after that there are questions and they can't be left alone. Mostly they just learn from experience.' And in a computer finance office it was admitted: 'The work requires little training, they learn as they go along just watching'.

Jack's

Over a period of months, Jack's always found it inconvenient for us to observe any off-the-job training or to interview tutors or trainees. It was 'not their policy' to give access to employers. (Early on, however, we were given lists of trainees and through them we gained access to employers.) One reason for Jack's wariness might have been that we accidentally witnessed an angry encounter between the managing agent and clerical tutors. From this it seemed that staff, though unqualified, were expected to design as well as teach their courses, but were given no allowance for preparation. The use of a large number of part-timers was said to disrupt teaching, any co-ordination having to take place off the premises, unpaid and in their own time. One tutor agreed to an interview at home. He claimed that lack of resources and the level of the trainees limited the clerical scheme to one exam in typing. The search for alternative exams were frustrated by lack of cash for entry fees. They were using old chairs discarded from the office 'which are the

wrong height and the kids fall off the back of them . . . It's always the
cheapest options. They think now we've got a set of coursebooks that's it, we
never need to update it any more.' Staff turnover was very high and the
senior tutor confided: 'I'm not long for this place myself.'

Our two clerical trainees (one employed) from Jack's were extremely
dissatisfied. One had got her employer to complain and had been trainee
representative at an acrimonious feedback meeting, but had got nowhere.
Lack of staff co-ordination had meant 'I must have been over the same unit
three or four times'. The other also complained of repetition, 'Boring, crap,
rubbish! You don't learn nothing . . . You ask any of the others, they'll tell
you the same.' Jack's employers were also vague about training off-the-job:
'They can't use it here . . . We don't need the qualifications but the young
people are glad to get it.' Any on-the-job training had been short and
unsystematic. One trainee said: 'After I started there the lady went on
holiday so I had to pick it up in two weeks.' An advertising agency said
frankly they wanted boys for media work but 'We prefer girls for clerical
work, understandably, because they don't mind the sort of dogsbody
position they're put in first.'

Dovers' catering scheme

Dovers' off-the-job catering training was specially sponsored at Southwich
College, but its FE tutor felt that 'Ultimately YTS has just got to lower the
standards of the College'. There was 'no comparison' between Dovers
trainees and full-time catering students or the HCITB trainees who 'do the
(second-grade City & Guilds) straight off but then they're much brighter'.
Some Dovers trainees failed even the multiple-choice first-level test: 'They
don't really want to do it. They have to do YTS so they're put on cookery.'
We observed a training session in a large purpose-built kitchen, with the
trainees following demonstrations by the tutor. There was a good atmosphere, although the tutor complained that a third of the trainees were away.
Theory, in the afternoon, created resistance and much clock-watching, and
by three o'clock the trainees all had their coats on because our visit had kept
them late. The tutor felt YTS was 'all geared to the employers . . . You get
so many who just use them . . . You need to be in a hotel really to do the
course . . . For some of these the only experience of cooking they get is
here.'

The best training was offered in an industrial canteen where the trainee
was supervised for main dishes and prepared vegetables on his own: 'The
staff show me and it was easy to learn . . . Most of it's the same every day.'
The supervisor felt that 'By the second year you need them, really . . . You
can basically leave them to get on with it.' He hoped to lecture in FE and
valued the training: 'They can take all day to learn to make perfect gravy –
here we have to teach them to cut corners.' The trainee, who had turned
down a college place, found Dovers' course 'a waste of time . . . If I'd known
this I'd've done it at college.' The only other trainee to do unsupervised

cooking worked mostly alone at a sports centre: 'Sometimes the boss will let me cook a steak but that's as difficult as it gets.' Otherwise he served meals and did kitchen and cellar work: 'Nothing took me more than about five minutes to learn.' He found the FE training too fussy: 'After all most places don't have home-made mayonnaise, only like the Hilton.' The employer merely put up with it to get the trainee.

The third trainee was clearly of low ability. He had failed first grade and been rejected by his placement in a function room, and now worked reluctantly in a sandwich bar: 'I mainly just wash up and do the sandwiches . . . butter the scones . . . It's the same every day and I do cleaning at the end . . . I could make a sandwich before I came on the scheme.' The supervisor painted a different picture: the trainee 'sets the tables, washes up, waits on tables, makes salads, soups, scones, etc.'. She complained he was slow and felt she was giving him badly-needed social skills and 'showing him what real work is about'. Both she and the trainee found FE training useless: 'We've got no time for that . . . The only kids who need to know how to cook like that are the ones who'll go and apprentice at the Dorchester.' The remaining trainee had also failed first grade and was content as a waitress in the tea-shop where she had washed up before YTS. The manager found her slow: 'Every day at the same time we have to say, "Biscuit-tray, Donna" '. He felt that he provided mainly compensatory education: 'The very first thing she had to do was to sit down with me and learn her tables.' Both he and the trainee felt that FE training was pointless – 'There's not a lot she can do with it here' – though meeting people at college had boosted her confidence.

These employers had little contact with the managing agent, and although all four catering trainees were now in effect working, none had employed YTS status.

'Multi-skill' schemes

The local authority (former Mode B) construction tutor complained that training 'used to be more specific . . . Now it's been knocked on the head by CITB, we've had to move into the realm of "multi-skills". Silly title, doesn't tell you anything.' The scheme was now called landscape gardening: 'That's why we do so many garden gates, we've got hundreds out there!' We observed the City & Guilds testing, which will be described in the next chapter.

The 'welding' course was a mixture of welding, fabrication, motor vehicle and motorcyle work, but the tutor said the trainees really wanted to be motor mechanics, 'Not all of it is engines but they can't see that.' Classroom time was minimal and the first year was spent in supervised repetition of a task, with testing of the more able as and when they became proficient: 'Out of a group of eight we're lucky if two pass on the City & Guilds.' The second year involved 'making something, not just practising the same thing over and over again'. However, training was difficult to observe in the cramped conditions of the welding shop.

According to the trainees, the reason we had been refused permission to observe second-year training on Jack's 'engineering'/industrial production scheme was possibly because there was none. One said: 'Don't talk to me about training! What a waste of time that is. We don't have classes, we just sit around chatting. They tell us we can do what we like, but we've come here to learn. I get cross about it. The tutors spend their time having tea.' Another insisted: 'No, really, we don't do anything. You think we're kidding, but we play cards or talk.'

The small employers with 'multi-skill' trainees proved most elusive. Builders (who change sites and work long hours) claimed they were too busy. A small garage owner was angry that we had traced his ex-directory number, and another, who was said to have physically attacked several of his trainees, seemed too dangerous to contact. Eventually for our 14 multi-skill trainees we interviewed nine employers, from two small building-firms, two tool-hire firms (on different schemes), two garages, a tyre and a windscreen replacement company, a signmakers and a small rural engineering firm.

The five construction trainees were labouring, digging, carrying hods, mixing cement or plaster, or cleaning up, and were only occasionally allowed to try anything more skilled: 'When they're rendering they leave a little hole and let me fill it in'; 'I get to do some of the bits that don't matter like undercoating'. One of the builders explained: 'We just haven't time for him to make mistakes.' Both builders found YTS superficial: 'They say they'll be semi-skilled in the end but in a small firm you [have to] be versatile'; 'It's nowhere near apprenticeship standard'. The trainees, too, felt they were merely dabbling: 'We've cut a bit of wood, cut a joint, did a little bit of bricklaying, half an hour of plumbing, and a little bit of painting'; 'The trouble is . . . it's general'; 'You should learn more than this in two years'.

The other nine multi-skill trainees and their employers would also have preferred in-depth training in one skill relevant to the placement. One employer summed up: 'We don't want exams, just a bit of nous.' However, although five placements seemed to offer some skills they were very varied and learning could depend on the trainees' confidence: 'There's always someone to ask. I don't know how they learn things but they do.' At best, one welding trainee ran a small rural garage single-handed, using skills picked up before his YTS placement and through training from the owner: 'He teaches me everything . . . He tells me once or twice, then I know. If it's a big job he'll stand behind me.' Another trainee was in charge of a mower repair workshops: 'It took me three months to settle to the job and six months to really get the hang of it.' Another had taken only two weeks to learn to dismantle machinery but 'Every day's different, I never know what I'll be doing when I get in'. A trainee using a pantograph in a sign-making workshop said: 'I'm still learning new aspects of it, but to get a grasp of it, I suppose it took nine or ten months.' Another trainee had learned to install telephones.

On their employers' statements, the remaining four trainees were doing unskilled jobs with employers who offered no training: 'The trainees help out with lesser skilled bits like clearing away', 'They cleaned the equipment, tidied up the yard, that sort of thing'. Without the trainee, 'The bosses would have to make the tea'. Although all 14 'multi-skill' trainees were now working rather than training, only two had employed YTS status.

'New-skill' schemes

Retail training

The LCU mother and baby chain store
In the LCU mother and baby chain, off-the-job training was centralized in one store for an area within about 60 miles. Based on City & Guilds, the first year covered general retailing skills including till use, second products and marketing, neatly packaged into 'customer relations', 'security' and so on, with additional work-based projects, visits, talks and demonstrations. The tutor had switched from management and was well equipped for training, which she felt was 'junior management level . . . much better than the usual staff get'. We observed a well-received session on 'security', with a video in the morning and the afternoon spent making posters, the best to be displayed at the work placements. In a group discussion these trainees were most positive about their training: 'They tend to spend more time with us and show us more', although 'They tend to baby us a bit. It's like being at home.' Our Southwich trainee was going to be employed and groomed for management: 'The training helps you know how the shop's run and gives you a better chance in it.' Her store supervisor said: 'I ask them all about it . . . It keeps it relevant and the enthusiasm going.'

The LCU grocers
The LCU grocers' training was also centralized. The YTS tutor had switched from management and had previous YTS experience with a health authority scheme and an entrepreneurial scheme in retail training. She now felt her principles 'less compromised' because she designed, taught, monitored and assessed the area scheme. Again it was based on City & Guilds, and the second year overlapped management training in production and marketing.

In the training session we observed, the tutor complained that a pilot project on tea, designed by the Accredited Training Centre, was 'too hard for them, it works in theory but not in practice'. She had to do most of the work herself, witness one exchange:

Trainee: 'What do you mean by tea chest?'
Tutor: 'You know, what you pack things in when you move.'
Trainee: 'Oh so then you put it on the shelves and sell it.'
Tutor: 'No, it's got to be blended and packaged yet.'

Trainee: 'You're just going round it the long way . . . You just buy it and drink it. That's all I need to know.'

The next exercise (on the life of an Easter egg) was met by moans: 'What a load of crap, eh!' Only a star trainee discussed shelf-life, while the rest yawned insistently or chatted. The tutor complained that the training was not valued by the branch managers, who would offer trainees jobs too late, only when they were leaving: 'How can [trainees] value it when . . . they work for someone that's antagonistic . . . [The managers] think because I'm a YTS tutor I'm one step removed from a YTS [trainee], so they treat me the same.' The scheme asked for homework after the long daily journey to the centre, but the tutor complained that trainees would do no written work for assessment and wanted only training immediately relevant to their placements. However, in a group discussion all but one of the trainees said they valued most of the off-the-job training because they hope to go into management.

Our Southwich trainee was enthusiastic about work supervision at his placement in the training centre: 'We have a film on how to do [packing] . . . where to put the eggs and that. Then we're till-trained for six weeks . . . The rest of it is in four-week blocks on provisions, etc.' Now employed, he found the second year a bit pointless because 'I can do all the jobs . . . but I do enjoy it'. In contrast, trainees from other branches complained bitterly that the managers' opposition to training made work experience like 'organized chaos . . . terrible . . . Like we were supposed to be put on different departments within the stores, but we weren't allowed on them.' 'Yeah, like I spent months on the trolleys . . . The only shit-work is supposed to be packing bags . . . for two weeks during the induction.' 'If there's anything they want doing, it doesn't matter what it is, the YTS has to do it.'

The Chamber of Commerce

We interviewed tutors at the Chamber of Commerce before the drastic fall in numbers reduced its training to general office and retail skills (which the managing agent felt were 'far too broad-based to mean much'). However, the tutors were already demoralized. Although they had had backgrounds in office and retail work, none had teacher training, yet they complained they had to design courses with no help beyond the qualification guidelines: 'You get no input or output from anyone here.' Usually they did not know where trainees worked: 'It's ridiculous to try to teach youngsters to be adapted to employers' needs when most tutors don't meet employers to know what their needs are.' They felt that they mainly provided compensatory social skills but that two years was too long: 'We think we're enlarging their potential, but quite frankly they think it's a waste of time.' All complained of poor pay: 'As you can see, the atmosphere here is awful.' We discovered later that most had left.

We observed a week's special project on setting up a shop. Day one produced 'a big argument, we couldn't agree on a shop . . . It was awful . . .

We all went home in the end.' On the second day the issue was shelved to prevent a renewed quarrel. They were given time alone to choose job descriptions, but merely chatted, made sexist comments and threw things. A further fruitless break exasperated the tutor: 'Well?' Silence, then a girl said: 'Why don't you just choose? . . . Please!' After refusing, the tutor tried unsuccessfully to co-opt a too-vocal trainee as managing director: 'You're the one with the mouth and ideas.' Finally, a girl gave in: 'I'm bored with this. I'll be managing director just to get moving. Otherwise we'll be here all week.' Each then stood on a chair to say why they wanted the post, most reluctantly, some disruptively. After a tea break they moaned about planning a board meeting: 'This place makes me want to go home'; 'When's teatime'. Next day saw renewed arguments between the boys who chose a bookshop when told they couldn't have a sports shop, and the girls who wanted a babywear shop:

'Books are boring.'
'So are babies.'
'I'm going home . . . This is stupid and boring and I'm not wasting my time.'
'We're bored . . . cross at the boys. They're spoiling it.'

By midweek, hostility had become indifference, with one girl sitting with her back to the group. They grew hostile when their designs for shop layouts failed to meet the tutor's standards. After all the arguments, writing-up had to be done at home, but protests that they were confused only brought warnings that they would fail that part of the course. During the week four trainees left for jobs, and the remainder seemed to see the training as punishment for not finding work.

Our seven trainees were very dissatisfied: 'It bears no relationship to what I do at work at all'; 'They take no notice if you say you've done it already at school. They just say, "So do it again" '. One girl found telephone practice 'just insulting'. Two years' extended training seemed to them well beyond reasonable limits – 'They're just filling in time now' – and they saw the qualification as useless. The Chamber sent employers regular bulletins to get them involved, but they were not interested. A china shop owner affirmed his belief in training but knew nothing of the scheme and told his trainee: 'It's all right, you don't have to go in.' Others found the training irrelevant: 'They don't need two years . . . They don't want to go either.'

Employers' comments also indicated that on-the-job training was minimal and unstructured: 'They don't need training as such. It's all quite easy to pick up'; 'After two months we could leave her to get on with it'. The few trainees who reported any supervision estimated it lasted under six months. One employer referred our questions on training to the trainee who ran a shop entirely alone. A boy whose job was heavy lifting had never been shown how to lift. Several trainees spent all day dusting. A fashion shop manageress said: 'Our job as we see it is to show them a sample of what work will be like. Punctuality, on your feet all day, that sort of thing . . . Their main job is to keep the shop tidy.' There was no time to train, which meant trainees could not be taken on and they were 'a bit of a nuisance . . . because there's nothing for them to do'. The trainee left because she was merely replacing clothes on hangers: 'They treat you like you're really thick and don't let you do anything.'

The local authority (former Mode B) and Dovers care schemes

The main local authority care tutor, a trained teacher, was deeply ambivalent about YTS: 'Sometimes I feel like a parasite on the unemployed, but I have to say to myself, "Maybe we do help people in a time of no work" . . . [The trainees] are my real priority, I do my best for them.' However, 'What they want is a job . . . that's far more important than any exam'. Second-year training consisted of diverse individual projects, so we observed a first-year session on mental handicap. The tutor and 15 trainees sat in a circle in a redundant school building (one girl joked, 'When I left school I thought I'd seen the back of it. Now here I am again!'). They began listing 'nasty' and sympathetic descriptions, until their hilarity led the tutor to ask one boy to read out the poem he had written down: 'Half a pound of nuts and bolts/Half a pound of plastic/Put it in the washing machine/Out pops a spastic!' The tutor was tight-lipped:

> 'Do you think that's funny, all of you? . . . That's what this is all about, getting rid of ignorance.'
> He tried again:
> 'Why aren't we sorry for handicapped people?'
> A girl replied:
> 'Because . . . it's easier to make it into a joke.'
> *Tutor:* 'Is that ignorant?'
> *Girl:* 'No, because it's done out of fear.'
> *Tutor:* 'Is that still ignorant?'
> *Another girl:* 'Yeah, 'cos they're still people just like us.'

They filled in questionnaires on prejudice and jokily discussed each other's answers. The tutor asked: 'What should you do if you're in a café and there's someone odd-looking who needs help?' 'I'd ignore them.' 'I wouldn't, I'd cut up their food for them.' They talked about how the group could pick on outsiders, and concluded they should try to be nicer to each other as well as to the mentally handicapped.

Our five second-year trainees had preferred first-year training: 'It's broadened my horizons'; 'It's not necessary for work, but it's helpful for life'. Their second-year projects took them out of the centre, and the tutor stressed the need for trust: 'Look, I know you'll sneak a look in Top Shop – I would, too – but you'll do what I ask as well.' However, the trainees said: 'We only come in for the morning, then we go up town and have coffee all afternoon'; 'There isn't really (a second year). They don't know what to do with us'. Most showed no interest in City & Guilds: 'No one fails them, I didn't even know we'd taken them.' However, two girls wanted to enter nursing and the tutor had taken them along to enrol in O-level evening classes (although one was discouraged because YTS participation meant she had to pay fees).

All the tutors at Dovers had nursing backgrounds, but only the head tutor had previous teaching experience, with Dovers' trainees at Southwich College: 'It was so fragmented at College. I didn't know where they [the trainees] were half the time. Also they were so frightened of the set-up . . . they wouldn't use the resources.' She stressed the trainees' need for social skills: 'Really they're just pacing the time until they get married . . . Some are so scruffy, and the language they use . . . they'd never get a job.' She felt that neither trainees nor employers valued the training or credentials, but during the second year 'You can certainly see a change . . . They're much more responsible'. At the training session at Dovers' centre, dressed in outdoor coats and gloves, the tutor and nine girl trainees sat in a bare cold bedroom round a large table. Although the girls seemed to like the tutor personally, one ostentatiously read a book and the rest periodically raised their eyes heavenward, tutted or yawned. The tutor tried to discuss last week's essay topic – 'Come on now, give me an advantage to taking handicapped people swimming' – but few had attempted it. After a silence her direct questions met with 'Dunno'; 'What was the question?'; 'What are you on about?' She gave up and answered herself. 'Special shopping evenings' for the handicapped caused a wave of laughter. 'What places might handicapped people like to visit?' brought 'Museums' and 'Art galleries', and when the tutor suggested a pub or a disco, there were further hoots of laughter. The tutor tackled them: 'All right, very funny, but just remember that handicapped people want to do the same things as you do.' The afternoon session was interrupted by wrapping sweets they had made for a local old people's home, but most of the trainees flounced out to watch TV: 'I ain't doing that'. We learned later that the afternoon session had been staged for our benefit.

Our five Dovers trainees were all very critical: 'It's rubbish, we do sod all if you ask me'; 'It's a waste of time coming here, I'd rather be at work'; 'It's so boring, I bring my book and do knitting. We go down and watch *Neighbours*.' General topics such as contraception were seen as repetitive, common sense or insulting: 'If we didn't know what they think they're telling us, we'd be pretty useless, wouldn't we?'

Placements for these schemes overlapped. We interviewed seven supervisors or employers for ten placements, including two private schools, a home for disturbed and mentally handicapped children (with two trainees), and two private and one council old people's homes. But no YTS supervisor could be found at two NHS hospitals and at one other private home. Some employers did not know their managing agent, and suffered off-the-job training merely to get a trainee, although several who might have been interested lacked information. None valued the YTS credentials, and training was criticized for lack of direct practical relevance. The matron of an old people's home complained that it was 'not 100 per cent about old people . . . Learning care out of a book is no good.' A children's home matron thought: 'They do a general residential care training which might be old people. That's very different from dealing with children.'

Few employers or supervisors could point to even minimal training: 'We supervise them for six weeks, then they're on their own. It's better they learn to handle responsibility and learn by their own mistakes'; 'We really haven't a lot of time, so we rely on people to ask . . . but they rarely do'. A matron complained that the trainee avoided doing commodes: 'He had a work routine which he more or less chose for himself, which as far as I know had nothing to do with training'. Another matron confessed: 'It was difficult telling the staff [that trainees] weren't just there to help out. With Jane it's still difficult because she's happy to do ironing all day.' Rather than providing skill training, supervisors saw themselves as helping the disadvantaged: 'We offer a small, non-threatening, supportive environment.' A school matron felt young people needed 'time to mature and to compensate for what the school's done to them . . . YTS is not about learning practical skills, it's about building a whole new person.' (Her trainee was learning her tables with the infants' class.) Another matron washed her trainee's clothes and provided a bath: 'You have to treat her like a child to rebuild on all the damage that's been done.'

Only one trainee, in a hospital, felt she received training: 'The nurse shows me how to do dressings, stitches and that . . . I've learnt something new every day.' But NHS auxiliaries were hostile to what they saw as job substitution. Other trainees confirmed that any supervision had ended after a few weeks, and felt that at best their placements offered experience and 'common sense' rather than training. Working with children, 'You just look after children. There's not a lot to know.' 'Every day's the same. I listen to the little ones read, do up their shoelaces, take them to the loo, just generally help out. There's no real skill involved.' A trainee in a private school had been put in charge of a class of six-year-olds several times when the teacher went sick: 'I was really scared to begin with.' Two trainees in a home for disturbed children had little supervision: 'We have the little ones on their own. It's not really right, is it? . . . If they start having tantrums and that, we just hold them. With the bigger ones it's difficult, we couldn't keep them down if they decided to go mad.' ('Training' from other staff had included advice that children who bit should be bitten in return.) A girl worried that on her training day there was nobody to do her work with elderly people in a day centre: 'I'm responsible for them. Mostly I just talk to them, but we do cooking, bingo, gardening, keep fit.' Another trainee had been wrongly blamed for an accident and was barred from close contact with residents: 'Now I'm just a dogsbody. It's just slave labour.' Ironically, the trainee who was said to avoid commodes complained: 'I'm not allowed to touch the old people at all apart from to take them to the commode. I wipe their bottoms and wash the commode . . . That's all I'm allowed to do all day long.' An official complaint failed because his work was controlled not by the employer but by the other care assistants: 'It's still commodes and more commodes, I'm the expert now.' Later he left.

Estimates of the time needed to learn the job varied from 'no time at all' to three or four months, and by the second year most trainees were included as staff in work rotas, working shifts and covering for staff who were sick, so that sometimes they were left in sole charge: 'They're useful members of the team. They do all the same sorts of care for the children as we do.' Yet none had been given employed YTS status.

Dovers' warehouse scheme

When we visited Dovers' warehouse scheme four months after it had started, senior staff joked about making up the training as they went along. They had not yet worked out whether or how to teach the costly RTITB fork-lift truck driving, the most tangible skill previously offered. Stock control would be taught by a retired marine engineer with experience in adult education. Meanwhile, health and safety was taught by a retired nursing sister with little teaching experience but great compassion for young people: 'If you steal you go to prison, if you can't get a job you go on the YTS. I'd rather teach in a borstal, at least they've done something wrong to be there.'

In the training session which we observed, for all their grimaces and jokes, the trainees (one girl and nine strapping lads) clearly liked the little old lady who told them off 'like yer gran'. She began by asking: 'What did we do last week, boys?' 'Get a bollocking' (hoots of laughter). 'Well, this week we're going to do how not to slip over, how to climb a ladder and not fall off, and good housekeeping . . . No, don't laugh boys, I don't mean you should rush and get your pinnies on. What I mean is to "keep your house in order" in the work-place.' The trainees found parts of her message ridiculously simple. 'What do we do if we find a pool of water on the floor?' Chorus, 'Mop it up!' 'Now remember boys, don't ever climb a ladder backwards'. (Heavenward glances of disbelief.) Though none of them worked on a laboratory, she seemed disappointed at their glazed response to her visual aids on lab safety, 'Is that it then? Not a comment? Not even a laugh at the funny drawings. So much for staying up till twelve o'clock colouring pretty colours on the bottles.' In the afternoon the tutor asked: 'What would you do if someone was facing you with a sawn-off shot gun?' The trainee paused a moment: 'I'd shit bricks and build myself a brick wall!' The resulting hilarity brought a threat to send him home without pay. The disruption was partly the trainees' response to being kept late for our benefit.

Among our warehouse trainees, only the girl felt the training would be useful, but she was unrealistically hoping the computer training would equip her to computerize the warehouse stock in the family business. The remaining four trainees found training irrelevant: 'I suppose it keeps you off the streets.' Only one trainee had been able to do the work assignment, locating fire points and describing fire drill at their work, because none of the placements had drill and most had no fire equipment. The tutor chided:

'You should go and tell your placements that it's against the law if they don't have a fire drill.' But trainees who wanted a job had not the confidence to challenge their employers: 'If my boss told me to go up a 50-foot ladder and I thought it didn't look too safe, I'd still have to go wouldn't I?' Already without the training two boys were driving forklift trucks.

Four of the trainees felt they already knew their job completely. The girl had worked in her parents' business before leaving school and could run the warehouse alone. A boy said it had taken only three weeks to learn his job in a wine warehouse where he, too, worked alone: 'It's too limiting . . . I unload the boxes, pack the boxes away and look after the warehouse . . . I clean up, wipe down bottles, sweep the floor, make up orders.' A trainee at a computer firm also ran the warehouse alone. A trainee in a dark, damp road-haulage warehouse described his job as 'the same every day mostly, we just load up the lorries with the tomatoes, but I've only just learnt how to unload the reels of paper . . . I suppose I might learn how to load tin plate next, that's it then.' The manager of a large sweet warehouse claimed the work 'may seem simple but we deal with up to 300 lines. You can't just go and get *All Gold*, there's fourteen different boxes of them.' But the trainee said the job had taken only a week to learn: 'Really, a kid of five could do it. All the boxes are labelled. You're given a list to get out, that's all.'

However, although trainees felt their work was simple, some of their managers complained. The wine firm's manager wanted more contact with off-the-job training and complained that the trainee would 'sit down once he's done the allocated job'. The computer firm's manager also complained of poor motivation: 'I told him to go once, but they pleaded with me to keep him on.' He blamed off-the-job training: 'When they're away it disrupts the team, so they're not so company-minded.' At the road haulage firm the manager thought that 'Basically they're, well, dross really . . . If they had any go in them they wouldn't be on YTS anyway . . . Their college days are like holidays, then they get holidays on top . . . We should get paid to take them on, they're a real liability.' His was the only trainee to prefer off-the-job training to work, 'It's a day off isn't it!' Again, not a single trainee had employed YTS status.

Conclusions

In this chapter, we have focused on a representative range of training from the more vulnerable entrepreneurial and new-skill schemes, which in Southwich provided the bulk of YTS placements. We need to remind ourselves that we have been describing what is officially claimed to be 'quality training' and ask if such claims hold water. With the exception of the somewhat mixed training at the LCU schemes (where training quality depended on support from branch managers), the only regulated training occurred where a small minority of employers paid extra for standard FE courses rather than use the entrepreneurs. (Even FE training had been partly 'colonized' by training specially sponsored for YTS.) Schemes with traditional craft labels had become *internally* stratified between apprenticeships and a wide range of training whose quality depended very much on the scope of the placement and the employers' commitment. The so-called 'multi-skill' schemes were the extreme example of the deskilling of traditional craft labels which has taken place in part of YTS.

To do them justice, the training entrepreneurs had been given the virtually impossible task of organizing a common off-the-job training for (mostly) low ability trainees in a wide variety of placements. They did not appear to have succeeded markedly better than the public sector FE described in Chapter 3. Trainees in placements with little scope or encouragement to practice skills still mostly resisted the training as irrelevant, as did almost all their employers who valued only practical skills directly linked to their placements. Indeed, the employers' comments were remarkably similar in tone to those of the small employers whom we interviewed for YTS 1. Usually, they were not only ignorant of the off-the-job training which the managing agents were attempting to provide. They were also hostile to formalized training off the job and they had no commitment to provide a structured programme of training on the job. The YTS 2 rhetoric of quality training had passed completely over their heads.

In short, our research bears out the fears of those most closely involved in YTS 1. Except for shrinking areas of established training the extension of YTS training to two years has too often been at best meaningless, at worst virtually a confidence trick. Although only a minority of trainees were employed, they were not 'training' but *working*. And the new administrative arrangements under YTS 2 seemed to have led to less contact with managing agents and the virtual ending of any pretence of controlling the quality of training on the job.

Chapter 13
Loss of control and deskilling in YTS 2

The previous two chapters indicate that, far from upgrading training, the further introduction of market forces in YTS 2 has led to a marked deterioration in quality. This raises the question as to what had happened to the quality controls supposedly built into the scheme. In this chapter we will describe how the MSC still lacked the financial backing of market intelligence to permit planning for the skill needs of both young people and employers, and YTS 2 continued to be undermined by pressures to mop up the unemployed. Training standards were further undermined by changes in MSC's role in YTS 2. Control of training shifted towards managing agents and employers, and the MSC began to monitor the managing agents' performance more indirectly. One important indicator of high standards was intended to be the new nationally recognized credentials of the NCVQ, and we will explore whether these were likely to meet official claims that they would guarantee quality training.

The reduction of the MSC's powers to control training

Under YTS 2, the MSC abandoned attempts to monitor and control the quality of the training *process*, and instead the *outcomes* of training were to be assessed by 'competence objectives' to be attained by trainees. The managing agents themselves now took over direct monitoring, but as a safeguard they first had to undergo MSC vetting to achieve recognition as ATOs. Apart from periodic financial monitoring, MSC surveillance was then relaxed for the three-year term of ATO recognition, during which ATO contracts were rolled over annually. Under MSC guidance the ATOs were required to prepare annual development plans, and other periodic quality checks were to be provided by employers and trainees via

Programme Review Teams (PRTs). Meanwhile, MSC surveillance continued more indirectly through various indicators of managing agents' performance, particularly those obtained from a 100 per cent follow-up postal survey of all former trainees.

The quality and relevance of training now depended on the stringency of the MSC's initial scrutiny of managing agents for ATO status, the effectiveness of the PRTs, and the MSC's general planning role, including the guidance it was able to offer ATOs for their development plans. To assist planning, the MSC had the trainee questionnaires, its new Regional Manpower Intelligence Unit and the Careers Service's survey of school leavers' destinations.

Changing relationships between the managing agents and the MSC

Our early approaches to the MSC (in 1983–4) had met with a cool indication that they would prefer us not to talk to managing agents. The local MSC manager continued to treat us with reserve, on one occasion referring to us as 'spies'. However, we were allowed to observe the managing agents' meetings, which involved the MSC and key Careers Service staff. (The local MSC still called the ATOs 'managing agents' to stress that they 'managed' YTS on the MSC's behalf). Later, the local MSC manager retired and we were now able to chat informally to the new managers at local and area level.

The meetings had their undercurrent of humour and drama, as the retiring local manager drily joked to distance himself from the latest bit of central MSC bureaucracy, or Dovers' managing agent sparred with his local authority rival and tried to 'talk up' the quality of his schemes. However, although these meetings had a surface *camaraderie* which was only occasionally disrupted, they remained essentially a top-down channel of information rather than a forum for any real discussion and exchange of views. Between 1986 and 1988 there were marked changes in the climate of relationships which mirrored threatening developments in the political, economic and demographic climate of YTS 2. For the managing agents, the message concerning YTS 2 was increasingly confusing and depressing.

The MSC's vetting for ATO recognition

Ironically, it was the most experienced trainers with the better-regulated schemes who were most wary of the rhetoric of 'quality' which launched YTS 2 in 1986. They feared they would be held accountable to deliver training which was too tightly specified in the new training agreements. Their distancing from the MSC and their shrinking commitment to YTS was signified by the fact that their attendance at the agents' meeting became patchy. Other managing agents (apart form Dovers) also worried about the legal status of the training agreements, and questioned the enormous detail required in ATO submissions to the AMB. Indeed, as we saw earlier, several smaller schemes were partly induced to close by the weight of YTS 2 paperwork.

However, gaining ATO recognition proved much less of a hurdle than the managing agents anticipated, and eventually only the local authority managing agent complained that MSC vetting was too stringent. The retiring local MSC manager reassured the meeting that the AMB had time to vet only summaries, although the detail was needed in case the unions objected. He advised how to describe placements in small firms so as to avoid union challenges on job substitution. He also brushed aside the accreditation criteria as 'a strange list of things . . . "Not satisfactory on equal opportunities" . . . It's all a bit silly, my staff will tell you I don't believe in equal opportunities . . . Oh, but there's a whole list of damn silly things.' In response, some managing agents merely copied out the MSC's model scheme: 'We don't want to waste a lot of time yet . . . If we did what the MSC thinks we're doing, it would be impossible.'

The truth was that the MSC feared a shortage of placements with second-year training coinciding with the Job Training Scheme for retraining unemployed adults and the coming of compulsion. It consequently remained dependent on the entrepreneurs and LCU multiples whose standards were most suspect. A tutor at Private Trainers had told us: 'The ATO idea worries the hell out of me because I can see it becoming a licence to kill . . . I know a large [multiple] managing agent in this country whose retail trainees are currently only having five weeks' off-the-job training, but . . . [the MSC] can't afford *not* to give approval to those agents . . . They don't consider things like staff turnover and leaving, or what they're going to pay which is a tremendous worry. I've just seen an advert for staff: "£6,000, No qualifications necessary"!' (Later he himself was made redundant by undercutting from other private trainers.) The managing agent of a stable 'umbrella' scheme found that ATO status had been 'easy to get – too easy. The assessment was a joke.' As soon as he had gained the required City & Guilds credential from the Accredited Training Centre, the MSC suggested that he could accredit his own staff but, 'I insisted we had an outside assessor . . . MSC weren't too happy but they had to agree . . . I could have simply pulled a piece of paper out and written "pass" to all my staff. I'm sure some unscrupulous managing agents will be doing just that.'

Nationally, only a minority of managing agents have failed to gain ATO status eventually. In Southwich, Jack's and Dovers were among the very first ATOs. Several of the experienced traditional trainers were wryly amused, commenting: 'That's "political".'

The ineffectiveness of Programme Review Teams

All the managing agents agreed that after ATO recognition, MSC visits were restricted to routine accounting inspections of their books, with periodic discussions of their development plans. However, they were also unanimous that as an alternative check on training quality, Programme

Review Teams were a sheer waste of time. The insurance company's managing agent said: 'I can't get [work sponsors] to the water, let alone get them to drink.' The hairdressers' managing agent pronounced them 'a farce', because of his own regular meetings with trainees and employers. Jack's had a very acrimonious Programme Review, but trainees' complaints were contradictory and could be discounted.

The motor vehicle association's trainer best summed up the problems of PRT meetings for umbrella schemes: 'To be quite honest, they're a bit embarrassing. We get a lot of people here and sit round not knowing what we're here for . . . The trouble with employers and training is that most are very narrow . . . Formalized training is completely different from what they know about . . . Our employers are too varied, we'd never get any agreement.'

Shrinking funds and falling numbers: towards accountability and marketing

The crisis of shrinking funds and falling numbers was slow to develop, and in mid-1987 there was little evidence of local attempts to gear YTS 2 more closely to real skill needs. Like ATO vetting, the requirement to produce development plans also proved a dead letter. One managing agent had been pressed for her development plan at very short notice, and in less than an hour produced a set of very general goals which was accepted by the MSC. The managing agent of an 'umbrella' scheme near Southwich, 'Victor', derisively refused to submit a plan: 'It's like designing a development plan in a fog . . . *You* [the MSC] don't bloody know what's happening any more than we do!' The retiring local manager agreed: 'Do you think *we* know what's going to happen? . . . [But] we still have to have a plan, even if it's on the back of a cigarette packet.'

Over the next year and a half, falling numbers and closer financial scrutiny forced the MSC to try to tighten up accountability, and to market YTS 2 more energetically. Some schemes found themselves unexpectedly short of trainees, and Dovers pleaded: 'Any more trainees please . . . Where are they?' The MSC's reply was not reassuring. With only a 25 per cent shortfall, Southwich had much better occupancy levels than neighbouring areas. The MSC now planned yearly cuts in trainee quotas, with initial payments for only 70 per cent of contracted places (or 60 per cent in the case of local authority schemes), with extra money only if more trainees were recruited. The incoming local manager's claim that 'the idea is to simplify the whole process' brought cynical laughter from the meeting.

The managing agents were further unsettled in autumn 1987 when they heard that an internal MSC discussion paper (which they did not receive), queried the need for managing agents' fees and asked whether employers were paying enough. There were renewed fears of a move towards self-funding, but the new area manager tried to reassure them: 'I think they know it won't work. Over time the government expect employers to contribute more, but more in terms of a sliding scale. At which point they'll stop I'm not sure.' He insisted a little desperately: 'We *do* have a long-term strategy. I agree with you the funding is difficult, in fact the MSC feel as frustrated as you do.'

In the event, the 1988 Funding Review brought what one craft trainer called 'a stay of execution' (pending, however, the autumn White Paper on training). The MSC's plans for expansion were turned down but with only a minor erosion of funding. The area manager now revealed: 'The Public Accounts Committee is on our backs . . . YTS money will be restricted, there's only a limited amount and it will go to the best, so we must show we're giving value for money . . . If you want the money you'll have to go along with us.'

The MSC now began to emphasize its marketing of YTS to trainees: 'We've just got to get at these kids somehow. *Encourage* them to see sense.' A careers officer was more tentative: 'Quite honestly, hardly any of them nowadays tick YTS . . . We must respect their decision. YTS is not right for everyone, is it?' But the area manager shrugged non-committally. The group set up a sub-committee to market YTS. Discussion assumed that YTS offered an attractive alternative to a job and mistrust was merely a problem of better publicity. The former Mode B managing agent complained it was getting 'increasingly worrying now with all the kids managing to get jobs'. Dovers said its fall-out rate was alarming and the manager asked uneasily about the ethics of its latest move: 'If someone announces they're going to leave us and they've got a job, we casually ask them which employer. Then we approach the employer to see if they will do it via YTS.' A careers officer said: 'I don't feel that's a problem.'

They felt that every school should be compelled to second a teacher to YTS, and the new local manager said that teachers 'are not the ogres you all think they are – they're just lacking information'. Examples were given of seconded teachers who had been impressed and 'had their eyes opened', although one still had a tendency to 'say the wrong things at the wrong time'.

Dovers was praised for inserting newspaper publicity which looked like editorial material on the entertainments page and elsewhere. Dovers' managing agent revealed triumphantly that it was 'way ahead of the rest of you', with afternoon tea invitations to teachers and Sunday lunch invitation to parents: 'We've got to bribe them somehow – they're just not going to be interested otherwise.' The MSC announced that it had arranged breakfast meetings to market employed YTS status to employers.

Towards a free market or planning in YTS 2?

During the run-up to the 1988 White Paper on training, the new area manager presented his own local consultative planning document. (When he had first tried out this paper on the regional meeting of managing agents, their response was reported as: 'Get away, we're desperate, we'll take anyone!') He said the need for his paper arose partly from complaints that the national LCU multiples were trying to poach from local schemes, and even local MSC staff did not know what was happening. Above all, with fewer school leavers and more jobs: 'We won't maintain the penetration of YTS into the labour market . . . The existing planning process was designed for a growth situation . . . It owed as much to accident as design . . . Arguably, if we were blunt, it's not really related to labour-market needs . . . To be quite honest, it's not been related to managing agents' performance.' Two different proposals were being floated at headquarters: a free-for-all where managing agents could do as much training as they wanted but the MSC would only pay for trainees recruited, or alternatively some kind of *planning*.

On the free-market proposal, he explained: 'There are papers floating about at [MSC headquarters], one called "Increasing Freedoms for Managing Agents' Choice".' (The meeting erupted in hysterical laughter.) A 'stable-skill' managing agent objected: 'Everybody will be fighting to keep up business, not putting money into training.' Another worried: 'You'll get rogue organizations coming in, but what about quality?' A public sector 'umbrella' agent agreed: LCU multiples 'are very big but not necessarily very good. LUCs can afford to make mistakes. We can't.' A careers officer worried: 'There are [now] some managing agents we've never heard of . . . It's bewildering, it takes the credibility out of it.' Only Dovers seemed slightly tempted: 'We could move into another [locality] . . . I'd think: "Got this super training programme that young people are not taking advantage of".' But when he asked innocently, 'Aren't we here for the training?', the area manager replied: 'That's the emotional bit, but we're also here for industry.' The most vocal critic, Victor, summed up: 'Then like running the bus services we'll go for the well-paying routes. The consequences will fall back on the youngsters and the managing agents who're the "rural routes". Managing agents who're bold enough and courageous are going to be struggling.' The area manager replied: 'Current thinking might be that if you choose to live in a rural area that's your choice.'

There was general agreement that a free market would let in the LCU multiples and kill off local schemes. The area manager conceded that while a free market had attractions for the MSC, there would be mismatching as managing agents went for easy pickings, and he did not want a local training monopoly. He personally favoured some sort of planning, where the MSC would 'decide what sort of places there should be in what sort of area and the main decision would then be who to contract'. This would need better information to decide on the numbers and distribution of placements. The area manager said that ATOs would then bid and win contracts on the strength of their past performance on six indicators: occupancy, completion, turnover, gaining vocational qualifications, finding employment after YTS, and employed YTS status.

At this the managing agents became distinctly worried. The former Mode B managing agent pointed out: 'We'll have to turn down the no-hopers. Already people's standards are dropping because of needs for bums on seats. People will go on schemes they're not suited for, they may not achieve the qualifications, and then you'll brand the schemes failures . . . Our completion rate is lower than anyone else's in this room. Our vocational qualifications are lower, our employment is lower and our employment status is lower. But I don't think that shows I run a worse scheme.' The area manager conceded (but without explaining how) that 'We'd take inputs into account. But I am clear we have for too long . . . focused on inputs and not much on *outputs* and their consequences.' Dovers complained: 'What I don't agree with is these 100 per cent follow-up surveys on the computer . . . They say we don't get many in employment . . . We're going to collect our own.' The area manager defended the reliability of the follow-up: 'Anecdotal evidence won't do in my book – if you give me hard evidence I'll look into it.'

The local manager gave a technical description of the MSC's new efforts to predict employers' skill demands. But Victor again derided the MSC's attempt to plan placements as 'deeply and fundamentally flawed . . . *You* don't have that information. And that's why the contracts we have are *meaningless*.' Jack's protested: 'The problem is the whole thing is funded on bums on seats . . . Somehow you've got to guarantee that you'll give us the trainees . . . From day one the philosophy . . . was to have too many managing agents, to build in choices . . . The "vacated places" rules provided the cushion. As soon as MSC moved the goalposts it should have rationalized, reduced the number of managing agents.'

The area manager came back: 'The real problem is that we're hampered in penetration (i.e. marketing the YTS to school leavers) by having a product that's not sufficiently flexible and can't be tailored sufficiently well to individual's needs . . . [Headquarters] is looking at individual experience and work placements which need not have 20 weeks as long as they're geared to a qualification . . . Promotion is the other key – focus on teachers and parents . . . We've got to plan what, where and how we're going to provide it . . . At the moment any resemblance [between placements and jobs] is, to put it bluntly, more by accident than design.' The local manager added: 'The overriding thing is that we're not running a social service, we're trying to give youngsters skills required in the local market.'

At the end of the meeting someone asked about prospects for merging YTS with Employment Training, but the area manager said: 'The most attention is devoted to getting ET off the runway without thinking where it's going to fly when it's in the air.' Jack's agent put in: 'That's what they did with YTS.' The area manager protested: 'Don't blame them . . . I suppose it was not for the love of training but as a way to reduce the unemployment figures. But now MSC are putting effort into changing it.'

To sum up, these meetings reveal how MSC policy was altering continuously under rapidly-changing conditions. The MSC now frankly admitted (at least behind closed doors) that YTS had been more concerned with employment than relevant training, and the training entrepreneurs revealed their activities as now driven by the need for 'bums on seats'.

Market forces and competition for scarce trainees had brought confusion, secretiveness, and less *informed* choice for trainees. The beleaguered MSC began to speak the language of market forces and accountability. A YTS free-for-all would lead only to a further fall in standards and choice as the LCU multiples undercut local training. Yet the MSC still lacked the ability to plan, and its crude proposals for monitoring schemes with such varied intakes and functions, rightly aroused managing agents' fears that any 'performance criteria' would be too crudely applied.

Not surprisingly, the managing agents, particularly those who had entered YTS with more altruistic motives, felt betrayed and demoralized. Few now believed that YTS would survive without cuts, scheme closures and a further deterioration of standards. Leaks began soon after the White Paper that after the death of the MSC, not only MSC staff but managing agents would now be cut (*Times Educational Supplement*, 23 October 1987; *Guardian*, 21 December 1988). As we go to press, cuts have begun – on the grounds that unemployment is falling.

The move to control by competence objectives and NVQ

The reduction in MSC's role was to be matched by monitoring the outcomes of training by 'competence objectives' and guaranteeing its quality by a new system of NVQ. The NCVQ was set up in 1986 to bring some order into the free-for-all of 'City & Guilds with everything' by rationalizing all sub-professional skill credentials under one national scheme (Thompson, 1989). The stated intention is to enable employers to match skills with jobs and so obtain greater productivity, and to offer workers open access to skills and credentials which will provide a clear route of promotion and motivation to train. The new schemes will be *employer-led, employment-based* and assessed where possible at the workplace. The weight of government training funds will be thrown behind the scheme to make it compulsory by 1991.

At a briefing meeting in Southwich, an NCVQ representative talked of 'getting rid of sacred cows', getting away from 'ideas of time-serving and traditional apprenticeship' and from the dominant role of BEC in FE. The NCVQ thought that employers should pay for NVQ as an investment. Industries with small businesses, such as hairdressing, could have trained part-time assessors who visited workplaces to test competence. Alternatively, in the new catering scheme, Caterbase, supervisors from the workplace would receive short training and become assessors. (Only the minimum of assessment would be under simulated work conditions.) To cope with the limited nature of much work, NVQ 'levels' would be broken down into modules, each made up of smaller tasks offering credits.

The NVQ scheme was first opened up to the Employment Training programme and YTS, and during our research, new 'nationally-preferred' schemes were being negotiated for YTS 2 by the Youth Training Council and the private technical exam boards, notably City & Guilds and the RSA but also others like Pitmans. For these opportunist exam entrepreneurs the new credentials offered a potential bonanza but also a threat, and there was squabbling as some boards tried to float their own alternatives in and outside NVQ.

During our research it was still early days, and nationally-preferred schemes were being introduced piecemeal in different skill areas. Sometimes negotiations were complete, as in motor vehicle or catering training, but other schemes had only provisional recognition, as in clerical training where there were five competing credentials from different technical exam boards. However, there were already troubling features about the involvement of the training entrepreneurs in assessment and accreditation.

'Competence objectives' and NVQ in Southwich

The more experienced trainers saw competence objectives and (to a less extent) NVQ as merely coming into line with existing ITB practice: 'MSC were adamant that they wouldn't get into bed with the Training Board so they created their own paperwork, but now they've accepted entirely our approach.' In fact, the NVQ motor vehicle scheme was adapted from the existing RTITB modular scheme, although the association's trainer found it now fragmented. The engineering trainers were irritated that assessment costs would triple for credentials less finely-graded than the existing EITB and City & Guilds scheme, and unless compelled they would not change over. They anticipated little problem of personal bias in work-based assessment and gauging 'competences', which resembled the clear-cut tasks of existing log-book practice in craft skills. Where they were training recruits for skilled jobs which carried extra pay, they probably had little personal incentive to pass inadequate training. For clerical assessment these trainers still used the RSA, but for work-based assessment, 'You have to have half a dozen standards and even then you end up saying, "She's a bit of this and a bit of that". It's a lot to expect of the supervisor.' They feared supervisors would resist work-based assessment and refuse trainees (a fear shared at Endowments).

In construction, the NVQ scheme had yet to arrive, but the managing agent suggested that his employers 'couldn't be bothered with' work-based assessment and preferred traditional FE assessment. But as the CITB nationally tightened its grip on apprentice and quality training the government announced its intention of abolishing the remaining ITBs.

The hairdressers' managing agent could use his own staff for work-based assessment and NVQ offered him independence from FE. Nevertheless, he feared that NVQ would increase costs and lower standards generally: 'Hairdressing salons . . . are not necessarily qualified or wish to . . . fit in with this.' Work-based assessors would need only minimal training: 'That's the problem, that's why the very bad schemes come up in favour.'

Lack of vested training interests in catering may explain why the NVQ Caterbase scheme was introduced early. However, there was much irritation with the HCITB, the lead body. Dovers was resisting NVQ as needless cost and disruption. An FE tutor also explained how the trainer's role in assessment posed problems: 'I'm a City & Guilds assessor but I'm with [the trainees] all the year round. There's obviously going to be some pressure on me to let them pass. Also two people could do it differently. But when I phoned up City & Guilds they said, "You're qualified, get on with it!".' With Caterbase, 'You have to assess the trainees at work, which is a lot more difficult and more arbitrary than at college'. The local authority managing agent complained: 'The tutors . . . have got to go out to sell trainees to employers. Now we've been put in the position of saying . . . "If you've got the right qualifications you can have a trainee" . . . It's a bit of a cheek when 94 per cent of HCITB employees are unqualified . . . I'm going to go out and get a Hotel and Catering management award so I can assess . . . just to show what a mockery it is.'

In retail training, the Co-op managing agent was quietly confident that his scheme would dovetail with the NVQ, and the mother and baby LCU felt it could easily switch and still use training material designed for the company. The Chamber of Commerce managing agent showed us the neat grids of Pitman's competence objectives. However, she admitted that checking by the Chamber's own staff might be a problem, and in any case the objectives were too broad and meant 'nothing at all' to employers. The chief tutor felt that NVQ were 'very much for employers' needs' and would lower and blur standards: 'MSC don't want kids to pass or fail.'

Jack's approach to competence objectives for multi-skills had a neat circularity: 'We say [to employers], "What jobs have you got a young person can do?", and feed those into the training programme . . . Then as we cover it we tick it off.' (Dovers gave a similarly circular description of how it set and assessed competences in its care scheme.) However, Jack's managing agent worried about NVQ: 'If they're going to say everyone takes the same level, the same qualification, there's no way they can do that.' He felt NVQ 'credits' would not be accepted by trainees as much as City & Guilds certificates. But also, 'The company are not going to pay unless they need them . . . Some employers, quite frankly, don't want that sort of thing. Will those sorts of young people be excluded from YTS?'

Government moves to break the CITB monopoly on construction training through privatization and NVQ would be popular with multi-skill managing agents. In the meeting someone complained: 'MSC have got into bed with the CITB model – it's too high-falutin' and too selective . . . Their power reduces opportunities for youngsters.' However, our observation of the assessment of some 'construction' trainees at the former Mode B scheme revealed most clearly the problems of assessment by trainers. The tutor explained that occasionally a moderator came from City & Guilds, 'But they warn us before they come'. Usually he did the tests (although another tutor was actually the only trained assessor), and he confessed: 'We should let them go through it all when they make a mistake, but if I see them going hopelessly wrong, I'll stop them.' Two bewildered first-year painting and decorating trainees were in the group by mistake, but they were urged to have a go. He told the group: 'I'll help as much as I can but it's as new to me as you'. They grew apprehensive because they had been out on placements for some months: 'You mean it's for real today!' They had handouts describing the tests and warning of the difficulties, and they would have a demonstration and practice before taking their own tests: 'I will be watching, monitoring while you have a go, but I can't help you'. Before this they had a half-hour lunch-break, but after an hour and ten minutes they had not returned. Asked if they valued certificates, the tutor replied wearily: 'I sometimes think they don't value anything at all, quite honestly.' When they came back one of the first-years withdrew to mend his scooter and then sat on a chair in the middle of the field facing away from events. For the test, the plan of a building had to be laid out by the trainees with a 'dumb labourer' who was to offer no advice. The tutor worried: 'They don't know what the hell is going on.' However, after a while a bolder trainee asked to take over the half-completed demonstration, and he was allowed to submit it as his test. He urged his 'labourer': 'You help me get through it today and I'll help you tomorrow.' Some trainees mixed concrete while others sat about, and the first-year painting and decorating trainee returned to mending his scooter. We later learned that he had passed the test.

Conclusions: the erosion of skill-training and accreditation standards by employer control and NVQ

At the end of Part Two, we identified control of training quality as a major source of segmentation and inequality in YTS, and we can now take our discussion a stage further to include the likely impact of NVQ. Before YTS, the quality and transferability of skills could be underwritten by the *external* accreditation of traditional vocational credentials taught in FE. In some instances standards were also upgraded and overseen by the public ITBs and defended (although also restricted) by the craft unions and apprenticeship system. With the coming of YTS 1, government policy deliberately weakened all of these external controls and, in particular, used the MSC to undermine the FE monopoly on vocational training standards. The MSC was helped by the collusion of the private vocational exam boards and, as a result, accreditation was rapidly extended and diluted to cover a range of dubious YTS 'training'.

NVQ's move to employer-led and employment-based assessment is presented as rationalizing and opening up skills training. It is claimed that NVQ will remove unnecessary barriers raised by formal taught courses, which tend to 'overskill' because they contain elements of selection and preparation for further progress, rather than just the 'competences' needed for specific tasks (Thompson, 1989). However, as our research has shown, training standards under YTS had polarized between skills backed by FE and the craft tradition, and the expanded newer training where control was lost to employers with very little interest in upgrading training quality. We

Table 13.1 Established skills versus NVQ training

Characteristics	Traditional training	NVQ
Goals	National standards	Individual employers
Means	Public intervention	Market forces
Funding	General levy	Individual employers
Content design	National	Local
Employer control	Relatively low	Relatively high
Union control	Relatively high	Relatively low
Validation	Universal external	Variable local
Main base	FE, ITB	Employers' premises
Theory content	High	Low
Theory validation	External exam board	ATO (external moderation?)
Practical content	Minor	Major
Trainees' production	Relatively low	Relatively high
Work context	Large firm/FE simulation	Small firm
Work experience	Varied	Limited
Practical supervision	Relatively strong	Weak
Practical assessment	External monitor	ATO/employee
Assessor's training	High	Low
Assessor's vested self-interest	Low	High
Credential level	Standard	Variable
Skills content	General	Specific
Transferability	High	Low

can schematize the likely impact of NVQ by contrasting, in a slightly idealized way, the established training and credentials with those of the new NVQ scheme (Table 13.1).

As we have shown in this chapter, the introduction of NVQ and competence objectives seems likely to lead to the setting and accreditation of 'skills' falling (to varying degrees) into the hands of employers or their trainers, or the training entrepreneurs. The assessment process in some schemes has a circularity which renders such accreditation useless as a guide to training quality. Under YTS 2, trainers increasingly have a vested interest in their training and trainees *appearing* to achieve a high pass rate, upon which will depend their reputation and profits. The fact that the training entrepreneurs are also accredited exam centres heightens the need for the external monitoring of any practical or written work. Here the vocational boards' eagerness for business does not inspire confidence.

We are not alone in this analysis. A recent comparison of mechanical and electrical craft training in Britain, France and West Germany concluded that there were no signs that YTS 1 had increased numbers with craftsmen credentials, and only employed YTS apprenticeships had prevented a sharper decline. Yet only one in six YTS 'engineering' trainees are on such credentialling courses and the rest attain *no* nationally-recognized skill credential (Steedman, 1988). Lower-level NVQ credentials will not remedy this, and another recent comparison of retail training in Britain and France concluded that NVQ will 'promote and perpetuate [what will ultimately be regarded as] a certificated semi-literate under-class, a section of the workforce inhibited in job-flexibility, and inhibited in the possibilities of progression' (Jarvis and Prais, 1988).

The not-too-hidden curriculum of NVQ seems to be to undermine any remaining defences against deskilling of training jobs and workers. Despite some union co-operation (at least from non-craft unions), a primary purpose is to erode still further the power of the unions, and to secure better access and a spurious legitimacy for the 'training' of the government's workfare programmes such as YTS and ET. The result of YTS and NVQ will be that not only training quality but the validity of the vocational qualifications by which it is supposedly guaranteed will be undermined by market forces.

Part Five
Conclusions

Chapter 14
Protecting
training from market forces

YTS set out to improve the skills and job prospects of young people and to promote equality of opportunity by relying on private employers and market forces. However, in our study of Southwich we have shown how YTS developed a commercial logic far more complicated than the free-market theories behind it predict. What we have called the 'surrogate labour market' of YTS proved to be 'segmented' into a range of very unequal training opportunities and it was, at the same time, a very inefficient means of promoting training and allocating skilled workers. It suited the needs of neither young people nor industry.

In this final chapter we will summarize and discuss the details of our findings on three levels: firstly, as a description of YTS at the grass roots, secondly in relation to academic debates about how Britain's social and economic structure has changed in the 1980s, and finally in relation to the government's general free-market strategy and what might be learned from YTS as a policy experiment.

A description of YTS at the grass roots

YTS was *not* a decisive break with the voluntarism which had held back industrial training in the past. It still left responsibility to provide training with individual employers and follows the *laissez-faire* tradition which equates markets with efficiency, and regulation with inefficiency. Existing research suggested that in the case of training this simple contrast is naive, misleading and counterproductive, because without intervention, markets cause employers to *avoid* costly training. Southwich offered a critical test-bed of the YTS blueprint. In the early 1980s it had a large and growing number of jobless school leavers, but also a relatively prosperous economy. As a result, most of the unemployed young people became trainees in the favoured employer-dominated 'private' sector of YTS. Yet we found that in Southwich YTS actually intensified and added to the defects of the 'voluntaristic' training tradition.

The failure of the subsidy to promote adequate skill provision

From industry's point of view, the most alarming defect of YTS was its continued failure to stimulate enough high-skill training, because it was too costly for 'the market' to bear and the YTS subsidy too low. Experienced trainers compared the MSC's efforts unfavourably with earlier reforms by the old ITBs. Large firms with a training tradition used YTS to support apprenticeships and real traineeships. YTS also encouraged a number of 'stable' schemes in recognized craft skills, some run by ITBs, using subcontracted training. Together these employer-led and stable-skill schemes offered good training that could be a genuine alternative to staying on at school. With the possible exceptions of construction and hairdressing, however, they grew out of the least dynamic sectors of employment which were still recovering from the shake-out of the early 1980s and were cautious about employing too many workers. At best, YTS encouraged firms to reopen limited surplus training capacity for business partners, although sometimes in obsolete skills. These schemes thus remained a small elite core.

If anything, YTS worsened the problem of skill shortages. The subsidy encouraged new and sometimes inexperienced entrepreneurial trainers to dress up and sell low-skill and insecure work as 'training', in a way which confused and deskilled both occupational labels and the trainees themselves. Their placements were in the flourishing shopping centres, warehouses, building societies, estate agents, hotels and new financial offices in Southwich, which mostly generated jobs with low training costs. The net effect was to create a rhetoric of training in jobs where it had previously been absent, but a surfeit of 'skills' never scarce in the first place. Whatever its commitment to training, the MSC lost control of the overall provision of training places because it was too weak to counter the commercial logic determining which schemes came forward. In any case the MSC continued to lack the statistical data to plan, and by 1988 it was admitted informally that to date YTS's priority had been to soak up youth unemployment.

Training also continued to be limited by the local employment structure, with serious consequences for trainees. Compared to Southwich, some areas have more large-firm and manufacturing placements such as those prominent in YTS advertisements. But in Southwich, what YTS could offer fell somewhere between the better schemes of the more favoured areas, and the dominant premium and public sector YTS of more depressed regions. Even nationally, as in Southwich, the distribution of YTS training relies too heavily on service trades and small firms.

The MSC's loss of control of training content

YTS also made control of the content of training both off and on the job more vulnerable to short-term commercial pressures. In Southwich, MSC policy bypassed the FE college and encouraged undercutting of its off-the-job courses by managing agents who set up their own lower-cost training. The traditional system of apprenticeship-based ITB training plus FE had been a source, albeit inadequate, of external standards until the government eroded (and now abolished) the remaining ITBs. This deliberate privatization of training lent more importance to the labour-market strategies of employers and private trainers, and as a result training, both off and on the job, was devalued and deskilled even in the best-regulated schemes. Increasingly exposed to market forces, the public sector and 'premium' YTS schemes have also had to become commercial and managerial (Chandler, 1989).

Control over the quality of private training has always lacked effective sanctions, and under YTS 2 it has been further undermined by the death of the MSC. Pressures to cut corners in on-the-job training were worse in the non-traditional schemes, and the MSC had much more difficulty in controlling work experience subcontracted in small firms. Here training was organized by the entrepreneurial trainers, and as the subsidy was reduced under YTS 2, their fortunes depended increasingly on cutting training costs and filling places. Yet as ATOs they have now been put in charge of training standards. At the same time the work-providers now pay for their trainees, which means that if external control becomes irksome they find it easier to offer young people jobs. NCVQ moves towards employer-led and employment-based credentials will erode the standards and credibility of skills accreditation.

Thus, in the attempt to improve on past defects in training, YTS offered no solution to the problem that the provision and quality of training varies with the state of trade, the size of firms and the health of local economies. Overall, it has done little to alter the well-documented failings of Britain's traditional *laissez-faire* policies on industrial training. If anything, market forces under YTS have made matters worse.

The failure to promote equality of opportunity

Opportunities in Southwich YTS schemes ranged from genuine training with good job prospects to low-paid and insecure work masquerading as 'work experience'. These limited and very unequal opportunities of good training, combined with high youth unemployment, meant that there was competition for the restricted placements of the best schemes which were oversubscribed. It then fell to the new non-traditional training to absorb the rest of the trainees, but this needed a hard sell by both the managing agents and the Careers Service.

However, despite the YTS goal of equal opportunities, managing agents and employers kept the right to select trainees, and administrative control over commercial pressures was weak. As a result, YTS incorporated the screening devices which employers have always used to discriminate by ability, gender, race or physical disadvantage. The intakes of individual YTS schemes (and even placements within schemes) became socially differentiated, varying from skill to skill. The most favoured schemes could pick and choose from the best-qualified and most 'respectable' school leavers. The worst-qualified and most disadvantaged trainees finished up with the most dubious schemes and employers.

Because Southwich had few trainees from ethnic minorities there were only hints of the racialism which is visible in inner-city labour markets. But gender divisions are all-pervasive, and in Southwich boys and girls faced two overlapping but distinct YTS surrogate labour markets with poorer chances for girls, which helped to lower their initial career expectations and their later earnings and prospects. Girl trainees were better-qualified and more middle-class, yet they had fewer opportunities in 'sponsorship' or 'credentialling' schemes, and generally met greater educational and social selectivity (including selection by appearance). Yet, apart from some hand-wringing, we met few efforts to challenge either selection by employers or the limited horizons which most girls, especially the lower achievers, brought to YTS.

Rather than promoting equal opportunities and radically altering trainees' life chances, YTS merely mediated between trainees' upbringing and the labour market. The overlapping influences of social and educational background re-emerged and even increased in work careers after YTS. As a result, YTS never overcame the burden that for many trainees it was thinly disguised unemployment relief. In Southwich, with the improvement in sixth-form opportunities many more young people chose to avoid YTS and stay on at school, while the local job boom meant also that they and employers voted with their feet, spurning YTS for traditional job offers. Falling numbers in the age group brought further financial headaches for the training entrepreneurs, as the supply of trainees dried up and the MSC withdrew grants for empty places.

YTS and economic and social change in Britain

At a wider level, our research also engages with recent academic debates about social class and other influences (including government training and YTS) which have shaped jobs and opportunities during the 1980s. Despite the rising living standards and social legislation of the post-war period, considerable research now supports the view that social class is still highly significant in Britain. A recent nationally-representative study of occupational stratification shows the persistence of widespread inequalities at work and in the labour market, and class continues to shape social and political attitudes and the prospects of children born with different social backgrounds (Marshall, *et al.*, 1988). Our research confirms that even in the narrow social stratum of our trainees, YTS, albeit in a complex way, reflects rather than challenges the stratification of British society by social class background. YTS has become absorbed into the wider processes through which inequalities of opportunity and life chances persist.

The widening gap between the 'educated' and the 'trained'

Nationally as well as in Southwich, YTS has not become a genuine alternative to continuing in education at 16, despite recent evidence suggesting that some young people would do better transferring to a good YTS scheme than resitting exams at school (Roberts *et al.*, 1989). As a result, the gap between those who stay on and those who leave has been perpetuated and emphasized. Our findings were in line with various national surveys, according to which, because on average working-class children do less well at school, they formed the bulk of the unemployed and low achievers who became YTS trainees. Young people from better-off homes mostly avoided YTS, seeing it as second best to staying on at school and college. Perhaps YTS now attracts marginally more high-fliers, but not enough to overcome Britain's long history of social divisions between the 'educated' and the 'trained'.

Unfortunately, economic change has worsened the chances of secure work careers for working-class early leavers, widening the social divide between the most and least successful. The collapse of manufacturing jobs during the recession of the early 1980s and the growth of service employment have reduced the 'middle range' of jobs once open to relatively able boys and girls who leave school (Ashton *et al.*, 1990). The causes of this 'disappearing middle' differ by gender. The recession mostly hit adult male jobs and cut the recruitment and training of apprentices and trainees. But the loss of jobs became permanent because widespread technological changes, especially in engineering, also made many older (mostly apprenticed) craftsmen redundant. However, the similar recession in female jobs in manufacturing was more than offset by growth in the largely female services sector. Clerical employers have opted for adults while retailing, hotels and other services have favoured youth. Overall, technical change and concentration of ownership have caused an increasing polarization between a core of highly educated, mostly male staff and a low-skill, mostly female labour force, increasingly adult part-timers.

The net result for young people is that better-qualified boys who once would have gained apprenticeships and traineeships have now been forced into less-skilled service jobs, pushing out the less able. On the other hand, girls are in intense group competition with married women part-timers. Although some apprenticeships and traineeships have been incorporated into YTS, too often it is the entry route to a growing stratum of low-skill, mostly service jobs, where trainees have displaced full- and part-time jobs for older workers. (Ashton *et al.*, 1990).

These national changes explain much of the development of YTS in Southwich, where the already small base in manufacturing and traditional crafts was static or shrinking, but there was an expansion of commuting, light industry and services which in turn supported a comfortably-off stratum of the self-employed. We could see large economic divisions between the poorer council estates and the surrounding commuterdom and affluence. The large number of poorly-qualified school leavers could find few permanent job openings. Instead, they were offered a range of entrepreneurial schemes in non-traditional 'skills', with placements which were in effect low-paid jobs, and girls were often substituting for adult workers.

Towards a 'flexible' work-force?

Some writers claim that employers have become increasingly willing to use so-called 'flexible' labour practices such as sub-contracting, part-time work, casualization and self-employment (see, for example, Atkinson, 1984; Hakim, 1987; Wood, 1989). The term begs the question of whose interests are served by such 'flexibility', and critics have questioned the concept or doubted any long-term trend (Pollert, 1988). However, few deny that British employers have always used non-standard forms of labour extensively and both groups accept that government trainees are a further source of 'flexible' labour.

The 'flexible' employment of young people can be seen as a result rather than a cause of the availability of YTS and other government trainees. Research on the setting-up of YTS and related programmes shows they are part of a deliberate campaign by government and state agencies to deregulate controls on wages and employment, and to replace traditional crafts with 'multi-skills' (which, as we saw, is deskilling), in order to prepare individuals (and in some cases whole communities) for the obsolescence of their jobs and generally to lower workers' expectations (Pollert, 1988; see also Finn, 1987; Ranson, 1984). Cuts and privatization in the public sector have also added to the range of insecure employment.

In Southwich, spontaneous demand for flexible labour and the use of YTS and other trainees seemed mutually reinforcing. YTS had brought a change in management tactics towards recruiting young people, which enabled firms to ride the recession. Managing agents reported rising demand for trainees and employers became aggrieved when the supply of trainees dried up and they had to contribute to YTS. But although, unlike less buoyant areas, a high proportion of Southwich trainees *continued* in work after YTS, we found many of them had a succession of not very exciting or secure jobs, indicating an underlying local demand for low-skill labour, flexible in that it could easily be laid off if need be.

The 'sub-employment' and 'civic exclusion' of young people

YTS is thus powerless to counter broader changes which are reducing the employment prospects of working-class youth, and indeed its role in deregulation shows every sign of reinforcing their disadvantages. It is dominated by the 'local labour-market effect' which results in a very unequal distribution of life chances, with a high proportion of school leavers joining YTS schemes in depressed regions as the start of a work history of *sub-employment*, where spells on government training programmes alternate with short-lived low-paid jobs and unemployment (Ashton *et al.*, 1990). Southwich had begun to resemble the opposite situation, where higher staying-on rates and plentiful jobs, combined with falling numbers of teenagers, are restricting YTS participants to two groups, an elite of sponsored trainees and a residue of 'problem' youth.

Clearly, the class stratification of youth differs by locality. But the 'workfare' principle has introduced a further factor. Young people's situation in depressed areas approximates to 'civic exclusion' (Lockwood, 1985), now that their civic right to social security has been removed even though they are also excluded from the labour market and have lost the right to work. On the other hand, the bulk of Southwich trainees experienced 'sub-employment' in the strict sense, where loss of citizenship rights could be hidden from them by the 'right to work' in low-skill, low-wage jobs. However, to this must be added the rider that, because of the emphasis on appearance in service jobs, a sizeable minority of girls suffered civic exclusion even in Southwich.

Evidence of young people's attitudes and values was sketchy, but it suggests that these Southwich young people were 'Thatcher's children'. Although only *relatively* more fortunate, they had little understanding of the situation of young people elsewhere, and they largely identified with the individualism of their parents and the Thatcher years. Acknowledging money as the basis of social position, they thought instrumentally and individualistically about their own lives, and they showed remarkably little sympathy for the unemployed from whose ranks they had been so narrowly 'rescued' by YTS.

The policy debate

The way YTS has been caught up in the social divisions of the 1980s is important because, arguably, sharp social inequalities between and within occupational classes have been a factor in Britain's long-term industrial decline. Traditional *laissez-faire* policies towards unemployment and welfare have undermined labour commitment, creating a disaffected, disadvantaged, divided, and above all undereducated and undertrained working class (Barnett, 1986: 187–200). By contrast, many other leading economies have sought to involve the labour force at a relatively early stage of industrialization through policies of state-sponsored education, externally-controlled training and schemes of employer and state paternalism.

YTS thus provides vivid confirmation that 'Thatcherism may not be the "cure" for the "British disease" but rather the latest manifestation of the disease itself' (MacInnes, 1987: 6). The more unregulated are market forces, the more difficult it becomes to provide the kind of skill training that will upgrade the long-term capabilities and living standards of the workforce. Nor will market forces do much to eradicate the costly social insecurities in young workers' home lives which decrease their ability and willingness to learn and be taught.

The government's White Paper on training

Consequently, it is strange that a government committed to halting the decline of British business should have pursued a deregulation policy so close to the *laissez-faire* voluntarism which created the problem in the first place. Yet there seems little prospect of a change of direction. On the contrary, the latest government White Paper claims that 'The Youth Training Scheme . . . has been a resounding success . . . standards of youth training have been improved to a point where there is now good quality youth training nation-wide for all 16 and 17 year old school-leavers who seek it' (DE, 1988: 46). This official verdict is the basis on which the latest White Paper states once again that 'the main responsibility for training rests with individual employers'. Helped by the TUC's withdrawal from the Training Commission, the government's policy is to place leadership and ownership of the training system 'where it belongs – with employers' (DE, 1988: 46). Further administrative changes will create Training and Enterprise Councils (TECs) in the local 'community' in place of the AMBs and local MSC/Training Agency offices (DE, 1988: 39–43). These will take charge of much of FE as well as contract with managing agents to run YTS and ET. 'By increasing employer responsibility for local training arrangements and enterprise support and development, TECs will ensure that training provision is more relevant to employers' needs and so improve the skills and enterprise of the workforces' (DE, 1988: 39–43).

These proposals merely accept and formalize the deregulated and inadequate arrangements for training which were virtually in place by 1988. The basis for a decentred, wholly employer-directed system of local labour management has been laid down throughout the 1980s, with YTS providing the pattern and structure for later adult training initiatives such as ET. Now the complementary growth of employer-based NVQ assessment will also bring the setting of skill standards and credentialling under employer control.

Our research strongly supports the view that the government is going in precisely the wrong direction in equating the behaviour of individual employers with the public good. It is useless in a system whose whole rationale is based on short-term competitive individualism to expect hard-pressed employers to behave altruistically with an eye to the long-term public interest. Investment in British industry as a whole suffers the disease of 'short-termism'. And as our findings confirm, individual employers will only invest in workers they intend to use for their own production needs.

Controls to protect training from market forces

Training standards will only be upgraded by insulating the training process from the short-term interests of individual employers, rather than by giving them more control. Of course, external control must not prevent responsiveness to the latest and best industrial practice. The primary task of external controls is rather to ensure that whatever syllabuses and training programmes are needed are visible, adhered to and not susceptible to manipulation by trainers or the trained as convenient. So external skill-setting and validation are vital to maintaining standards if skills are to be genuinely transferable. For this public intervention and more cash are essential.

The government has adopted a rhetoric of vocational training but has not taken on board the evidence that other countries use public intervention and resources to provide such independent training safeguards. There is an ongoing debate about which of two alternative models Britain should follow. One is the employment- and occupationally-based apprenticeship training system of West Germany. The other is the state-provided vocational education developed in France (Maurice *et al.*, 1986; Steedman, 1988; Jarvis and Prais, 1988). However, both have defects. The German system has not altogether escaped the problems of market-led training or bureaucracy (Casey, 1986; Chandler and Wallace, 1989) while French curricula tend to lose touch with industrial practice. Arguably, with legally backed external standards, effective integration into the further education system and different funding, the NTI proposals for a youth training scheme (and similar adult retraining) could still enable Britain to combine the merits of both systems. In any case, it would take many years to switch Britain to either alternative because it is difficult to transplant particular national policies without more wide-ranging institutional change. The economic and social problems to be tackled by training reform are too urgent for such delay.

We have therefore considered what might be done in the short term with the new administrative arrangements proposed in the White Paper, even though further legislation would clearly be required for our recommendations to be followed thoroughly. The government intends to give the TECs 'real powers to take real decisions' and wishes to attract to them senior industrialists (DE, 1989). Such individuals, in our experience, tend to take a more sceptical view of free-market dogma. We urge them to seek ways of protecting training from market forces by all means in their power.

The first priority, after adequate government funding, would be the return to some form of regulation of training standards mandatory on individual firms, including adequate representation on the TECs for the public interest, the unions and the rights of young workers. In West

Germany, the law obliges *all* employers to conform to training standards. The newly-constituted TECs could move in this direction using the civil law of contract at least to control the conditions for releasing adult and youth trainees for work experience. This will require the TECs to exercise more powerfully the role FE once played towards trainees in the NTP, helped by existing FE and Careers Service staff and resources. Even though the climate towards local authorities and unions was not favourable, under YTS a number of more pioneering authorities had begun to recognize that they could influence policy, through their role as large employers and providers of funds to the voluntary sector, and also through FE, the youth services and social services.

Equally vital is improving the general educational level of all young people (where national standards are now under further threat from the government's so-called reforms (Simon, 1988)). The current real skill shortages are in occupations requiring extended education, so the TECs' use of resources and design of training programmes needs to counter the fact that too many young people give up formal learning too early. The suggestion we have encountered that they might become overskilled or overtrained seems, in the British context, to be ludicrous. But although generally the picture was discouraging, a few YTS schemes were able to use the transition from school and task-related 'experiential' learning to remotivate young people who had been put off by school. In a few areas outside Southwich, local councils and voluntary organizations, too, have been more adventurous and have taken advantage of the opportunities offered by YTS for structured work experience, social and life skills and sheltered workshops. To widen the supply of scarce educated talent, TEC training needs to boost this 'retrieval' role, making schemes trainee-centred rather than firm-centred, with clear rights to further study built into training contracts. Again TECs could use their new powers to ensure that contracts with work providers allow young (and other) trainees to progress from one course module to another and maximize their potential. Vocational preparation could become a genuine alternative route for those who have rejected school as too academic, and could enable many to move back into some form of further education later on. Such second chances are more widely available in other countries, and TECs could use their promised resources to counter the too-rigid hurdles which British education raises against re-entry. They should also push for a complete rethinking of administrative boundaries between 'employment', 'training' and 'education', and the various associated funding such as YTS, day release and education maintenance allowances. If schools have become too remote from 'industry' it is also true that, in a disastrous way, too much of British industry has the wrong attitudes to learning.

A third priority, then, is to educate employers and managers themselves. Many have grown up in a culture that devalues scholarship and science and favours the 'practical'. In our research we often met training 'supervisors' who were actually hostile to training and seemingly ignorant that YTS required employers to train. They knew even less about alternative models available in other more successful capitalist economies, where employers must themselves be credentialled before being allowed to train. They were equally unaware of any social science research on training and management. Ideally, the new Councils should seek through short courses and programmes of continuing education to disseminate information and knowledge about good training.

The 'immorality' of political claims for YTS

Sociological explanations are sometimes misleadingly accused of bias against business, but in this book we have found that the real danger to the long-term interests of Britain's business as well as to its training standards and young people lies in neo-liberal dogma, not least the currently fashionable version of it which has come to be called 'Thatcherism'. The government saddled the MSC with the impossible task of setting up a system of quality training without adequate resources or regulatory powers, meanwhile deliberately undermining traditional controls. Even as we went to press it was reported that ministers were planning yet another revamping of the scheme to make it more attractive to school leavers. Once again employers will be expected 'to assume a fuller share of costs' (*Guardian*, 24 May, 1989).

Throughout our research we have wrestled with the moral problems posed by YTS. After all, it looked better than what had gone before or the alternative of unemployment and, freed from neo-liberalism, still might be used as the basis for genuine change. How far was the MSC to be 'blamed' for selling unemployment relief as 'training'? Some of the Commission's documents and individual officials have revealed ambivalence about its role. Similarly, although Careers Service management resolutely pushed the official line, staff who were forced to operate the scheme were racked with doubt. How deeply are individual managing agents and employers implicated in or victims of the YTS confidence trick? Some of the training entrepreneurs too easily fell into their role yet here, too, were individuals who remembered an element of altruism in the early days of YTS and deplored its decline as funds were cut and market forces intensified.

We conclude that the real 'immorality' of YTS lies with a government so blinded by its own rhetoric of the 'enterprise culture' that it is prepared to conceal the scheme's failure and to exclude young people from their basic rights if they refuse to join. Until they provide adequate funds and regulation, government ministers should stop making the bogus claim that all YTS provides quality training.

Appendix
Sources and methods

Quantitative information on Southwich and its school leavers and YTS comes from three main sources: background statistics comparing the town with elsewhere in Britain; a two-stage postal survey of the 1984 cohort of 16-year-old Southwich school leavers; and a two-stage interview survey of over 200 Southwich young people participating in YTS in 1984–5.

Background statistics
Background material was supplied by the MSC Regional Manpower Intelligence Unit, Southwich Planning Department, the Local Education Authority, and the Southwich Careers Office. However, problems of obtaining good official data about local school-leaving patterns, always difficult, worsened with the discontinuation in 1975 of the National Insurance Card system and, since 1983, with cuts in the data submitted by LEA careers services. Also, Southwich Careers Office refused, even for statistical analysis, to disclose any information or collaborate where records on individual school leavers were involved.

Leavers survey
Used to supplement official local sources, this survey covered every school leaver who had left the fifth form of Southwich non-selective schools during or at the end of 1983–4. It aimed to provide a very simple biography of the cohort between the date of their leaving and December 1985. This necessitated a separate approach to the headteacher of each secondary school within the Southwich educational catchment area because of LEA policy on personal information about pupils. Despite LEA backing, co-operation varied, but eventually the total of names and addresses we were given correspond closely to the total held by the Careers Office (Table A.1). We also obtained accurate school-leaving examination results for 98 per cent of the cohort (pupils' memory of their own exam attainments is often inaccurate). As a cross-check, we contacted all Southwich YTS managing agents listed by the MSC, and so were able to compile an early listing of the names and addresses of Southwich leavers signed up for the main YTS schemes. The lists from schools and managing agents enabled us to distribute two short written questionnaires to every member of the cohort. The first of these were distributed in December 1984 (purposely adapted from similar enquiries being conducted at national level notably by the MSC and the

Table A.1   Southwich leavers survey: analysis of coverage – type of respondent destination in relation to Careers Service returns

Destination	Careers Service estimate (October)	Returned questionnaires December 1984		Cohort biographies (collected 1984–6)
Boys				
FE college	78	58		72
Full-time job	169	106		128
YTS	261	199		257
Unemployed	90	31		39
Moved	–	–		17
Not known	95	–		186
Total	693	394	(57%)	699
Girls				
FE college	103	94		101
Full-time job	104	71		85
YTS	277	233		290
Unemployed	86	38		56
Moved	–	–		13
Not known	150	–		131
Total	720	436	(61%)	676

Scottish School Leavers Survey). Questions covered respondents' experiences since leaving school, attitudes to school and work, social background and home circumstances. The second followed in December 1985, requesting an update on the labour-market experiences and current attitudes of the same individuals. Those listed as having joined the YTS received questionnaires personally wherever possible through their managing agents and completed them either under our supervision during off-the-job training or at home. The rest of the cohort were sent questionnaires to be returned by freepost. In the 1985 survey all questionnaires were distributed and returned by mail. On both occasions, reminder letters went out to non-respondents in January. National surveys of school leavers have regularly reported rates of at least 60 per cent, sometimes higher. Our own 1984 questionnaire was returned by 57 per cent of the school leavers (Table A.1) and the 1985 questionnaire by an estimated 54 per cent.

Outline biographies for a substantial proportion of non-respondents were obtained in two ways. Some were included in the interview sample drawn from managing agents' trainee lists (see below). We also carried out doorstep sample surveys of non-respondents, the most important of which was carried out in March and April 1986. Smaller ones, targeted at former YTS trainees and those who had gone straight into jobs, were carried out by telephone and doorstep contacts in September 1986. These indicated that approximately 17 per cent of non-respondents had moved away during the period of our enquiries. Table A.1 shows that basic labour-market biographies were eventually obtained from just over 75 per cent of the original cohort. Other background and attitudinal data are based on the postal questionnaire replies only. Because of our deep reservations about standard reweighting procedures for non-response, only raw numbers are reported in the text.

Table A.2   Representativeness of target and achieved trainee interview samples

Exam attainment	Cohort YTS Trainees		Target sample	Achieved			
				'Core'		'Extended'	
	N	(%)	(%)	N	(%)	N	(%)
No passes							
Boys	9		9	9	(10)	15	(15)
Girls	9		10	8	(8)	17	(14)
CSEs only							
Boys	60		62	55	(59)	55	(53)
Girls	58		55	58	(59)	58	(47)
1–4 O levels							
Boys	25		24	25	(27)	25	(24)
Girls	27		30	28	(29)	28	(23)
5 O levels							
Boys	2		3	4	(4)	4	(4)
Girls	5		4	4	(4)	15	(12)
No information							
Boys	3		–	–		4	(4)
Girls	0.1		–	–		5	(4)
Total							
Boys	257		100	93		103	
Girls	290		100	98		123	

Interview survey

In-depth information about YTS 1 was based on personal interviews with a sample of 226 trainees listed on YTS schemes in late autumn 1984. They were first interviewed in the spring of 1985 during their YTS year and were then followed up by means of home visits a year later. Though members of the 1984 cohort, the sample was not selected from school registers because these rarely gave any indication that a pupil had joined YTS. As a sampling frame, therefore, we had to use managing agents' lists. According to these lists, at the time 197 boys and 238 girls had become YTS trainees. This compares with an eventual number in the cohort of 257 and 290 plus non-respondents and those who joined YTS schemes outside Southwich. The list used for sampling also underrepresented those who started YTS late in the year as well as those on LCU schemes. One hundred boys and 100 girls were selected at random with stratification to ensure representation in the sample of each school and educational level in correct proportions. This procedure produced very small numbers with more than five O levels and, at the other extreme, those with no exam passes at all.

To maximize within-sample comparisons of selectivity on YTS schemes we decided to extend the sample by including all who fell into these two extreme educational categories and the handful of trainees who had been at the selective secondary schools. This overweighted sample is the base for Chapters 8–10; except for Table 7.1, however, where we make a direct inference from the unweighted 'core' sample of 200 back to the cohort 'population'. Adhering strictly to the sample list proved difficult in practice: we found that some young people had changed their intentions or left town. Where this happened the lost sample member had to be replaced by another, usually during the course of fieldwork, but we did our best to ensure that the 'new' cases matched the 'old' ones as closely as possible. Table A.2 shows that we actually interviewed 93 boys and 98 girls or their matched replacements (teenage boys proved an elusive group to 'pin down' for interview). The resultant core sample was representative in educational attainment of YTS trainees in the cohort as a whole. The extended sample differed as between boys and girls, the number of high-achieving boys on YTS schemes being in any case very small. There were more high-achieving girls and interviewing low-achieving girls was an easier task, so the girls' extended sample is larger.

References

Ashton, D. N., (1988), *The Youth Labour Market and the 1979–1982 Recession: The Effects of Cyclical and Structural Change*, Labour Market Studies, University of Leicester.

Ashton, D. N. and Maguire, M. J. (1983) *The Vanishing Youth Labour Market*, Youthaid, London.

Ashton, D. N. and Maguire, M. J. (1986) *Young Adults in the Labour Market*, Research Paper no. 55, Department of Employment, London.

Ashton, D. N., Maguire, M. J. and Garland, V. (1982) *Youth in the Labour Market*, Research Paper no. 34, Department of Employment, London.

Ashton, D. N., Maguire, M. J. and Spilsbury, M. (1990) *Restructuring the Labour Market – the Implications for Youth*, Macmillan, Basingstoke.

Atkinson, J. (1984) *Manning for Uncertainty: Some Emerging UK Work Patterns*, Institute of Manpower Studies, University of Sussex.

Banks, M. and Ullah, P. (1989) *Youth Unemployment in the 1980s – its Psychological Effects*, Routledge, London.

Barnett, C. (1986) *The Audit of War: the Illusion and Reality of Britain as a Great Nation*, Macmillan, London and Basingstoke.

Burghes, L. (1987) *Made in the USA: a Review of Workfare, the Compulsory Work for Benefits Regime*, Unemployment Unit, London.

Burton, J. (1987) *Would Workfare Work? A Feasibility Study of a Workfare System to Replace Long-term Unemployment in the UK*, University of Buckingham, Buckingham.

Casey, B. (1986) 'The "Dual Apprenticeship" System and the Recruitment and Retention of Young Workers in West Germany', *British Journal of Industrial Relations*, Vol. 24, no. 1; 63–84.

Central Statistical Office (1988) *Regional Trends*, no. 23, HMSO, London.

Chandler, J. (1989) 'Youth Training and the Limits of Vocationalism', paper presented to the British Sociological Association Conference, Plymouth, April; mimeo, Plymouth Polytechnic.

Chandler, J. and Wallace, C. (1989) 'Some Alternatives in Youth Training; Franchise and Corporatist', mimeo, Plymouth Polytechnic.

Chapman, P. and Tooze, M. (1987) *The Youth Training Scheme in the United Kingdom*, Avebury, Aldershot.

Cockburn, C. (1987) *Two Track Training*, Macmillan, Basingstoke.
Courtenay, G. (1988) *England and Wales Youth Cohort Study – Report on Cohort 1, Sweep 1*, Manpower Services Commission, Sheffield.
Craig, R. (1986) *The Youth Training Scheme: a Study of Non-participants and Early Leavers*, YTS Evaluation Series, no. 2, Manpower Services Commission, Sheffield.
Deakin, B. and Pratten, C. (1987) 'Economic Effects of YTS', *Employment Gazette*, 95, 1, 31–53.
Department of Education and Science (1986) English School Leavers, 1983–4, *Statistical Bulletin* 4/86, February 1986, DES, London.
Department of Employment (1981) *A New Training Initiative – The Government's Response*, Cmnd 8455, HMSO, London.
Department of Employment (1985a) *Employment: the Challenge for the Nation*, Cmnd 9474, HMSO, London.
Department of Employment (1985b) 'A Survey of Youth Training Scheme Providers', *Employment Gazette*, 93, 8.
Department of Employment (1987) 'Education and Labour Market Status of Young People', *Employment Gazette*, 95, 9, 459–64.
Department of Employment (1988) *Employment for the 1990s*, Cm 540, HMSO, London.
Department of Employment (1989) 'Setting up a TEC', *Employment Gazette*, 97, 4, 155–8.
Dutton, P. A., (1987) *The Impact of YTS on Engineering Apprenticeship – a Local Labour Market Study*, Engineering Industry Training Board and Institute for Employment Research, University of Warwick, Coventry.
Finn, D. (1987) *Training Without Jobs*, Macmillan, Basingstoke.
Further Education Unit (1985) *Supporting YTS: Evaluation of the FE Role in YTS*, Further Education Unit, Department of Education and Science, London.
Gleeson, D. and Mardle, G. (1980) *Further Education or Training? A Case Study in the Theory and Practice of Day Release*, Routledge & Kegan Paul, London.
Gray, D. and King, S. (1986) *The Youth Training Scheme – the First Three Years*, YTS Evaluation Series, no. 1, Manpower Services Commission, Sheffield.
Gray, J. and Jesson, D. (1987) 'Exam Results and Local Authority League Tables' in A. Harrison and J. Gretton (eds), *Education and Training UK 1987 – an Economic, Social and Policy Audit*, Policy Journals, Newbury, Berks.
Hakim, C. (1987) 'Trends in the Flexible Labour Force', *Employment Gazette*, 95, 11, 549–60.
Jarvis, V. and Prais, S. J. (1988) *Two Nations of Shopkeepers – Training for Retailing in France and Britain*, Discussion Paper no. 140, National Institute of Economic and Social Research, London.
Keep, E. (1986) *Designing the Stable Door – a Study of How the Youth Training Scheme Was Planned*, Warwick Papers in Industrial Relations, no. 8, Industrial Relations Unit, University of Warwick.
Lee, D. (1966) 'Industrial Training and Social Class', *Sociological Review*, 14, 3, 269–85.
Lee, D. (1975) 'Neglected Territory: the Regional Factor in Further Education' in W. van der Eyken, *Learning and Earning*, NFER, Slough.
Lee, D. (1979) 'Craft Unions and the Force of Tradition', *British Journal of Industrial Relations*, 17.
Lee, D. (1983) 'Social Policy and Institutional Autonomy in Further Education' in

D. Gleeson (ed.), *Youth Training and the Search for Work*, Routledge and Kegan Paul, London.

Lee, D., Marsden, D., Rickman, P. and Hardey, M. (1986) 'How YTS Tied Itself in Knots', *The Guardian*, 19 September.

Lindley, R. M. (1983) 'Active Manpower Policy' in G. S. Bain (ed.), *Industrial Relations in Great Britain*, Basil Blackwell, Oxford, 339–60.

Lockwood, D. (1985) 'Civic Stratification', mimeo, University of Essex.

MacInnes, J. (1987) *Thatcherism at Work: Industrial Relations and Economic Change*, Open University Press, Milton Keynes.

Manpower Services Commission (1980) *Outlook on Training: Review of the Employment and Training Act*, MSC, London.

Manpower Services Commission (1981a) *A New Training Initiative – an Agenda for Action*, MSC, London.

Manpower Services Commission (1981b) *A New Training Initiative – a Consultative Document*, MSC, London.

Manpower Services Commission (1982) *Youth Task Group Report*, MSC, London.

Manpower Services Commission (1988a) 'Skills Supply and Demand', *Labour Market Quarterly Report*, October, 5–6.

Manpower Services Commission (1988b) *The Funding of Vocational Education and Training: Some Early Research Findings*, Background Note no. 2, MSC, Sheffield.

Manpower Services Commission (1989) *YTS Progress Report*, MSC, Sheffield.

Marsden, D. (1986) *The End of Economic Man – Custom and Competition in Labour Markets*, Wheatsheaf, Brighton.

Marsden, D. and Ryan, P. (1986) 'Where Do Young Workers Work? Employment by Industry in Various European Economies', *British Journal of Industrial Relations*, 24, 1, 83–102.

Marshall, G., Newby, H., Rose, D. and Vogler, C. (1988) *Social Class in Modern Britain*, Hutchinson, London.

Maurice, M., Sellier, F. and Silvestre, J.-J. (1986) *The Social Foundations of Industrial Power: a Comparison of France and Germany* (trans. A. Goldhammer), MIT Press, Cambridge, MA and London.

National Association of Teachers in Further and Higher Education (1986) *Planning for Change in Further Education – Towards an Alternative Strategy*, NATFHE, London.

National Audit Office (1985) *The Manpower Services Commission: Report by the Comptroller and Auditor General*, HMSO, London.

Perry, P. (1976) *The Evolution of British Manpower Policy*, British Association for Commercial and Industrial Education, London.

Pollert, A. (1988) 'The Flexible Firm: Fixation or Fact?', *Work, Employment and Society*, 2, 3, 281–316.

Raffe, D. (1984) 'YOP and the Future of YTS' in D. McCrone (ed.) *Scottish Government Yearbook*, University of Edinburgh Unit for the Study of Government in Scotland, Edinburgh.

Raffe, D. (1987) 'The Context of the Youth Training Scheme – an Analysis of its Strategy and Development', *British Journal of Education and Work* 1, 1, 1–31.

Raffe, D. and Smith, P. (1987) 'Young Peoples' Attitudes to YTS – the First Two Years', *British Educational Research Journal*, 13, 3, 241–60.

Raffe, D. (1989) 'Longitudinal and Historical Change in Young Peoples' Attitudes to YTS', *British Educational Research Journal*, 15.

Ranson, S. (1984) 'Towards a Tertiary Tripartism: New Codes of Social Control and the 17 plus' in P. Broadfoot (ed.), *Selection, Certification and Control*, Falmer Press, Lewes.

Rees, G. and Rees, T. (1982) 'Juvenile Unemployment and the State between the Wars' in T. Rees and P. Atkinson (eds), *Youth Unemployment and State Intervention*, Routledge Direct Editions, London.

Roberts, K., Dench, S. and Richardson, D. (1986a) *The Changing Structure of Youth Labour Markets*, Research Paper no. 59, Department of Employment, London.

Roberts, K., Dench, S. and Richardson, D. (1986b) 'Youth Labour Markets in the Eighties', *Employment Gazette*, 94, 6, 241–6.

Roberts, K., Parsell, G. and Siwek, M., (1989) 'Britain's Economic Recovery, the New Demographic Trend and Young Peoples' Transitions into the Labour Market', paper presented to the Annual Conference of the British Sociological Association, Plymouth Polytechnic; mimeo, Dept. of Sociology, University of Liverpool.

Ryan, P. (1984) 'The New Training Initiative after Two Years', *Lloyds Bank Review*, April.

Ryan, P. (1986) 'Apprenticeship and Industrial Relations in British Engineering: the Early Interwar Period', mimeo, King's College, Cambridge.

Sako, M. and Dore, R. (1986) 'How the Youth Training Scheme helps Employers', *Employment Gazette*, 94, 1, 195–204.

Sheldrake, J. and Vickerstaff, S. (1987) *The History of Industrial Training in Great Britain*, Aldershot: Avebury.

Simon, B. (1988) *Bending the Rules: The Baker Reform of Education*, 3rd edn, Lawrence and Wishart, London.

Steedman, H. (1988) *Vocational Training in France and Britain; Mechanical and Electrical Craftsmen*, Discussion Paper no. 130, National Institute of Economic and Social Research, London.

Stoney, S. and Lines, A. (1987) *YTS: the Impact on FE*, NFER-Nelson, Windsor.

Taylor, R. (1982) *Workers and the New Depression*, Macmillan, London and Basingstoke.

Thompson, P. (1989) 'NVQs – What They Mean', *Employment Gazette*, 97, 1, 14–16.

Tipton, B. (1973) *Conflict and Change in a Technical College*, Brunel Further Education Monographs no. 6, Hutchinson, London.

Turbin, J. (1988) 'State Intervention into the Labour Market for Youth: the Implementation of the Youth Training Scheme in Three Local Labour Markets, unpublished Ph.D., University of Leicester.

Wood, S. (ed.), (1989) *The Transformation of Work? Skill Flexibility and the Labour Process*, Unwin Hyman, London.

Youthaid (1981) *Quality or Collapse? Youthaid Review of the Youth Opportunities Programme*, Youthaid, London.

Youthaid (1986) 'YTS Leavers Survey', *Youthaid Bulletin*, no. 29.

Index